Euro-Asian Studies

Series Editor
Christoph Bluth
Department of Peace Studies
University of Bradford
Bradford, UK

The transition of the countries in Euro-Asia is one of the most important developments affecting the international system since the end of the Cold War. The development of market economies after decades of central planning, the formation of new states and national identities, the creation of new, democratic institutions of state and the reintegration into the world economy poses enormous challenges. While some countries have progressed relatively well and are in the process of joining the European Union, others have experienced severe economic and social dislocations, to the point of political disintegration and armed conflicts. The Centre for Euro-Asian Studies at the University of Reading is dedicated to the academic study of the political, economic, social and cultural aspects of this process. This series presents the most recent contributions from leading academics in the field. With an interdisciplinary focus, it seeks to provide a substantial, original and ongoing contribution to our understanding of the region which is of vital importance for academics and of high policy relevance for governments and businesses.

More information about this series at
http://www.palgrave.com/gp/series/14973

Irina Heim
Editor

Kazakhstan's Diversification from the Natural Resources Sector

Strategic and Economic Opportunities

palgrave
macmillan

Editor
Irina Heim
Henley Business School
University of Reading
Reading, UK

ISSN 2662-625X ISSN 2662-6268 (electronic)
Euro-Asian Studies
ISBN 978-3-030-37388-7 ISBN 978-3-030-37389-4 (eBook)
https://doi.org/10.1007/978-3-030-37389-4

This Palgrave Macmillan imprint is published by the registered company Springer Nature Switzerland AG.
The registered company address is: Gewerbestrasse 11, 6330 Cham, Switzerland

To the new generation of academics

Foreword

In 1998 I published the first book in English on the Kazakhstani economy, where I clearly stated that, at that time, there was a lack of economic rationalism in the policy of the government. Under the misconception that the oil and gas sector could save Kazakhstan from all its troubles, the country had deliberately moved toward resource-rich sectors. Twenty years later, it is frantically trying to find ways of escaping from the vulnerabilities of such a dependency, through diversification, better management of revenues and spending, and longer-term fiscal planning.

A range of mechanisms have been proposed to achieve this goal, including the creation of an oil fund, a cluster program, and local content policies. Nevertheless, the country's hydrocarbon sector is still a main source of government revenue, a fact which clearly puts pressure on the state budget. The structural reforms needed to make the Kazakhstani economy more robust comprise the diversification of revenue sources, an effective management of the revenues from oil, good fiscal policies, and medium- and long-term planning of public finances. In order to achieve this, different aspects should be considered, namely institutional and infrastructural challenges, entrepreneurial ecosystem, and local industrial base.

On reading this volume, I was struck by the complexity of what was required to make the economic system work. This book identifies opportunities for diversification, highlighting the fact that the economy of Kazakhstan is still heavily dependent on natural resources. The contributors discuss the possible avenues for future development, arising not only from within the economy but also from the Belt and Road Initiative (BRI), trade and investment initiatives of the Chinese government, Eurasian Economic Union, and so on. Finally, the book depicts internal sources of diversification of the economy, with an emphasis on the development of local oil and gas firms, small and medium-sized enterprises, and the tourism industry.

I congratulate the editor, Irina Heim, for overseeing such a large international research project and making possible the publication of a book that promotes a deeper understanding of the Kazakhstani economy.

Reading, UK Yelena Kalyuzhnova

Preface

In December 1991, leaders of the republics in USSR—Russian, Belarusian, and Kazakh—signed an agreement (the Belovezha Accords) establishing Russia, Belarus, and Kazakhstan (and 12 others) as independent states as well as establishing the Commonwealth of Independent States (CIS) as a successor entity of the Soviet Union. This book is about the transition Kazakhstan made since this time on its way from planned economy to build a strong presidential republic with parliament, as well as market-based economy. The book expands on the need for further economic diversification from resource-based to a new modern economy built upon multiple comparative advantages, among all a strong tertiary sector. Successful economic diversification can be defined as the rise of new industries and the creation of jobs (McMillan & Rodrik, 2011), which occurs when a substantial and sustained investment in activities that are close to a country's existing areas of comparative advantage exists (Gelb, 2010). Defying the comparative advantage and missing out the steps on the ladder can stimulate sustainable development of the economy (Rodrik, 2011). This book analyzes different development and diversification programs, including the opportunities provided by the Belt and Road Initiative (BRI).

Today, Kazakhstan is still a young independent state. Significant changes took place during the period since 1991; however, the economy still significantly differs from a sustainable one—diverse economy is based on a wide range of sectors. Since foreign direct investment (FDI) is considered to be an important component of policies for development (Buzdugan & Tüselmann, 2018), Kazakhstan has focused on becoming a leader among post-Soviet countries in attracting foreign direct investments (FDI). Yet these investments are directed in a single, natural sector of the economy building the economy based predominantly on this sector. This means, according to the definition given by the International Monetary Fund (IMF), that at least 20 percent of their total exports are natural resources, or at least 20 percent of their revenue are derived from the exploration of natural resources (IMF, 2007, 2012). Secondly, in resource-rich countries, especially transition countries (like Kazakhstan, Russia, and Azerbaijan) and developing ones, the state and resource sectors still play important roles in the economy. However, they made progress in the transition to the market economy and now attract foreign investors due to their abundance of natural resources, cheap labor force, and/or strategic geographical position.

However, in 2014, the oil and gas sector faced the prospect of a long-term low-price environment, with other sectors of the economy experiencing a new industrial revolution in developing and emerging economies. At some point in time, resource-rich countries in Central Asia, such as Russia and Kazakhstan (and recently Azerbaijan), embraced *diversification* as "a national idea" with the aim of co-financing a wide range of development projects from small business support to infrastructure, with a focus on the oil and gas sector, high technology, and agriculture (Guriev, Plekhanov & Sonin, 2009).

This book is also about an important geopolitical position of the country on the way between China to the EU and how it can be used by Kazakhstan in an attempt to build a modern, robust economy. Geopolitical and institutional factors play an important role in the decision of foreign businesses to invest in the country. After their declaration of independence, as a part of their development strategy, Kazakhstan has adopted changes in their institutional environment in order to attract more foreign investments and the country has succeeded in this way. However, most of the investments are done in the extractive industries and particularly in the exploration of the oil and gas reserves.

Recently, the government of Kazakhstan has realized the importance of information and communication technologies (ICT) in the development of modern economies and diversification from primary sectors of the economy into new service industries. As state-owned enterprises still play a crucial role in the economy of Kazakhstan, the government has created new trends by establishing the state-owned information technology company Zerde National Infocommunication Holding JSC, wherein the Ministry of Information and Communications of the Republic of Kazakhstan is the sole shareholder. This holding company was created with the aim of enhancing the competitiveness and cost-effectiveness of the industry, the development of information and communication resources and standards, the promotion of investment and innovation in ICT, and the promotion of multilateral cooperation among the CIS member states in the field of information and digital technologies.

At the same time, Kazakhstan is considered a special zone of interest for China, especially in transportation and ICT infrastructure. In 2013, China introduced an initiative to build the Silk Road Economic Belt and the 21st Century Maritime Silk Road (jointly referred to as the Belt and Road Initiative or the BRI). In Central Asia, a core region along the Silk Road Economic Belt, the implementation of the initiative is generating more FDI from China in industries other than natural resources and helping diversify the economies of various host countries. Chinese companies already own a large part of the FDI stock in extractive industries in countries such as Kazakhstan and Turkmenistan. The ongoing planning of new Chinese investments in the region, however, has focused on building infrastructure facilities and enhancing industrial capacities. In addition, agriculture and related businesses are targeted. For example, Chinese companies are in negotiation with local partners to invest US $1.9 billion in Kazakh agriculture, including one project that would relocate tomato processing plants from China.

This book is about the opportunities for diversification of the economy of modern Kazakhstan, which is still heavily dependent on the natural resources, as well as the opportunities for the economy of the whole Central Asian region arising from the BRI and trade and investment initiative of the Chinese government.

Academics from different countries working on research in the field of economics and international business, as well as policymakers and business, have been invited to make contribution in this book. It comprises three parts.

Part I considers the first main theme of the book—development of the economy based on the resource sector on the example of Kazakhstan. Chapter 1 (by Baldakhov and Heim) gives an overview of the economic development in Kazakhstan since 1992 and the main economic trends that have an impact on the country's goal to become one of the top 30 developed countries. They consider GDP growth and FDI inflows, Kazakhstan's investment policy and regulatory framework, protection of intellectual property rights, an approach to development of local suppliers and industrial competitiveness, diversification and development policy, country's technological capability, recent national development initiatives, as well as compare regional governance indicators (Kazakhstan, China, and Russia). Chapter 2 (by Heim and Romanov) discusses the oil and gas industry, a core of the Kazakhstani economy, and elaborates on how Kazakhstan can diversify its economy to build a more sustainable economy, including the modern service sector. This chapter includes an overview of the oil and gas industry, the distribution of oil and gas reserves by regions, main international companies operating in the country, data on proven crude oil reserves, and FDI by country and by period. Authors discuss the evolution of investment regime in Kazakhstan, international law on foreign investment in the oil and gas (O&G) industry, and results of the research on the shaping forces for FDI in Kazakhstan: guarantee of legislation stability, guarantee against government interference and nationalization, principles of compensation and guarantee of free use of dividends, and transparency of investment activity. Chapter 3 (by Heim and Salimov) explains how the oil and gas industry as a primary sector of the economy in resource-rich countries influences the economic development and why diversification is necessary. This includes economic development in the post-Soviet period, the effects of oil rent on socio-economic development, the issue of redistribution of oil rent, and recent socio-economic reforms: National Development Program *Strategy 2050*, the Modernisation Program *Nurly Zhol*, and *One Hundred Concrete Steps* concept.

Part II changes the focus of discussion from national development initiatives to international, introducing the Belt and Road Initiative of the

Chinese government to invest in transportation and digital infrastructure in the Central Asian countries, mainly Kazakhstan, a new transportation hub in the region. Chapter 4 (by Ribberink and Schubert) is looking at the BRI as a large-scale transportation and infrastructure policy. They consider types of infrastructure investments, regional integration through BRI, and private sector opportunities. Chapter 5 (by Ambalov and Heim) discusses the second important focus of BRI (after transportation infrastructure development), namely digital connectiveness alongside the New Silk Road. The authors define new digital economy, define digital technological divide between countries, and argue that digital Silk Road can help Kazakhstan to overcome growing technological gap. The authors consider current development of the ICT industry in Kazakhstan and suggest starting with the digitization of the oil and gas industry and expanding digital technologies to other sectors such as financial, transportation, and so on. Case studies of cooperative projects between Kazakhstani and Chinese partners are discussed.

Part III explores the view from China on the perspectives of regional development—the economic reasons for the launch of this program, investments, and planned effects.

Chapter 6 (by Han and Ghobadian) gives an overview of Chinese investments in Kazakhstan as a trade hub in Eurasia. The authors give an overview of Chinese investment flows in Kazakhstan, including mergers and acquisitions, and explain the BRI and its motivation from the Chinese side: the pressure for sustaining economic growth for Chinese economy and opportunities for Kazakhstani economy. The chapter considers the case study of Khorgos, the biggest dry port at the border between China and Kazakhstan, and a case study of Huawei, a leading global provider of ICT technology in Kazakhstan. Chapter 7 (by Selmier) discusses Kazakhstan's strategic position on the New Silk Road, between China and Russia, East Asia, and Europe. It argues that geopolitical position of the country in the region catalyzes the development and promotion of a regional headquarters hub and integration. The chapter argues that sophisticated planning and development is necessary, and this will require integration and coordination between Kazakhstan and China. The author considers various factors including geography as logistic destiny, Kazakhstan's geographic location on the BRI, shipping costs, containerization, and capacity and then discusses the main issues involved in becoming a logistic linchpin.

Part IV discusses internal sources for diversification of the economy based on development of local industry (Chap. 8), small and medium-sized enterprises (Chap. 9), and tertiary sector of the economy (Chap. 10). Sabirov and Shakulikova argue that government policy to support the development of national industry in the oil and gas sector is necessary to avoid *resource curse*. Jumasseitova explores the effects of economic integration on the development of the entrepreneurial ecosystem in Kazakhstan. Ziyadin, Doszhan, and Akybayeva consider the potential of the tourism industry development based on the internet.

Overall, this book gives an overview of the economy of Kazakhstan, a major player in the Central Asian region, and the recent trends in its economic and institutional development. It also explores the need for diversification in resource-rich economies and discusses one of the opportunities to diversify the economy to infrastructure and communication projects. The book will be interesting for students, academics, policymakers, and practitioners focused on the investments in the region, as well as those who deal with the problem of diversification in their countries. The particular contribution of this book is its overview of the recent development of the economy of Kazakhstan integrated with new trends in the world economy such as digitalization and China's trade and investment policy, Belt and Road Initiative (BRI). Although this book is written by academics, it is an accessible read for a non-academic audience. It is recommended for researchers of economic development and industry practitioners seeking to understand the role of BRI and how it will affect their companies, and it is also of interest to policymakers working on the design of instruments for economic development in their countries, as well as for students studying economic development and business.

The editor would like to thank Professor John Dilyard and Associate Professor Joan McCormack for reading and editing this book, the publisher Palgrave Macmillan for agreeing to publish it, anonymous reviewers, and the editorial board of *Euro-Asian Studies* book series and Rachel Stranger of Palgrave Macmillan for her cooperation.

Reading, UK Irina Heim

Bibliography

Buzdugan, S., & Tüselmann, H. (2018). Making the most of FDI for development: New industrial policy and FDI deepening for industrial upgrading. *Transnational Corporations*, 25(1), 1–21.

Gelb, A. (2010). Economic diversification in resource rich countries. *Center for Global Development*, 1–23.

Guriev, S., Plekhanov, A., & Sonin, S. (2009). *Development based on commodity revenues*. European Bank for Reconstruction and Development. Working paper 108. http://www.ebrd.org/downloads/research/economics/workingpapers/wp0108.pdf.

IMF. (2007). *Guide on resource revenue transparency*. Washington, DC: International Monetary Fund.

IMF. (2012). *Macroeconomic policy frameworks for resource-rich countries*. Washington, DC: International Monetary Fund.

McMillan, M. S., & Rodrik, D. (2011). *Globalization, structural change and productivity growth*. Working paper No. w17143. National Bureau of Economic Research. https://www.nber.org/papers/w17143.

Rodrik, D. (2011). Comments on "new structural economics" by Justin Yifu Lin. *The World Bank Research Observer*, 26(2), 227–229.

Contents

Notes on Contributors

Gulvira Akybayeva is an associate Professor at Astana IT University, Nur-Sultan, Kazakhstan.

Vitaly Ambalov is an advisor at Republican Confederation of Entrepreneurship, Minsk, Belarus.

Ulan Baldakhov is a recipient of the International Scholarship of the President of the Republic of Kazakhstan BOLASHAK, at Henley Business School, University of Reading, Reading, UK.

Raigul Doszhan is an associate Professor at Al-Farabi Kazakh National University, Almaty, Kazakhstan.

Abby Ghobadian is a Professor of Management at Henley Business School, University of Reading, Reading, UK.

Tian Han is a doctoral researcher at Henley Business School, University of Reading, Reading, UK.

Irina Heim is a post-doctoral fellow at Henley Business School, University of Reading, Reading, UK.

Assel Jumasseitova is an associate Professor, and the Vice-Rector for Academic Affairs at Kazakh-British Technical University, Almaty, Kazakhstan.

Yelena Kalyuzhnova is a Professor of Economics and the Vice-Dean International at Henley Business School, University of Reading, Reading, UK.

Natalia Ribberink is a Professor of Foreign Trade and International Management at Hamburg University of Applied Sciences, Hamburg, Germany.

Maxim Romanov is a research fellow at the Kazakh-British Centre for Competitiveness, Almaty, Kazakhstan.

Beibit Sabirov is a business professional at the Karachaganak Petroleum Operating BV, Nur-Sultan, Kazakhstan.

Kairat Salimov is a senior expert at the Department of International Financial Relations of the Ministry of Finance, Nur-Sultan, Kazakhstan.

Lisa Schubert is a researcher at Hamburg University of Applied Sciences, Hamburg, Germany.

Gulzada Shakulikova is a Professor of Economics and the Rector at Atyrau University of Oil and Gas, Atyrau, Kazakhstan.

W. Travis Selmier II is a visiting scholar in Political Science at Indiana University, Bloomington, USA.

Sayabek Ziyadin is a Professor of Economics at Al-Farabi Kazakh National University, Almaty, Kazakhstan.

Abbreviations

ADB	Asian Development Bank
AIIB	Asian Infrastructure Investment Bank
BIT	Bilateral Investment Treaty
BRI	Belt and Road Initiative
CBR	Central Bank of the Russian Federation
CEEC	Central and Eastern European Countries
CEF	Connecting Europe Facility
CIS	Commonwealth of the Independent States
COSCO	China Ocean Shipping Company
CPC	Caspian Pipeline Consortium
EBRD	European Bank for Reconstruction and Development
EEA	Eurasian Economic Union
EIB	European Investment Bank
ERDF	European Regional Development Fund
EU	European Union
FDI	Foreign Direct Investment
GDP	Gross Domestic Product
HKTDC	Hong Kong Trade Development Council
ICT	Information and Communication Technology
IEA	International Energy Agency
IEF	Index of Economic Freedom
IIC	Industrial Internet Consortium
IMF	International Monetary Fund

IPO	Initial Public Offering
JSC	Joint Stock Company
MNE RK	Ministry of National Economy of the Republic of Kazakhstan
MoU	Memorandum of Understanding
MSR	Maritime Silk Road
NADLoC	National Agency of Local Content Development, now QAZINDUSTRY
NBK	National Bank of Kazakhstan
NFRK	National Fund for the Republic of Kazakhstan
OBOR	One Belt One Road
OR	Oil Revenues
PPP	Public-private partnership
QAZAQSTAN	Name of the country after switching to the Latin alphabet
QAZINDUSTRY	Qazaqstan Industry and Export Center JSC
RI	Return on Investment
RR	Rate of Reinvestment
SME	Small and Medium Enterprises
SREB	Silk Road Economic Belt
UN	United Nations
USSR	Union of Soviet Socialist Republics
WB	World Bank

List of Figures

List of Tables

Part I

Development of the Economy Based on Resource Sector: Economic Opportunities for Diversification

The authors of the chapters in this section provide an overview of the recent economic development of Kazakhstan since the declaration of independence in 1991 based on the natural resource sector. Baldakhov and Heim give an overview of institutional reform in the new country's transition from a post-soviet economic system to a market-lead economy. They suggest considering it through the lens of the institutional theory applied to the settings of emerging countries. Heim and Maximov overview the oil and gas industry, the heart of the Kazakhstani economy. They discuss different FDI regimes, applying an institutional theory view to foreign investments. Heim and Salimov apply an institutional theory view to sustainable development of resource-driven unbalanced economies.

1

Institutional Reform in Kazakhstan

Ulan Baldakhov and Irina Heim

Introduction

In December 2016, the Republic of Kazakhstan (RK) celebrated its 25th anniversary as an independent nation. By historical standards, this period of time has not been enough for the young state to have built a sustainable economy and become competitive at the international level. In 2008, the global economic crisis and the decline in oil prices—the main financial source for Kazakhstan's economy—raised the question of how the economy of Kazakhstan could be diversified to reduce vulnerability to particularly volatile sectors and products such as commodities. In 2012, the former President of Kazakhstan, Nursultan Nazarbayev, put forward an ambitious goal for the government to enter the group of the top 30 developed countries by 2050. Recent political and economic changes in the world, such as sanctions against Russia, Brexit, the election in the United States, the rise of China as a global player, and coronavirus COVID-19 pandemic will certainly have a significant impact on the achievement of this goal. In such an economic environment, one of the

U. Baldakhov • I. Heim (✉)
Henley Business School, University of Reading, Reading, UK
e-mail: irina.heim@henley.ac.uk

I. Heim (ed.), *Kazakhstan's Diversification from the Natural Resources Sector*, Euro-Asian Studies, https://doi.org/10.1007/978-3-030-37389-4_1

main instruments for economic development of a young state remains foreign investments and the development of formal and informal institutions aimed at the facilitation of foreign investments (Narula & Dunning, 2000). Although the country has attracted significant FDIs since its independence in 1991, most of them were concentrated in the natural resource sector. The challenge for the country is therefore to diversify[1] the economy and create an institutional environment to facilitate investments in the new, predominantly service sectors of the economy. This chapter will discuss the main changes in the institutional environment of Kazakhstan between the years 1991 and 2019, as well as the effectiveness of efforts that have been undertaken to improve the investment environment.

Economic institutions can be defined as informal business rules and laws regulating economic and business behavior, such as constitutional laws, government decrees, regulations, and others factors, as well as economic actors, such as industry association, development, trade unions, and so on, which can affect the economic and business behavior of the other economic actors. Numerous economic studies in recent years have highlighted the institutions' importance for economic development; in this context, institutions are important to any country, regardless of whether it is a developed country or a country in a transitional period (Acemoglu, Johnson, & Robinson, 2005). The most striking example of the importance of institutions for countries' economic development can be seen in the former Soviet Bloc countries. Obviously, the failure of socialism has led to significant institutional changes in these countries, but with different outcomes. The relative success of the countries of Central and Eastern Europe, in comparison to the former Soviet Union countries, is a result of their histories, cultures, and internal systems (Aoki, 2001), but also a result of their specific geographical positions. The newer members of the EU, such as Estonia, Poland, and Hungary, have managed to adopt the institutional framework of the EU, while Russia and Ukraine have faced significant challenges in the development of their new institutional environments (Berglof & Bolton, 2002).

[1] Diversification is defined in this research as a long-term change in economic structure.

Kazakhstan, being resource-rich, has built its economy around the oil and gas (O&G) industry that had been increasingly dominating its economy and became an O&G export-oriented country. Therefore, a major part of FDI is concentrated in this sector of the economy. As O&G projects can be very investment-intensive and Kazakhstan had none of its own financial resources to fund these projects, the Government of Kazakhstan has adopted a series of reforms to liberalize its economy and facilitate foreign investment, first and foremost in the O&G sector, since obtaining independence in 1991. As a next step in its development, the country needs to move out of this middle-income trap, defined as the inability to sustain growth, and transition from resource-driven growth, which is based on low-cost labor and capital, to productivity-driven growth (Khakas & Kohli, 2011). To diversify its economic structure, Kazakhstan has embarked on an ambitious program of economic change, innovation, investment in human capital, international trade, and attraction of FDI for job creation (UNCTAD, 2003).

Neo-institutional Theory and Emerging Economies

Emerging economies are characterized by, among other features, inefficient markets, active government involvement, extensive business networking, and high uncertainty (Xu & Meyer, 2013). Institutional theory is the prevalent approach in international business and management studies for explaining the strategic challenges businesses face in the context of emerging countries. For instance, institutional theory holds that norms and values of a given country are used to formulate formal and legal aspects of government directives (Kraft & Furlong, 2007). This can be helpful in an explanation of environments where market failure[2] is widespread and governments attempt to substitute for

[2] Market failure is an economic term covering all circumstances in which the market equilibrium is not efficient (Begg & Ward, 2013).

market-coordinated mechanisms more frequently and directly than the governments of developed countries (Kalyuzhnova, Nygaard, Omarov, & Saparbayev, 2016).

The applications of institutional theory include (1) conceptualizing national environments in terms of regulatory, cognitive, and normative "pillars," introducing constructs such as country institutional profile; (2) conceptualizing processes of large-scale transformation of national systems through the notions of institutional transition, upheaval, and imperfection; (3) explaining comparative national business systems based on institutional embeddedness; (4) explaining similarities in practices across organizations resulting from isomorphic pressures; (5) studying constraints on the diffusion and institutionalization of organizations' practices across borders and organizational units; and (6) explaining the relationship between foreign companies and their host environments (Kostova, Roth, & Dacin, 2008).

Institutional theory with an organizational focus has emerged from the works of Meyer and Rowan (1977), Zucker (1977), Meyer and Rowan (1983), DiMaggio and Powell (1983), Tolbert and Zucker (1983), and Meyer and Scott (1983). These works introduced the view of an organization as an actor responding to the environmental context. It explains that firm behavior is determined by the external institutional environment which includes formal institutions such as law, regulations and rules, and informal institutions such as norms, cultures, and ethics.

Before the emergence of organizational institutional theory, prevailing neo-classical theories assumed that the coordination and control of activity were the critical dimensions on which formal organizations have succeeded in the modern world. Meyer and Rowan (1977) challenged this view and defined formal organizations as systems of coordinated and controlled activities that arise when work is embedded in complex networks of relations and boundary-spanning exchanges. They supposed that organizational structures arise in a highly institutionalized context, and as a response, organizations conform to this context by reflecting the myth of their institutional environments—that is becoming isomorphic with their institutional context—by incorporating the practices and procedures defined by prevailing rationalized concepts of organizational work and institutionalized in society to increase their legitimacy and survival prospects. However, conformity to institutionalized rules may often conflict with efficiency criteria (Meyer & Rowan, 1977; Zucker, 1987); therefore, organizations' coordination and control activity to promote efficiency undermines an organization's ceremonial conformity and sacrifices its support and legitimacy. In their later paper, Meyer and Rowan (1983: 84) defined institutional context as "the rules, norms and ideology of the wider society." Table 1.1 outlines the main concepts of the institutional theory with an organizational focus.

Williamson (2000) proposed consideration of the four levels of social analysis: social theory (informal institutions), political theory (institutional environment), transaction cost economics (governance), and neoclassical economics (resource allocation). The second level according to Williamson (2000) is referred to as the institutional environment. Here "formal rules" such as constitutions, laws, property rights, and policies are introduced. Legislative, judicial, and bureaucratic functions of government as well as distribution of power across different levels of government are included. At level two research is concerned with normative design of better policies, the economics of property rights, changes in established economic and political procedures, breakdowns and development of the old and new political and economic systems, and so on. The institutions of governance are located in the third level. The concept of embeddedness[3] helps to understand network relationships in society and business.

In this chapter, the development of the economy of Kazakhstan will be considered through the lens of its institutional context (Meyer & Rowan, 1983) or environment (Williamson, 2000), that is the economic rules and norms of Kazakhstan in comparison to other countries, and institutional change (North, 1994), focusing on the institutional evolution of an economy in the post-Soviet period.

[3] Extent to which economic action is linked to structures of social relations in modern industrial society (Granovetter, 1985).

Table 1.1 Key concepts of institutional theory with organizational focus

Notion	Definition	Indicative literature
Legitimacy	Congruence of an organization with social laws, norms, and values which provide survival benefits	Parsons (1956), Parsons and Jones (1960)
Institutional context	The rules, norms, and ideologies of the wider society	Meyer and Rowan (1983)
Rationalized myth (rule)	Social understandings of appropriate organizational behavior	Meyer and Rowan (1977)
Institutionalization	The process by which social processes, obligations, or actualities come to take on a rule-like status in social thought and action	Meyer and Rowan (1977)
Isomorphism	Conformity of organizations with institutions	DiMaggio and Powell (1983)
Organizational field	Community of organizations that shares a common meaning system and whose participants interact more frequently and closely with one another than with actors outside the field	Scott (1991)
Institutions	The cultural-cognitive, cultural-normative, and cultural-regulative structures that provide stability and collective meaning to social behavior The humanly devised constraints that structure human interaction are made up of formal constraints (e.g., rules, laws, constitutions), informal constraints (e.g., norms of behavior, conventions, self-imposed codes of conduct), and their enforcement characteristics. Together they define the incentive structure of societies and specifically economies	Scott (1995), North (1994)

(*continued*)

Table 1.1 (continued)

Notion	Definition	Indicative literature
Institutional change	The interaction between institutions and organizations that shapes the institutional evolution of an economy. If institutions are the rules of the game, organizations and their entrepreneurs are the players	North (1994)
Organizations	Organizations are made up of groups of individuals bound together by some common purpose to achieve certain objectives. Organizations include political bodies (e.g., political parties, the Senate, a city council, regulatory bodies), economic bodies (e.g., firms, trade unions, family farms, cooperatives), social bodies (e.g., churches, dubs, athletic associations), and educational bodies (e.g., schools, universities, vocational training centers)	North (1994)

Source: Heim (2019)

Main Trends in Institutional and Economic Development of Kazakhstan in Recent Years

Since gaining its independence, Kazakhstan has made significant progress in terms of its economic development. With the separation of its economy from that of the Soviet Union, the first few years proved to be an extremely difficult period for the country (Hoff & Stiglitz, 2004). Within the 11 years since the beginning of the new millennium, economic growth has averaged slightly more than 8%, the main reason for this being the rapid increase in crude oil production. From 1995 to 2016, GDP per capita increased annually by an average of 5.2% (OECD, 2017).

The correlation between oil prices, production, and the GDP growth rate can be clearly recognized in the period between 1991 and the 2008 global economic crisis, after which moving up the income ladder lost its momentum (Fig. 1.1) and GDP growth declined substantially as compared to the early 2000s. The growth in GDP for 2015 was only 1%, while the same figure was 6% in 2013 and 4.1% in 2014 (OECD, 2017).

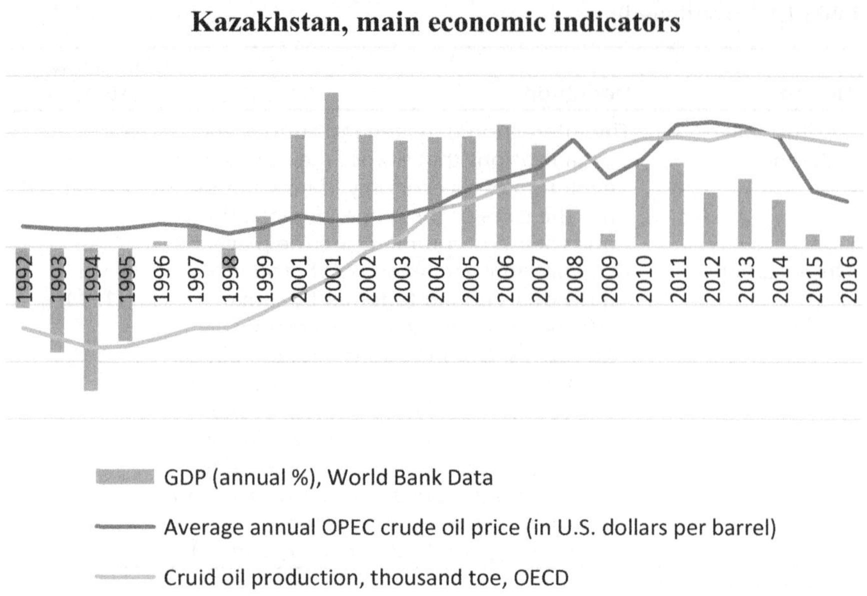

Fig. 1.1 Annual GDP growth, crude oil production in Kazakhstan, and world oil prices, 1992–2016. (Source: Own processed data based on WB, OECD, and OPEC)

These data show that since 1991, FDI inflows in the country have significantly increased (Fig. 1.2), with most investments in the natural resource sector. According to OECD (2017) data, one-third of state revenue, 16% of all value-added activities, 30% of GDP, and, ultimately, two-thirds of the country's total exports are derived from the oil and gas sector.

FDI inflows to Kazakhstan have fluctuated considerably over the past ten years. FDI reached several peaks since 2001 and declined after the financial crisis in 2008, only to rise again in 2016. The recent rise in FDI can be explained by new investment opportunities in major exploratory projects in the O&G industry. In this respect, Kazakhstan remains significantly ahead of most post-Soviet countries, even Russia, a country considerable larger in terms of territory and population. Because the domestic consumer market size of Kazakhstan is very small and the country is abundant in natural endowments, the main motive for foreign investments remains to be resource seeking.

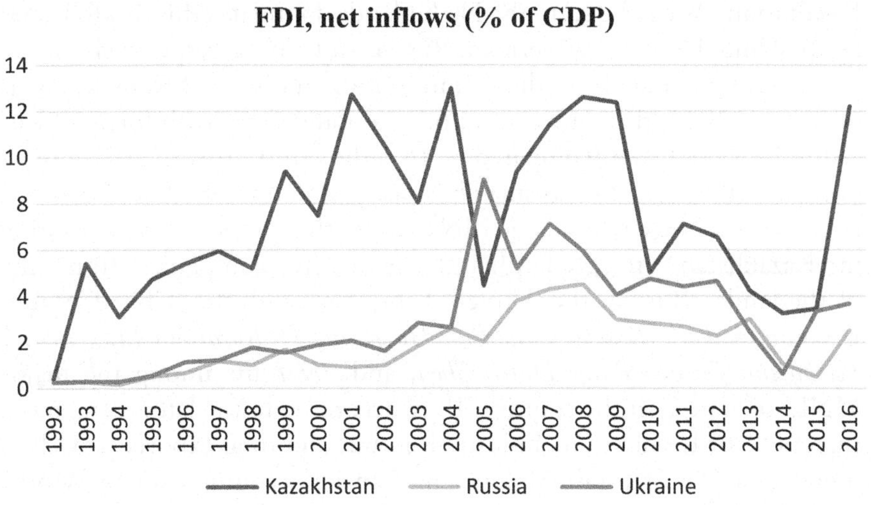

Fig. 1.2 FDI, new inflows as % of GDP in Kazakhstan, Russia, and Ukraine, 1992–2016. (Source: Own processed data based on WB)

Table 1.2 Top ten FDI inflows in Kazakhstan, by country, 2018

Country	FDI inflow, Mln USD	Share of total, %
Netherlands	7350.0	34
United States	5342.8	24
Switzerland	2540.8	12
Russia	1499.2	7
China	1476.2	7
Belgium	1049.0	5
France	916.1	4
United Kingdom	593.1	3
South Korea	478.9	2
Luxemburg	470.1	2

Source: Own processed data based on NBK

Analysis of the investment environment shows that Kazakhstan is closely connected with various countries of the EU, as they are the country's main investors. Additionally, powerful countries, such as the United States, Russia, China, and Japan, are currently actively investing in Kazakhstan. Table 1.2 shows a list of the ten largest investing countries in

Kazakhstan. As can be seen, the Netherlands dominates this list, followed by the United States, Switzerland, Russia, and China, respectively.

According to data from the Committee on Statistics of Kazakhstan, as of January 2020, there are about 26.7 thousand firms with foreign ownership in Kazakhstan (compared to 14.6 thousand firms in 2010): most of them can be classified as small businesses, some are medium-sized and large MNEs. The data on large MNEs notes that of these firms operating in Kazakhstan are predominantly extractive companies from the Netherlands, Russia, the United Kingdom, and the United States. *Chevron*, *Lukoil*, *Texaco*, *Canadian Hurricane Hydrocarbon Ltd.*, *British Petroleum*, *Exxon*, *Royal Dutch Shell*, and *Total* are among the major MNEs operating in the country. Thus, according to the latest data, more than 60% of Kazakhstan's industrial output and total exports, as well as more than 5% of total employment, can be accounted for by MNEs (OECD, 2017).

Kazakhstan's investment policy itself represents a flexible form of regulatory policy. Kazakhstan guarantees the legal protection of investments to create more favorable conditions for existing and potential investors. The Washington Convention of 1966, which was concerned with legal dispute resolution and conciliation between international investors, is applicable to the territory of Kazakhstan. As such, all foreign arbitration decisions regarding disputed investment issues between foreign citizens and states must be recognized by Kazakhstan. Moreover, more than 40 bilateral investment treaties are currently valid in Kazakhstan. This gives foreign investors confidence in the security of their rights. Such steps show the desire of the Government of Kazakhstan to provide an institutional environment that is equal in terms of international norms and rules. These documents are important to investors, especially if their home institutional environment is more developed than that of the host country. The greater the difference between the institutional development in the MNE's home country and in the host country, the more *liability of foreignness*[4] investors face (Peng & Meyer, 2011). Investors' competitiveness will be lower in comparison to local firms, which are

[4] Additional costs arising from the unfamiliarity of the environment, from cultural, political, and economic differences, and from the need for coordination across geographic distance (Zaheer, 1995).

used to working in a local institutional environment. Accordingly, the ratification of the above international documents has helped Kazakhstan to reduce the institutional gap between the state and the home countries of potential and existing investors.

According to the World Bank (2019), Kazakhstan has recently made a significant leap in the *Doing Business* rankings, improving its position from 51st in 2015 to 28th by the end of 2018. The significance of this jump cannot be underestimated, given that this rating evaluates more than 190 countries. Kazakhstan was able to achieve these results due to the fact that it had ratified a number of international agreements to improve its investment environment. These agreements, in turn, demanded the country carry out various institutional reforms. Obviously, such changes can have a positive impact on the strategic decision-making process of investors regarding a potential country as a location for their activities. The higher the rating of the state, the more investors will be interested in investing in the country. Ultimately, investors are interested in those countries in which they face fewer barriers for doing business. If it was not consistently receiving feedback from both existing and potential foreign investors, Kazakhstan is unlikely to be capable of finishing these reforms. To attract more investment, the Foreign Investors' Council (FIC) was created in 1998, with the main objective of creating conditions for bilateral dialogue between investors and the government. The most acute problems investors face are raised during meetings with the FIC, and possible solutions are discussed.

Low levels of protection on private and intellectual property rights reduce the country's attractiveness for investment (Acemoglu, Johnson & Robinson, 2005). This is mainly because companies, when planning to enter a new market, must be sure that their competitive advantages will be protected in the host country (Peng & Meyer, 2011). This problem is directly linked to the low level of development of legal norms and their effectiveness, as well as law enforcement. Many studies in this field have confirmed that the stronger and more developed legal institutions are, the more investors will be interested in doing business in the region, and some economic sectors will be developed more effectively and speedily (La Porta, Lopez-de-Silanes, & Shleifer, 1998). Therefore, protecting investors' interests in the host country is of paramount importance. The

Government of Kazakhstan has signed and ratified various agreements on the protection of intellectual property rights as part of its move toward improving the investment environment. The main laws regulating intellectual property in Kazakhstan include the Agreement on Trade-Related Aspects of Intellectual Property Rights, the Civil Code of Kazakhstan, the Law on Patent, and the Law on Copying and Neighboring Rights.

The presence of competitive local suppliers and buyers is of crucial importance to the country, as these conditions create jobs and improve the competitiveness of the whole economy. Importing intermediate goods and services, especially if the country is relatively distant, can significantly increase transportation costs for companies producing final goods in Kazakhstan. Therefore, Kazakhstan has made a number of changes to the formation of its competitive local business environment. The government established the Agency for Protection of Competition and allocated significant amount of money to the agency's budget. Therefore, for example, if the budget totaled US $4.5 billion in 2012, it then increased by more than double, equal to US $11.7 billion, in 2014 (Kazakh Invest, n/d). To achieve this, the agency had employed more than 190 full-time specialists. Recently, the World Bank published its report on Global Competitiveness Index (GCI) 2017–2018 where Kzakhstan is ranked 57th among 137 countries, and is positioned at 114th according to the intensity of local competition criteria and also ranked 84th in terms of the effectiveness of anti-monopoly policies. This shows that further improvements are still necessary.

The report notes that Kazakhstan is, at present, in transition from stage 1 to stage 2 of development, according to the well-known economic theory, distinguishing three specific stages of development—factors-driven, efficiency-driven, and innovation-driven (Porter, 1990; Porter, Sachs, & McArthur, 2002). This means that the competitiveness of the economy hinges primarily on well-developed institutions, a robust infrastructure, a stable macroeconomic environment, and a healthy workforce that has received at least a basic education. Kazakhstan has begun to invest in higher education and training, developing markets for goods (both domestic and foreign), labor, and finances that are harnessing benefits of different technologies. However, although these positive changes have not yet promoted Kazakhstan into a leading position according to the criteria of the competitiveness of the local business environment, innovation, and the competitiveness of the country as a whole, the indicators show a continuing trend toward further improvements. Furthermore, developmental efforts need to be put into the GCI's business sophistication pillar of competitiveness, including quality of business networks at the country level, as well as quality of individual firms' strategies. Development efforts also need to be placed into the innovation pillar of economy, specific for stage 3 of a country's development, namely innovation-driven growth, in order to catch up with advanced economies.

With this aim, Kazakhstan has begun to support and develop local companies in the O&G industry. With the introduction of the Law of the Republic of Kazakhstan "On Subsoil and Subsoil Use" in 2010, a local content policy (LCP), which is an industrial development policy specific for resource-rich counties, was launched in Kazakhstan. This policy includes procurement, labor, and technology transfer policies, as well as social projects. Special economic zones (SEZ) were created in 2011 in accordance with the Law of the Republic of Kazakhstan. Among the ten SEZ, three were created for the petro-chemical industry and one for the information and communication technology (ICT) industry. All these arrangements are considered to be part of LCP. Financial support is provided by a number of organizations, including the JSC *National Management Holding Baiterek* (founded in 2013). The company offers financial and investment support for the non-O&G sector, cooperates with the private sector, and develops business clusters, defined as "geographic concentration of interconnected companies, specialised suppliers, service providers, firms in related industries, and associated institutions (for example universities, standard agencies, and trade associations) in particular field, that compete but also co-operate" (Porter, 1998: 197).

With the launch in 2010 of the State Program *Business Road Map 2020*, the Entrepreneurship Development Fund *Damu* (established in 1997) has developed a range of tools to support small and medium enterprises (SMEs). This includes subsidization of interest rates on loans, credit guarantees, training, and consulting services. The mission of the *Development Bank of Kazakhstan* (DBK), which was founded in 2001, is "to promote sustainable development of the national economy by investments into non-resource sector of the country" (DBK, n/d).

<table>
<tr><th></th><th colspan="3">Internal domain</th><th colspan="3">External domain</th></tr>
<tr><th>Level</th><th>Infrastructure (tax incentives for local enterprises)</th><th>Finance (local enterprises support)</th><th>Market (opportunities for domestic companies)</th><th>Labor (local skills)</th><th>Technology (local capabilities)</th><th>Procurement (local goods)</th></tr>
<tr><td>Extractive</td><td>SEZ Atyrau
SEZ Taraz
SEZ Pavlodar</td><td rowspan="2">Entrepreneurship development fund (DAMU), Development Bank of Kazakhstan</td><td>Public procurement by NOC KazMunayGas</td><td>Local labor employment requirements
Training</td><td rowspan="2">The state program for Accelerated Industrial and Innovative Development</td><td>Local procurement requirements</td></tr>
<tr><td>Non-extractive</td><td>SEZ Aktau (seaport)
SEZ Ontustik (textile)
SEZ Park of Innovative Technologies (ICT)
SEZ Khorgos (logistics)
SEZ Saryarka (metal)
SEZ Astana (urban)
SEZ Burabay (tourism)</td><td>Public procurement by state enterprises</td><td></td><td>Local procurement Requirement in ICT</td></tr>
</table>

Fig. 1.3 Building blocks of local development policy in Kazakhstan. (Source: Heim, 2019)

The building blocks of LCP in Kazakhstan are presented in Fig. 1.3.

First, the *State Program of Local Content Development in the Republic of Kazakhstan in 2010–2014* was launched for the period of 2010–2014, and currently the *State Program of Accelerated Industrial and Innovative Development* of the Republic of Kazakhstan for 2015–2019 is in operation. The measures to promote local content[5] (LC) were also envisaged by the RK's sectoral development programs for 2010–2014. These are programs to promote LC in the chemical, nuclear, and electric engineering industries, as well as in information and communication technologies, the O&G industry, mining and metallurgy, mechanical engineering, agricultural industry, tourism, light industry, construction industry, and production of building materials. A list of the main legal regulations on LC in the O&G and ICT industries in RK can be found in Table 1.3.

[5] Value-added activities in which local businesses compete with foreign companies for contracts in the industry, as well as broader social participation by the foreign investors (Kalyuzhnova, 2008).

Table 1.3 Selected regulations on LC in O&G and ICT industries of the RK

Regulation	Number/ Date	Title
Decree of the President of the RK	№ 922 01.02.2010	Strategic Plan for Development of the RK until the year 2020
Decree of the President of the RK	№ 957 19.03.2010	List of State Programs
Decree of the President of the RK	№ 958 19.03.2010	The State Program of Accelerated Industrial and Innovative Development of the RK for 2010–2014
Law of the RK	№ 291-IV 24.06.2010	On Subsoil and Subsoil Use
Decree of the Government of the RK	№ 964 20.09.2010	Uniform accounting treatment to Kazakhstani LC by organizations when purchasing goods, works, and services
Decree of the Government of the RK	№ 1038 09.08.2012	Rules of conducting examination according to LC
Decree of the President of the RK	№ 874 01.08.2014	State Program of Accelerated Industrial and Innovative Development of the RK for 2015–2019
Decree of the President of the RK	№ 986 26.12.2014	Anti-corruption Strategy of the Republic of Kazakhstan for 2015–2025
Decree of the Government of the RK	№ 1418 31.12.2014	Map of industrialization
Decree of the Minister of Investments and Development of the RK	№ 87 30.01.2015	Single calculation procedure by the organizations of LC when purchasing goods, works, and services
Joint Decree of the Minister of Investments and Development of the RK and the Minister of Energy of the RK	№ 538, № 330 30.04.2015	Forms and rules of creation and submission of annual, medium-term, and long-term programs of purchase of goods, works, and services, reports of subsoil users on goods purchased, works, and services, and on obligation fulfillment on LC in personnel

(continued)

Table 1.3 (continued)

Regulation	Number/ Date	Title
Law of the RK	№ 438-V 07.12.2015	On Astana[a] International Financial Center
Decree of the Government of the RK	№ 827 12.12.2017	State Program "Digital Kazakhstan"

Source: Own processed data based on Legal information system of Regulatory Legal Acts of the Republic of Kazakhstan available at http://adilet.zan.kz
[a]The capital city of Kazakhstan has been renamed to Nur-Sultan in March 2019 to honor outgoing ex-President Nursultan Nazarbayev

Despite all these efforts, however, an analysis of technological capabilities in Kazakhstan shows that main technological capability indicators of Kazakhstan, in comparison with other emerging countries, remain low (see Table 1.4). This is why emerging countries like Kazakhstan need to be willing to encourage activities that enable firms to choose and use technology from abroad (if it does not exist within the country), to create a competitive advantage, as well as to develop local technological capabilities (Yu & Li-Hua, 2010).

In January 2014, the Government of Kazakhstan announced *The Strategic Plan for development of the Republic of Kazakhstan until the year 2020*. The Kazakh government has also introduced the *State Program of Accelerated Industrial and Innovative Development 2015–2020* (SPFIID) in order to implement the main provisions of these strategic documents.

Another important national document is the *Plan of the Nation 100 Concrete Steps* to implement the five institutional reforms proposed by the former President of Kazakhstan in 2015. It is designed to support the effort to join the top 30 developed countries by 2050. This document is closely linked to improvements in the investment environment, as its main goals are the development of a professional civil service, ensuring the rule of law, industrialization, economic growth, identity and unity, and establishing an accountable state. One example of such improvements is that Kazakhstan, over the past three years, has eased the process of acquiring a license; for example, the license to conduct business

Table 1.4 Technological capability in selected emerging countries in 2018

Indicator	Czech Republic	Hungary	Kazakhstan	Russian Federation	Ukraine	China
FDI stock, % of GDP	64.10	57.01	89.43	25.00	35.12	11.96
R&D expenditure, % of GDP	1.8	1.4	0.1	1.1	0.4	2.1
Researchers in R&D, per Mln people	3690	2924	662	2852	994	1235
Patent applications, non-residents	54	36	193	13,031	1861	148,187
Patent applications, residents	678	407	789	24,926	2207	1,393,815

Source: Own processed data based on WB and UNCTAD statistical databases

activities can now be obtained within two weeks, when three years ago obtaining it could take more than a month. This improvement is directly related to the introduction of the *Concept of the Further Reforming of the Licensing System of the Republic of Kazakhstan for 2012–2015*. Over this period of time, a system of e-licensing was introduced, which has significantly reduced the time, and simplified the process, of obtaining a license for such activities as business registration or obtaining a special permit for construction work (OECD, 2017). The section *Ensuring the Rule of Law* in the *Plan of the Nation 100 Concrete Steps* forms the main part of the document describing specific actions required on the part of the state in terms of institutional reforms. In recent years, Kazakhstan has significantly improved its processes of enforcing contracts and resolving disputes between the state and investors through its local and national courts. According to the World Bank's *Doing Business Report* for 2019, Kazakhstan currently ranks at 28th place among 190 countries. This progress is also reflected in the World Bank's survey of large MNEs. In 2013, less than 10% of all large MNEs operating in Kazakhstan considered the main problem and limitation to doing business in the country was the judicial system. These improvements are directly associated with the implementation of special procedures to resolve issues with investors and a result of the introduction of mandatory qualification requirements and training, as well as the procedure of revision activities for judges at all levels (OECD, 2017).

Kazakhstan's state strategy until 2050 identifies and underlines the paramount importance of combating increased levels of corruption in the country. Corruption can be defined as the deliberate abuse of power or illegal use and distribution of resources for personal gain (Shleifer & Vishny, 1993). High levels of corruption in a country increase the uncertainty of doing business, which in turn leads to increased costs (Cuervo-Cazurra, 2006) and decreased exports (Lee & Weng, 2013). At the end of 2014, the former President signed the *Anti-corruption Strategy of the Republic of Kazakhstan for 2015–2025 years*, designed to be the most effective solution to this problem.

The Government of Kazakhstan has recently made several attempts to establish quasi-public authorities that attract and support foreign investors in particular, as the main problem of the country remains to be access to financing, so investment opportunities are still limited. As such, organizations like the *Development Bank of Kazakhstan*, the National Holding *Baiterek*, the Entrepreneurship Development Fund *Damu*, and *KazAgro* have been created, in addition to special programs for subsidies and financing projects in the country. These companies provide advisory and financial support for investment projects; the Entrepreneurship Development Fund *Damu*, for example, offers low credit rates and flexible loan terms for companies that are engaged in local content (LC) development (Kazakh Invest, n/d).

So-called "one-stop shops" were established across the entire country of Kazakhstan; they were created in consultation with PricewaterhouseCoopers and with funding by both central state bodies and local executive authorities (Kazakh Invest, n/d). They are special institutions accountable to the Ministry for Investment and Development of the Republic of Kazakhstan (MID), the main purpose of which is to provide advisory support to investors. These initiatives are particularly important for foreign investors unfamiliar with business administration rules in foreign markets. The provision of financial and advisory support for foreign firms from the state helps to minimize the costs associated with liability of foreignness.

The Entrepreneurial Code of the Republic of Kazakhstan (EC) came into force in 2016 and is the main document regulating issues on the interaction of the state with investors and issues on competition, among others. This code is an update of the *Law on Competition*, adopted in 2008, and it replaced the previous *Law on Investment*, as well as other normative acts on regulating and protecting the rights of investors. The main aim of the EC is to protect the rights of investors who are facing direct confiscation of their firm's property by the government. Moreover, the EC ensures complete compensation in the case of damage that arises from illegal actions by the state; in such instances, the amount of indemnification is calculated according to current market value. In addition, the EC is different to previous laws in that it provides increased rights and safeguards for the protection rights and property. The application of such new regulatory codes and laws helps resolve any problems associated with ambiguities in legal documents that may lead to the wrong interpretation of the implemented laws (Peng & Meyer, 2011).

Kazakhstan's accession to the World Trade Organization (WTO) in 2016 has led to a new stage of institutional reforms. As such, Kazakhstan needs to adapt its institutional environment to the requirements of WTO standards by 2020. This will require removal of some restrictions, for example, most performance requirements, such as local content rules, restrictions on ownership of fixed telecommunications for foreign legal entities, the ban on the activities of subsidiaries of foreign banks, and restrictions on hiring foreign employees. Thus, in the subsequent and coming years, the state needed to and needs to re-design institutional policies according to WTO requirements.

In 2014, Kazakhstan joined the EAEU. This fact may also have contributed significantly to the revision of the local institutional system. Many of the economic barriers faced by Kazakhstani businesses may be reduced or eliminated in the future through the activities in international economic organizations. In the era of globalization, the role of such international organizations cannot be underestimated. They create a favorable framework for the free movement of capital, knowledge, labor, and other critical factors that stimulate market mechanisms.

The Astana International Financial Center (AIFC) was established as a part of the *100 Concrete Steps* Plan of the Nation, the government's attempt to modernize the financial sector. The main purpose of the center is to create unique and favorable conditions for the development of financial and banking services. A special judicial system, formed on the basis of the English legal system (common law), will operate in all territories of the AIFC. The AIFC will adopt all the best practices that other international financial centers[6] employ, such as minimal regulation and taxation of residents, as well as a favorable social environment.

To summarize, the main governance[7] indicators developed by the WB demonstrate the most important institutional changes carried out in Kazakhstan between 1996 and 2016, especially in comparison with its neighbors, Russia and China. As can be seen from Fig. 1.4 (a and b), the Government of Kazakhstan significantly increased its effectiveness and regulatory quality in the period between 1996 and 2016. Compared

[6] Such as London, Singapore, Dubai, Paris, Toronto, and New York.

[7] That is, the traditions and institutions by which authority in a country is exercised.

a

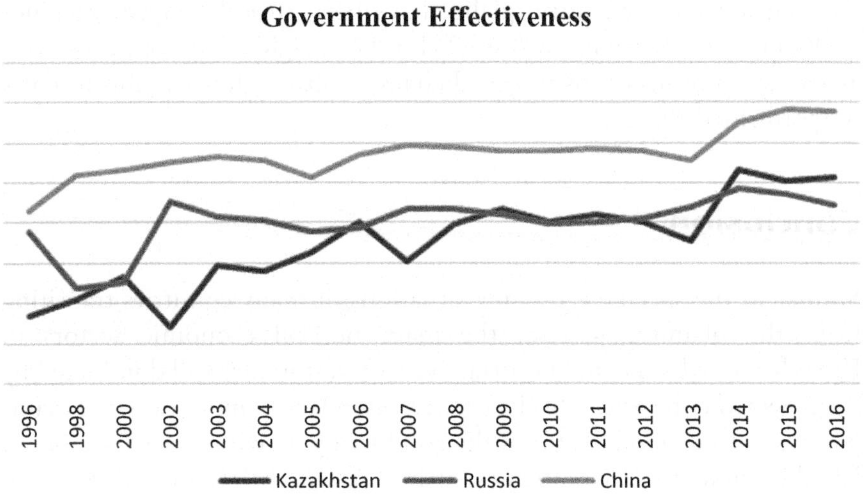

b

Fig. 1.4 (a and b) Governance indicators in Kazakhstan, Russia, and China, 1996–2016. (Source: Authors' own processed data based on WGI, World Bank)

to the 1990s, the criteria regarding the government effectiveness, rule of law, and overall regulatory quality have been steadily improving since 2006; however, Kazakhstan is still behind its neighboring countries, such as China, in terms of institutional changes, although it has also recently outperformed Russia.

Conclusion

Similar to the specific economic situations of many countries transiting from the planning system, the main non-oil economic sectors in Kazakhstan, which could be attractive to investors, are still dominated by state-owned enterprises (SOEs). SOEs often lack competition; for example, there were about 1200 SOEs conducting activities in 15 sectors in Kazakhstan in 2016. Companies, such as *Temir Zholy* (railways), *Samruk-Kazyna* (national welfare fund), *KazAgro* (agriculture), and others, are some of the largest SOEs operating in Kazakhstan. This obviously has a constraining effect on the whole economy, as competition stimulates supply. With the aim of giving an economy a new impetus for growth, as well as to reduce state ownership, the government launched an active program for privatization of SOEs in 2015. In total, 65 state-owned companies and 175 of their subsidiaries are in the process of being transferred partially or entirely to the private sector via a combination of negotiations, auctions, and IPOs by 2020 (O'Casey & Batchilo, 2016). Regardless, an additional effort might be necessary to develop competition in some industrial and economic sectors of Kazakhstan where the share of the quasi-public sector is still high, and foreign companies may have increased costs due to their liability of foreignness, causing difficulties for foreign newcomers to compete with SOEs that have legal and financial support from the state. On the other hand, the SOEs may have additional transaction costs due to their size, as well as their inability to react to changing market demands. This will also allow broader groups of investors to benefit from the Kazakh economy, especially local private investors.

In addition to the large share of state participation in the economy, there are challenges associated with the implementation of government initiatives in Kazakhstan. The main reason for the failure of these projects is often unqualified and untrained human resources, as well as a lack of effective management. This results in low wages for local workers, in comparison to foreign labor. In order to further develop a sufficient qualified local labor force, the country needs to make more investment in the educational system. The RK government introduced a limit on the share of foreign specialists in the category of corporate employees; however, this can make hiring foreign specialists with specific knowledge currently absent from the local labor market difficult. For example, a foreign specialist must obtain a special work permit in order to be transferred to work in another region of the country. Each region of the country has its own specific quota for the number of foreign workers. Under such restrictions, foreign companies often consider alternative locations for their activities; for example, China National Petroleum Corporation decided to open a new ICT service center in Dubai, in addition to Kazakhstan, as Dubai has no such restrictions on hiring foreign specialists.

The local economy in Kazakhstan needs to be further developed. Compared to countries such as Turkey, for example, where small and medium businesses account for 60% of GDP, local companies in Kazakhstan make up almost three times less. Therefore, the economy currently perceives a low ability of its SME sector to benefit from new information, technology, and innovation and cannot apply new knowledge within their own business practices. Consequently, local firms do not increase their production and do not create new jobs. All this leads to the fact that local citizens remain heavily dependent on the state and foreign firms in terms of employment, wages, and savings. Finally, because the level of domestic investment cannot be increased and the country remains dependent on foreign investments, Kazakhstan has limited ability to grow its financial sector.

Kazakhstan's government has attempted to make various institutional reforms and allocates funds for the development of the country's infrastructure, as well as to improve the legal and judicial system. Overall, there is a positive trend in government efforts regarding the importance of business institutions in the country, in such a way as to further improvements in the investment environment. Still, the main problem remains the effectiveness of these governmental initiatives, which need to be improved in order to reduce state budget expenditures in a new economic situation of low oil prices. The problems that investors face in practice need to be recognized; for example, not only large MNEs but also small foreign firms need to be represented in the most important discussion platform that exists between the government and such investors. This means that the opinions of foreign SME representatives are not taken into account. This assertion is confirmed by the cooperation between legislators and investors. Consequently, this broader participation will give the government proof, with more detailed feedback from foreign firms regarding the effectiveness of its institutional reforms.

Even though a wide inventory of natural resources blesses Kazakhstan's economy, especially in the initial stages of development, these resources currently constrain the country's level of investment attractiveness. Kazakhstan has only made feeble attempts to diversify its economy, and efforts to further development in other sectors of the economy need to be made. Thus, Kazakhstan is not fully utilizing its locational advantages to make it attractive to investments that could accelerate its entry into the top 30 advanced countries of the world. The next steps in economic advancement require improvement of the country's educational system, with the aim of training specialized personnel, strengthening the accountability of public initiatives, and developing projects by integrating private investment to them. A change in cultural perception, especially toward corruption and bureaucracy, is also necessary. Kazakhstan must also facilitate broad participation of investors in its rule-making process, as well as strengthening local industry and continuing the further diversification of its economy. The main location advantage of Kazakhstan is its strategic position between China, Russia, and the EU, on this so-called *New Silk Road*. These potential future developments arising from the geopolitical and internal factors and initiatives will be considered in detail in the next chapters.

Bibliography

Acemoglu, D., Johnson, S., & Robinson, J. (2005). Institutions as the fundamental cause of long-run growth. In P. Aghion & S. N. Durlauf (Eds.), *Handbook of economic growth* (pp. 385–472). New York, NY: Elsevier.

Aoki, M. (2001). *Toward a comparative institutional analysis*. Cambridge, MA: MIT Press.

Barney, J. (1991). Firm resources and sustained competitive advantage. *Journal of Management, 17*(1), 99–120.

Begg, D., & Ward, D. (2013). *Economics for business*. Maidenhead, UK: McGraw-Hill Education.

Berglof, E., & Bolton, P. (2002). The great divide and beyond: Financial architecture in transition. *Journal of Economic Perspectives, 16*(1), 77–100.

Cuervo-Cazurra, A. (2006). Who cares about corruption? *Journal of International Business Studies, 37*(6), 807–822.

DiMaggio, P. J., & Powell, W. W. (1983). The iron cage revisited: Institutional isomorphism and collective rationality in organizational fields. *Economic Journal, 65*(4), 691–716.

Granovetter, M. (1985). Economic action and social structure: The problem of embeddedness. *American Journal of Sociology, 91*(3), 481–510.

Heim, I. (2019). *Local content policy and value co-creation: Adopting information technologies in the oil and gas industry* (Unpublished doctoral dissertation). Reading, UK: University of Reading,

Hoff, K., & Stiglitz, J. E. (2004). *The transition from communism: a diagrammatic exposition of obstacles to the demand for the rule of law*. The World Bank.

Kalyuzhnova, Y. (2008). *Economics of the Kaspian oil and gas wealth: Companies, governments, policies*. New York, NY: Palgrave Macmillan.

Kalyuzhnova, Y., Nygaard, C., Omarov, Y., & Saparbayev, A. (2016). *Local content policies in resource-rich countries*. London, UK: Palgrave Macmillan.

Kazakh Invest. (n.d.). *Why Kazakhstan?* Retrieved from: http://invest.gov.kz.

Khakas, H., & Kohli, H. (2011). What is the middle-income trap, why do countries fall into it, and how can it be avoided? *Global Journal of Emerging Market Economies, 3*(3), 281–289.

Kostova, T., Roth, K., & Dacin, M. T. (2008). Institutional theory in the study of multinational corporations: a critique and new directions. *Academy of Management Review, 33*(4), 994–1006.

Kraft, M. E. & Furlong, S. R. (2007). *Public Policy*. Washington, D.C.: CQ Press.

La Porta, R., Lopez-de-Silanes, F., & Shleifer, A. (1998). Law and finance. *Journal of Political Economy, 106*, 1115–1155.

Lee, S.-H., & Weng, D. (2013). Does bribery in the home country promote or dampen firm exports? *Strategic Management Journal, 34*(12), 1472–1487.

Lusch, R. F., & Vargo, S. L. (2014). *Service-dominant logic: Premises, perspectives, possibilities*. New York, NY: Cambridge University Press.

Meyer, J. W., & Rowan, B. (1977). Institutionalized organizations: Formal structure as myth and ceremony. *American Journal of Sociology, 83*(2), 340–363.

Meyer, J. W., & Scott, W. R. (1983). *Organizational environments: Ritual and rationality*. Beverly Hills, CA: Sage.

Meyer, J. W., & Rowan, B. (1983). The structure of educational organizations. In J. W. Meyer & W. R. Scott (Eds.), *Organizational environments: Ritual and rationality* (pp. 71–97). Beverly Hills, CA: Sage.

Moe, T. M. (1984). The new economics of organization. *American Journal of Political Science, 28*(4), 739–777.

Narula, R., & Dunning, J. (2000). Industrial development, globalization and multinational enterprises: New realities for developing countries. *Oxford Development Studies, 28*(2), 141–167.

Nelson, R. R., & Winter, S. G. (1982). The Schumpeterian trade-off revisited. *American Economic Review, 72*(1), 114–132.

North, D. C. (1994). Economic performance through time. *The American Economic Review, 84*(3), 359–368.

O'Casey, E., & Batchilo, A. (2016, July 28). Kazakhstan: Privatization versus control. *Forbes*. Retrieved from: https://www.forbes.com/sites/riskmap/2016/07/28/kazakhstan-privatization-versus-control/#4777d547ede6

OECD. (2015). *Policy framework for investment*. Retrieved from OECD website: doi:https://doi.org/10.1787/9789264208667-en

OECD. (2017). *OECD investment policy reviews: Kazakhstan 2017*. Retrieved from OECD website: doi:https://doi.org/10.1787/9789264269200-4-en

Parsons, T. (1956). Suggestions for a sociological approach to the theory of organizations – I. *Administrative Science Quarterly, 1*(1), 63–85.

Parsons, T., & Jones, I. (1960). *Structure and process in modern societies*. New York, NY: Free Press.

Peng, M. M. & Meyer, K. E. (2011). *International Business*. London, U. K.: Sengage Learning.

Penrose, E. T. (1959). *The theory of the growth of the firm*. Oxford, UK: Basil Blackwell.

Porter, M., Sachs, J., & McArthur, J. (2002). Executive summary: Competitiveness and stages of economic development. In M. Porter, J. Sachs,

P. K. Cornelius, J. W. McArthur, & K. Schwab (Eds.), *The global competitiveness report 2001–2002* (pp. 16–25). New York, NY: Oxford University Press.
Porter, M. E. (1990). *The competitive advantage of nations*. New York, NY: Macmillan.
Porter, M. E. (1998). *On competition*. Cambridge, MA: Harvard Business School Press.
Scott, W. R. (1991). Unpacking institutional arguments. In P. J. DiMaggio & W. W. Powell (Eds.), *The new institutionalism in organizational analysis* (pp. 164–182). Chicago, IL: The University of Chicago Press.
Scott, W. R. (1995/2014). *Institutions and organizations*. Thousand Oaks, CA: Sage.
Shleifer, A & Vishny, R. W. (1993), Corruption. *Quarterly Journal of Economics*, 108, 599–617.
Tolbert, P. S., & Zucker, L. G. (1983). Institutional sources of change in the formal structure of organizations: The diffusion of civil service reform, 1880-1935. *Administrative Science Quarterly, 28*(1), 22–39.
UNCTAD. (2003). *Foreign direct investment and performance requirements: New evidence from selected countries*. Retrieved from United Nations Conference on Trade and Development website: http://unctad.org/en/Docs/iteiia20037_en.pdf
Vargo, S. L., Wieland, H., & Akaka, M. A. (2015). Innovation through institutionalization: A service ecosystems perspective. *Industrial Marketing Management, 44*(1), 63–72.
Williamson, O. E. (2000). The new institutional economics: Taking stock, looking ahead. *Journal of Economic Literature, 38*(3), 595–613.
World Bank (2019). Doing Business 2019. Retrieved from: https://www.doingbusiness.org/en/reports/global-reports/doing-business-2019
Xu, D., & Meyer, K. E. (2013). Linking theory and context: Strategy research in emerging economies after Wright et al. (2005). *Journal of Management Studies, 50*(7), 1322–1346.
Yu, J., & Li-Hua, R. (2010). *China's highway of information and communication technology*. London, UK: Palgrave Macmillan.
Zaheer, S. (1995). Overcoming the liability of foreignness. *Academy of Management Journal, 38*(2), 341–363.
Zucker, L. G. (1977). The role of institutionalization in cultural persistence. *American Sociological Review, 41*(5), 726–743.
Zucker, L. G. (1987). Institutional theories of organization. *Annual Review of Sociology, 13*(1), 443–464.

2

The Oil and Gas Industry in Kazakhstan's Investment Regimes

Irina Heim and Maxim Romanov

Introduction

After Kazakhstan's declaration of independence, foreign investors, the majority of whom had been attracted to petroleum production activities, contributed US $146,064 billion of FDI (UNCTAD, 2017). Since 2000, oil production in Kazakhstan has increased rapidly due to foreign investment and improvements in production efficiencies, which were contributions from firms with some of the world's best practices who were attracted to the country. Today, a landmark foreign investment in Kazakhstan's oil industry is the TengizChevroil joint venture, owned 50% by ChevronTexaco, 25% by ExxonMobil, 20% by the Government of Kazakhstan, and 5% by LukArco of Russia. International companies

I. Heim (✉)
Henley Business School, University of Reading, Reading, UK
e-mail: irina.heim@henley.ac.uk

M. Romanov
Kazakh-British Centre for Competitiveness, Almaty, Kazakhstan

I. Heim (ed.), *Kazakhstan's Diversification from the Natural Resources Sector*, Euro-Asian Studies, https://doi.org/10.1007/978-3-030-37389-4_2

such as Shell, Agip, Chevron, and Lukoil have developed the Karachaganak natural oil and gas condensate field. Recently, Chinese, Indian, and Korean oil companies have also entered Kazakhstan's oil industry.

Since its independence in 1991, Kazakhstan has never ranked higher than 82nd for its human development index and thus is in the middle of the list of developing countries (see Baldakhov & Heim, 2020, this volume). Worth noting is that Kazakhstan has been referred to as one of the *countries in transition*, being a former Soviet Union country according to IMF classification. At present, Kazakhstan has been widely regarded as an *emerging* nation. What does it mean for the investments in the O&G sector, and how can these dynamics be explained?

Institutional theory is increasingly applied to the study of foreign investments since it provides a rich theoretical foundation for examining a wide range of critical issues and also allows for theorizing at multiple levels of analysis, which is essential for this research (Kostova et al., 2008). In this chapter we will discuss the evolution of the investment regime in Kazakhstan with a focus on the O&G industry investments.

Evolution of the Investment Regime, Subsoil Legislation, and Petroleum Fiscal Systems in Kazakhstan

Early post-Soviet Times: 1991–1993

The period of Kazakhstan's emergence as a new independent state was extremely challenging. Additionally, low hydrocarbon prices contributed to the rupture of existing economic ties, exacerbated by a lack of experience in managing the economy, which led to a sharp drop in GDP (see Fig. 1.1) and an increase in poverty. The decisions taken by the government in these years, and the history of the creation of institutions (see Baldakhov & Heim, 2020, this volume), are examples of the lesson of recent economic history that creative interventions can be remarkably effective even when the investment climate, judged by standard criteria, is poor (Rodrik, 2003). Moreover, to create an attractive environment,

Kazakhstani institutions had to simultaneously solve the issues of supporting small cities, depending on the load of enterprises near which they were located, while also launching privatization programs, creating a new financial system, and so on.

By the time Kazakhstan achieved independence in 1991, the country had inherited Soviet legislation along with Soviet problems. A negative total factor productivity, which exacerbated the political and economic tensions of the late Communist society, was not recovered after the reforms of the mid-1980s, leaving the countries of the USSR in poor economic conditions. Over the decades of Soviet rule, the administrative system implemented consistent cutbacks in investment, which finally led the country to a period of stagnation. The revision of economic policy introduced by Gorbachev's government in the 1980s could not resolve the problem of ineffective distribution. The reforms of so-called *Perestroika* revealed that any attempts to redirect investment from unjustified productive projects to non-productive social projects failed due to weak input-output relationships built into the economic structure over the course of decades. The economic reforms of *Perestroika* could not solve the crisis of the internal investment system, which showed that the economy needed significant resources, along with modern technologies. Such technologies, however, were not available inside the country nor were there conditions for attracting business from the outside. Since this fact revealed the need to create conditions that could allow foreign capital to enter the country, legislation shifted toward the establishment and operation of joint enterprises, with the participation of Soviet organizations.

Post-Soviet Times: Most Favorable Investment Regime and the "Free Entry" Model—1994–1997

Post-Soviet republics, in their first steps toward independence and autonomy, had to face the crucial need of attracting foreign investment, along with creating a welcoming investment regime within the conditions of a fierce rivalry in the post-Soviet arena. As suggested by classical theories of foreign investment, the free-entry model can meet all these goals. In this model, the guarantees provided by the host government should prevail over requirements set for them (Sornarajah, 2004, 2017). Based on these ideas, Kazakhstan adopted the first *Law on Foreign Investment* in 1994.[1] For the first time, it provided foreign investors with a sound national regime that covered all investment activities. The national law guaranteed equal treatment for foreign investors and residents of the country. The promise of equal treatment was reflected in other legal documents, such as *the Civil Code* and *the Tax Code*. Along with this, it provided several significant guarantees as was suggested by the classical theory on foreign investment law. This reduced investment risks, ranking the country one of the tops among developing states for its favorable foreign investment entry model. The government was seriously concerned about attracting foreign capital into the economy in short-term, rather than in long-term perspective. Thus, those guarantees were assumed to promise a risk-free investment environment by introducing a system of safeguards that complied with the requirements of the free entry model.

There were seven principal initial guarantees outlined in the first law on foreign investment, covering promises of legal stability, protection from state interference, and freedom of financial flows.

1. The first and the foremost was the guarantee of stable legislation. Stability was meant to assure foreign investors that their investment would not be subject to changes in the host country's law. As will be discussed further, however, this guarantee did not really come into effect until ten years later in 2004.
2. The guarantee against expropriation provided a clause stating that the international practice of expropriation could be undertaken by the state only in cases explicitly defined in the statute and, if so, only in accordance with a particular legal procedure and with payment of adequate, prompt, and adequate compensation.
3. In addition, the law defined the principles of compensation for the cases of illegal action of the state or its officials, guaranteeing full compensation for the damage. At the same time, for the claims of damage

[1] Law of the Republic of Kazakhstan dated December 27, 1994, No. 266-XIII *On Foreign Investments*.

to foreign capital caused by *force majeure*, the compensation was to be paid in accordance with the national law.

4. Another important guarantee was that against interference by the state institutions and its officials in the activities of foreign investors. This guarantee was dedicated to the normative acts issued by the state and its officials against compliance with the law, thus worsening the conditions of foreign investment, which would be considered void. This aspect also included the guarantee against unauthorized state inspections, which meant that any state agency or official could inspect foreign investors' activities, but only within the scope of authority vested upon them by law. In this respect, foreign investors had a right not to respond to orders which were issued by the state or an official beyond the duties defined by law. They could also refuse to present information to them that is outside the scope of their authority.
5. Further guarantees were dedicated to the freedom of financial flows associated with investment activities. One of these was the guarantee of free use of dividends earned in the territory of the republic, which gives foreign investors the right of free reinvestment of the dividends received through initial investment for any other objectives which would be not prohibited by the national legislation of the country.
6. Following on from the previous rights listed above, the guarantee of the free transfer of currency abroad was introduced. All payments stipulated by law were guaranteed to be freely undertaken by a foreign investor. Furthermore, foreign investors were entitled to use hard currency to make payments for transactions occurring in the territory of the republic, as well as to pay salaries to the employees.
7. Finally, the law on foreign investment pretended to provide transparency for investment activity, which meant that foreign investors were guaranteed to have open access to all statutes and regulations, as well as court decisions, relevant to foreign investment. The law specified that foreign investors could have free access to information about the registration of juridical persons, on their charters, on the registration of real estate transactions, and on issued licenses. Free access to information did not apply to the data, which would constitute a commercial secret of another business entity or individual. With regard to the oil and gas business, all interested persons were allowed access to

information on the procedures for investment tenders and on their results, as well as information on a contract concluded between the state licensing authority and a winner of a bid. The information, which was agreed by the winner of the bid and a state organization to be confidential, could not be disclosed.

Moreover, the Law on Foreign Investment of 1994 took into account applicable law, which indeed allowed investors to choose an investment regime in favor of a more advantageous relationship between local laws and those in their home country, in the case that a bilateral treaty would be signed between their country of origin and Kazakhstan. At that time, Kazakhstan signed bilateral investment treaties, the vast majority of which were negotiated on so-called mutually beneficial clauses, with major capital exporting developed countries soon after their independence. This attempt to create a favorable investment regime was welcomed by international oil and gas companies, since it allowed them to strive for negotiations of conditions that benefitted them in terms of contract timeframes and production sharing agreements (PSAs), which were mostly based on the Indonesian model (Maulenov, 2005).

The concept of applicable law was reflected to a large extent in contracts in the petroleum sector since the early 1990s (Dosmukhamedov, 2003). At this stage of opening up the economy and attracting foreign investment, investors were understandably wary of Kazakhstan when choosing a recipient country because it had appeared on the world market as a new, previously unfamiliar subject of international economic relations (Esembayev, 2010). As a result, at the first stage, the range of investor countries was somewhat limited, as shown in Fig. 2.1.

Thus, the proclamation of the national regime of treatment of investments, along with the aforementioned guarantees, demonstrates Kazakhstan's willingness to adhere to an open and optimal model of regulation. The focus of the regulator on structural factors, rather than on conduct and control, sets up a facilitative institutional environment in which a foreign investor anticipates a longer commitment on the part of the state. The investing firm is therefore more willing to put down deeper

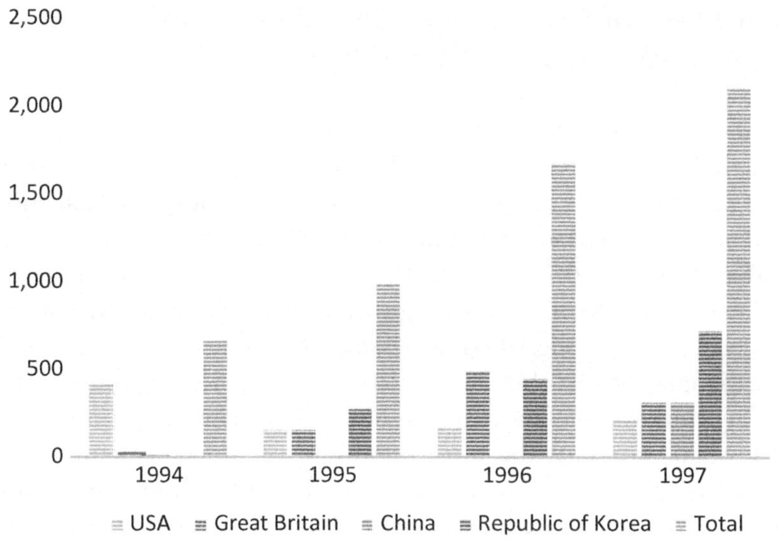

Fig. 2.1 Gross foreign investment inflows 1993–1997, billions USD. Source: Authors' own processed data based on the National Bank of Kazakhstan

roots in the host country. Accordingly, a predicted *spillover*[2] effect is likely to be more rooted in the sense of quality and the spread of knowledge-based assets to be diffused in the local economy. Nevertheless, further examination of the above clauses leads to the opposite conclusion. The first legislation on investment activities at that time was designed with the primary purpose of appearing favorable to foreign investors. In this regard, the government had to create as many guarantees, incentives, and preferences for the entry and presence of foreign capital as was possible within the bounds of adhering to national interests, all while making the climate for overseas capital a priority.

[2] Spillovers (or externalities) are impacts on third parties not directly involved in an economic transaction (Pigou, 1920 in Eden, 2009)

An Increase of Government Bargaining Power: "Negotiation Model"—1997–2003

The next step toward improving the country's investment climate was taken three years later in 1997, when the *Law on the State Support of Direct Investment* was adopted. The government announced that this law was designed to attract investments, borrowing the best international experience of transitional states. The investment legislation undertaken by Malaysia, as one of the fastest growing Asian countries with a transition economy, was suggested as a sample pattern for this purpose. As such, the goal of this shift in legislation was to create a framework for boosting inflows of investments into the backbone sectors of the Kazakhstani economy, the most important of which remained oil and gas. At the same time, a significant shift toward strengthening government bargaining power could be observed in this legislation amendment, with three important signs as evidence of such a shift. In fact, not only do these aspects represent the change in the investment regime, they also show change in the investment regime as a whole.

First, the law defined changes toward ensuring the interests of the state regarding foreign investment activities. Instead of providing guarantees of treatment in line with the national regime to all foreign investors, the new law carried these guarantees out within the boundaries of the national legal system, thus creating a distinctly separate regime for the regulation of foreign investment activities. First and foremost, this confirmed a swing toward the negotiation nature of the investment regime. This meant that, from that time, not all foreign investors were allowed to enter the country, but only those chosen and approved unilaterally by the government. Moreover, the initial terms of the contracts could be negotiated only by the government.

Second, the law replaced the procedure of granting foreign investors incentives, preferences, and grants, which were previously equally available for all foreign investors. From the initiation of this law onward, incentives, preferences, and grants not only became available solely for investors approved by the government, but the terms and volume of them could be varied with such approval.

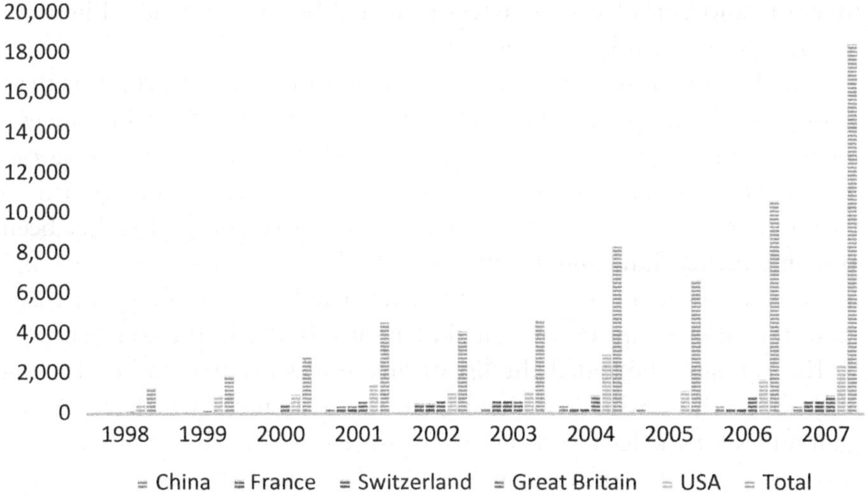

Fig. 2.2 Gross foreign investment inflows 1998–2007, billions USD. Source: Authors' own processed data based on the National Bank of Kazakhstan

Third, the law of 1997 undermined previous attempts to develop equal tax systems throughout all sectors of the national economy and origin of ownership. On the contrary, the law established the basis for so-called "contractual taxes" for individual investors, with particular emphasis on investors in the oil and gas and natural resources industries.

In this period, gross foreign investment inflows demonstrated a moderate increase, as depicted in Fig. 2.2.

Crisis and Post-Crisis Period: "Approval Model"—2003–2014

Since 2003, foreign investment activities in the Republic of Kazakhstan have been governed by the *Law on Foreign Investment*, issued that year.[3] This latest law generally combined contents of the two previous laws of 1994 and 1997; however, it significantly restricted the rights of foreign

[3] The Law of the Republic Kazakhstan from January, 8th, 2003 Nr. 373-II *On Investments.*

investors and curtailed preferences provided by the state, all while reinforcing government bargaining power.

Thereby, the most important amendment of the law of 2003 was that, as opposed to its predecessors, it no longer separated delimited investments into foreign and local categories. Abolishment of these categories meant the elimination of any preferences that were dedicated to attraction and free entry of investments in the country and had earlier been available for foreign capital. Likewise, the difference between direct and portfolio investment in the law was eliminated, thus leveling out treatment for different means of capital being invested into the country.

The law also shortened the list of guarantees ensured earlier, leaving only four. Thus, what remained were the assurances which embraced guarantees for the legal security of investment within the territory of the country, warranties of free use of dividends earned through investment activities, and for transparency of the state authorities' involvement and against nationalization and expropriation. Such an investment policy contributed to a rise in investment inflows and, more importantly, to an increase in the number of investor countries, combined with a decrease in the share of each state in gross investment. As such, the economy's resilience to external shocks was increased.

Regarding preferences, the law of 2003 indicated only the possibility of providing preferences, emphasizing, however, that from that time on, the latter would be negotiated and levied on a common basis for specific investment projects. Three types of preferences remained available with the most recent law, related to taxation, customs fees, and state on-location grants.

The beginning of the period of formation of Kazakhstan's investment regime coincided with the global economic crisis in 2008, followed by the sharp decline in hydrocarbon prices, which led to stagnation and a significant slowdown in growth rates. This did not, however, affect the flow of investment into the economy, including non-primary sectors (see Fig. 2.3). This is the best evidence of the success of Kazakhstan's investment strategy. After 2012, there was a slight decline in investment, but the average annual level for the entire period was kept at around US $20 billion.

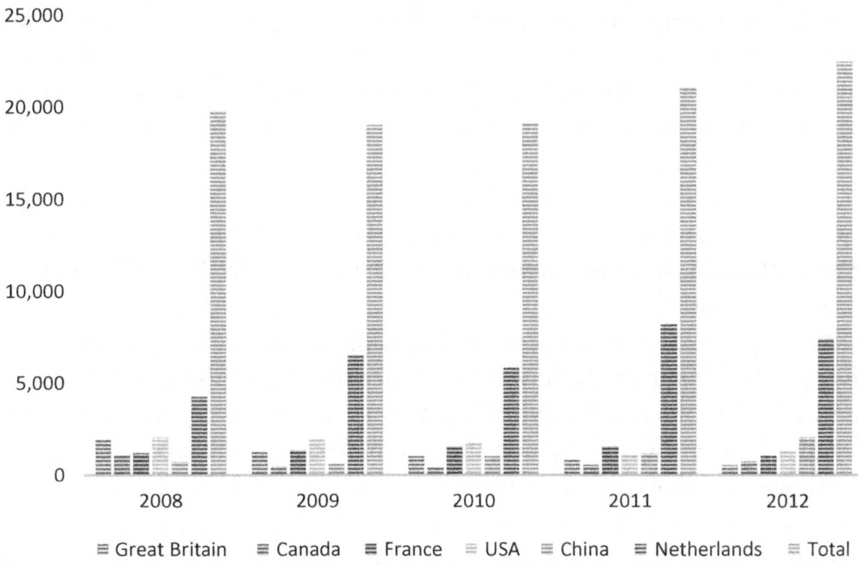

Fig. 2.3 Gross foreign investment inflows 2008–2012, billions USD. Source: Authors' own processed data based on the National Bank of Kazakhstan

The main priority of Kazakhstan's industrial strategy in this period was the introduction of a local content policy (see Baldakhov & Heim, 2020, this volume), reflected in the relevant statutory act.[4] Following this act, the Ministry of Investment and Development of the Republic of Kazakhstan established the *National Agency for the Development of Local Content NADLoC*,[5] which was delegated the authority to form the LCP and monitor the share of local content in procurement and projects. The objective function of the LCP is to mitigate the conflict between the country's need for FDI, the source of which is MNEs, and the need to increase domestic employment, wherein experience and knowledge often do not meet the MNE's requirements. The core of the LCP consists of appropriate and robust host country institutions that can enable the

[4] The Decree of the President of the Republic of Kazakhstan from January 27, 2009, Nr. 733 *On some issues of local content in the procurement of goods, works, and services to be procured by organizations and Government agencies.*

[5] NADLOC has been merged to Qazaqstan Industry and Export Center JSC (QAZINDUSTRY) in 2018.

indigenous labor force to attain a suitable level of training and skills for participation in the global economy. They also help to ensure that the quality and use of human resources, which are inevitable as a country moves up its development path, can be restructured (Dunning & Lundan, 2008).

Currently, the parties participating in investment activity consider the LCP to be standard practice. For example, Chevron invested about US $50 million in the construction of two factories to produce polyethylene pipes and more than US $40 million in a plant to produce valves. There are enough other examples of MNEs adopting the rules established by Kazakhstani institutions; however, practice shows that there are still many unresolved problems that will likely require special attention in the next stage. These problems include the complexity of analyzing oil and gas contracts or supply chains in general, due to limited information and the difficulty of accessing contracts that govern the relationship between operators and main contractors. The parties actively discuss the problem of information asymmetry, since the adequacy of local content assessment depends on this information being available. Even the authors of the policy themselves admit the difficulties associated with the process of collecting data and verifying the conformity of estimates of local content at all levels of contract chains (Ospanova, 2012).

The starting point of the fourth stage of investment reforms in Kazakhstan was the adoption of *The Code on Subsoil and Subsoil Use* in December 2017, which simplified the procedures for granting subsoil use rights, while also increasing the availability of geological information, information on subsoil users, subsoil use conditions, and final beneficiaries. The new code aimed to reduce the risks of non-users due to changes in terms of previously signed contracts. The priority right of the state is retained only in relation to strategic sites for hydrocarbons and uranium. In general, the expert community highly appreciates the investment climate of Kazakhstan, predicting that in the next 3–4 years, the country will receive more than US $100 billion of FDI. At the same time, the share of FDI in sectors oriented toward efficiency growth remains low, and the percentage of reinvested income is low (Muminov, 2018).

The character of the fourth stage of Kazakhstan's investment development will become clearer over time, but there is no doubt that digitalization will lead to its mainstreaming. While going digital has mostly become the norm, it perhaps makes more sense for O&G companies to seize the opportunity and scale up its impact, especially in today's lower-for-longer environment that requires new operating and capital cost models. With a comprehensive roadmap in hand, the journey may not be so cumbersome after all (Deloitte, 2017). At this stage, we can expect an increase in the influence of state institutions and the stimulation of projects outside the oil and gas sector. One such industry is the information and communication technology (ICT) sector, the development prospects of which are suggested in Ambalov & Heim, 2020, this volume.

Evolution of Subsoil Legislation and Petroleum Fiscal Systems, 1991–2015

The economic literature (i.e., Esembayev, 2010) distinguishes three stages of the investment development of Kazakhstan:

- The first stage (1992–1997) is the transition from a planned, centralized economy to an open market economy and the first attempt to attract FDI.
- The second stage (1998–2007) is the intensification of processes related to investment activities, accompanied by the improvement of legislation.
- The third stage, ongoing at present, began with a period of stagnation and a noticeable slowdown in growth rates (2007–2008). This stage is characterized by the improvement of legislation and the creation of particular quasi-state institutions designed to ensure the harmonization of the interests of MNEs and local enterprises. Such institutions are the *National Welfare Fund Samruk-Kazyna* and the *JSC National Agency for the Development of Local Content.*

At the same time, the government implemented reforms of tax legislation on subsoil use alongside the creation of these institutions, such as the following:

1. 1991–1995: mining contracts determined all tax conditions;
2. 1995–2004: adopted *Tax Law* and Kazakhstan *Tax Code* consolidated basic terms and conditions of the taxation of mineral resources users (principle of tax regime stability, etc.);
3. 2004–2008: tightening of tax legislation (rental tax levy, cancelation of a principle of tax regime stability, etc.);
4. 2008–present: export duty and the enactment of new *Tax Code and Transfer Pricing Law.*

The International Law on Foreign Investment and Reinvestment in the O&G Industry

The O&G industry is one of the most capital expensive in the natural resources business. At the same time, petroleum projects give the highest return on invested capital. High returns create a favorable premise for the involvement of foreign capital in the development of oil and gas deposits all over the world. The most broadly represented form of foreign capital in the petroleum sector is FDI. Foreign direct investment involves the transfer of tangible or intangible assets from one country to another for the purposes of generating wealth under the total or partial control of the owner of the assets (Sornarajah, 2004, 2017). In contrast to portfolio investment, which is normally considered to be the movement of money to buy shares or undertaking overseas investment through other instruments, international law protects direct investments at least in terms of physical property and assets invested through principles of diplomatic protection and the state's responsibility.

The evolution of the term *investment*, which was first initiated with the principal of providing an alien nation with a minimum standard of treatment in order to minimize the responsibility of the state in case of their absence, consequently led to three principal concerns. These concerns are, first, to protect the physical property of the foreign investor; second, to extend protection to intangible rights, giving them the same status as the property; and, third, to include the administrative rights needed for the operation of the investment project within foreign investment.

The formation of the international law on foreign investment appeared during the transition from the colonial to the post-colonial historical periods and the liberation of former British and European colonies in Asia and Africa. Looking back at the history of the phenomena helps to gain an understanding of how emerging countries, which had recently lost centralized command governance of their former dominion, acted according to the reality of the market economy. In the majority of cases, soon after having seceded from a commonwealth or being set free from a protectorate, former colonies or union states joined the list of the developing nations, thus facing the severe problem of searching and attracting foreign investment for reconstructing the damaged economies. Sornarajah (2004, 2017) outlines two alternative views on the approach toward alien nations by the host state that existed during the colonial period. Both of them—whether that state would strive for equal treatment of the nationals or even for some external standard, which was higher than the national one—were alien friendly (see Fig. 2.4). Further development of the self-consciousness of foreign investment hosting states, however, led to two types of taking over of foreign property for political and economic self-determination. These two types included either capricious grabbing of property for the personal advancement of elite groups, as happened in many Latin American states, or the taking of property by a government for the institution of economic reform.

During the post-colonial period, developing countries have been introducing far more welcome policies on foreign investment. The reason here lies in the competition for a limited amount of foreign investments. The successive economic crises that followed in the developing nations of the former Commonwealth of the Independent States (CIS), Asia, and Latin America boosted liberalization, demonstrated as a speedy outflow of foreign funds when the situation turned bad. For many of these investments, this dilemma highlighted the idea that cyclical changes, which would differ on issues such as rights of access, types of treatment of investment, and dispute resolution, were necessary. This aspect has, to some extent, a lot in common with the situation that Kazakhstan faced immediately after having seceded from the USSR and declared its independence in 1991 (Dosmukhamedov, 2003).

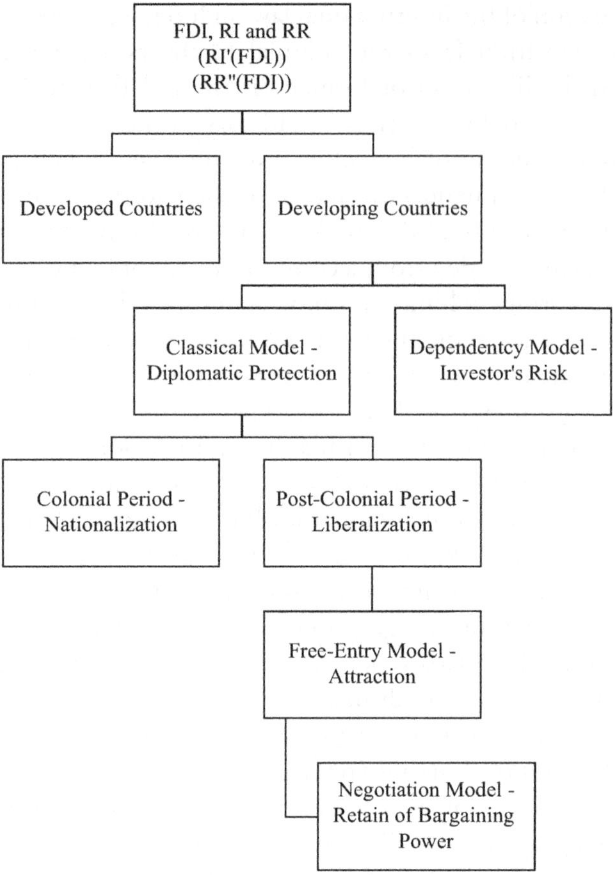

Fig. 2.4 International law on foreign investment and reinvestment. (Source: Adapted from Sornarajah, 2004, 2017)

Governments of resource-rich countries and foreign investors negotiate their interests in one of two primary systems: concessionary and contractual (see Fig. 2.5). The fundamental difference between them stems from different attitudes toward the ownership of mineral resources. The Anglo-Saxon and the French concepts of ownership of mineral wealth are the root beginnings. This ownership issue drives not only the language and jargon of fiscal systems but the arithmetic as well (Johnston, 1994).

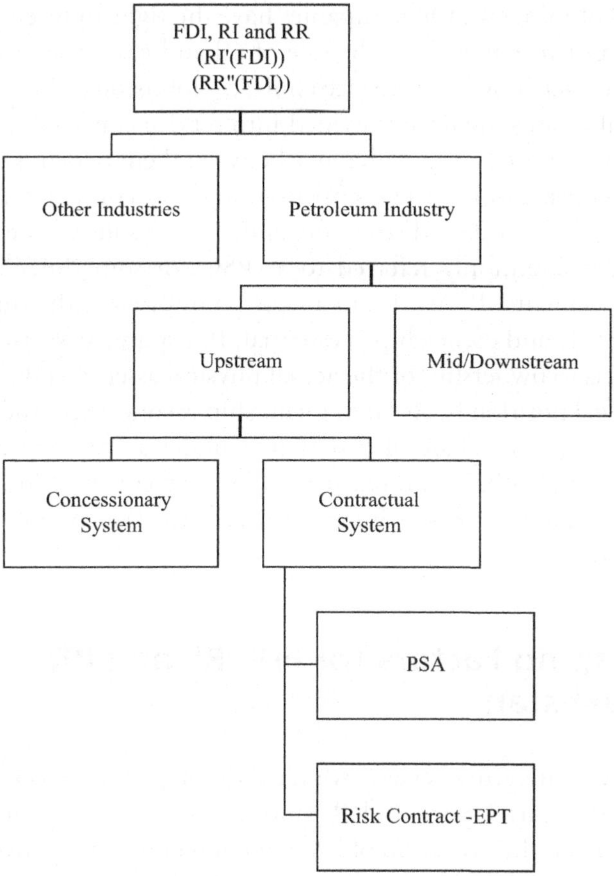

Fig. 2.5 Petroleum fiscal systems and FDI, RI, and RR. (Source: Adapted from Sornarajah, 2004, 2017)

Concessionary systems, as the term implies, allow private ownership of mineral resources. This concept comes from the Anglo-Saxon legal tradition. In most countries, the government owns all mineral resources, but under concessionary systems, it will transfer the title of the minerals to a company once they are extracted. The company is then subject to paying royalties and taxes. Under contractual systems, the government retains ownership of minerals. Oil companies have the right to receive a share of production or revenues from the sale of oil and gas under a production sharing contract (PSC) or a service contract (Johnston, 1994). Therefore, contractual arrangements are divided into service contracts and production sharing contracts. The difference between them depends on whether or not the contractor receives compensation in cash or in extracted crude. This is a rather modest distinction and, as a result, systems on both branches are commonly referred to as PSCs or sometimes production sharing agreements (PSAs). From a legal point of view, the timing of the transfer of title and ownership is essential. If disputes arise, the closer the contractor is to ownership of the actual physical assets (crude), the stronger their legal position is. As far as ownership is concerned, the contractor ultimately receives a share of production under a PSC and thus claims title to the crude oil. The transfer of title is effectively shifted from the wellhead, under a concessionary system to the point of export, under a PSC.

The Shaping Factors for FDI, RI, and RR in Kazakhstan

Based on the literature review, we have developed a conceptual framework for the correlation of RR amounts in the upstream sector of Kazakhstan and the evolution of investment regimes and petroleum fiscal systems utilized in the country (see Fig. 2.6). Its aim was to empirically explain the fluctuations of the share of RR in the petroleum industry, which were fluctuating cyclically over time, either with peaks or with troughs, falling in the middle of each investment regime. Structured questionnaires completed by legislation scholars, lawyers, and tax and legal consultants in Kazakhstan proved the robustness of the model (Sekaran, 1992; Tharenou, Donohue, & Cooper, 2007).

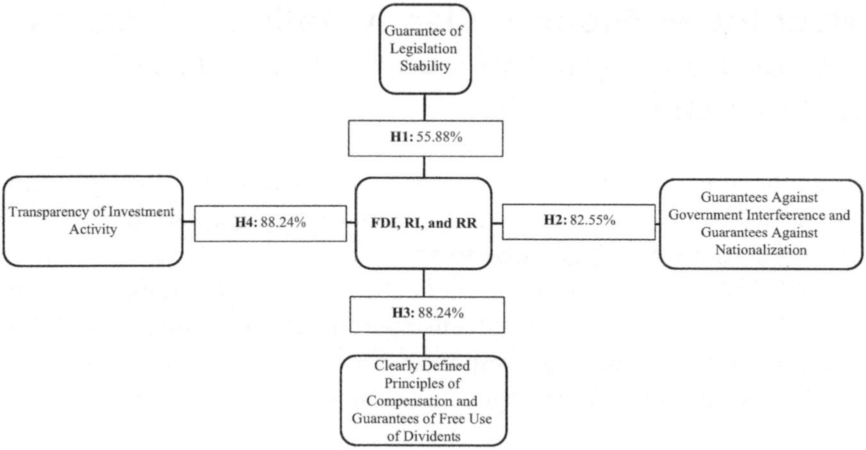

Fig. 2.6 The shaping factors for FDI, RI, and RR. Source: compiled by the authors

Hypotheses Group 1: Guarantee of Legislation Stability

From the group of questions dedicated to the general provisions of relationships between a host country and foreign investors, we generated hypotheses in the form of positive statements. The hypotheses addressed some turning points of the conceptual framework. For this hypothesis group, the responses from the questionnaires revealed the following results: an average "agree" factor of not less than 55.88%.

Hypotheses Group 2: Guarantees Against Government Interference and Nationalization

This group of hypotheses was dedicated to the examination of whether the classic theory of foreign investment could be applicable for Kazakhstan, particularly regarding drafting its investment legislation and developing its framework for FDI attraction. For the second subject group, the responses from the questionnaires revealed the following results: an average "agree" factor not less than 82.55%.

Hypotheses Group 3: Clearly Defined Principles of Compensation and Guarantees of Free Use of Dividends

The following subject group of questions was dedicated to the legal regulation of investment activities and consisted of nine questions. Seven of these questions were dedicated to the general aspects against which an investment regime is assessed, while the last two questions were concerned with some factors of influence within the investment model. For the third subject group, the responses from the questionnaires revealed the following results: an average "agree" factor not less than 88.24%.

Hypotheses Group 4: Transparency of Investment Activity

This subject group of questions was dedicated to the assessment of the evolution of oil and gas legislation regarding contractual bases and fiscal regimes. As derived from the literature review and presumed in the conceptual framework, oil and gas legislation, along with these two significant parameters, are the tools for varying relationships between the government and investors within the invariable investment model and, thus, the primary tool of increased governmental bargaining power (Johnston, 1994). This subject group consisted of four questions, which were meant to trace the whole evolution of Kazakhstan's petroleum legislation, starting from concessions owned entirely by investors, through the period of production sharing contracts shared with the government, and, finally, to the abolition of PSAs and their replacement by service contracts. For the fourth subject group, the responses from the questionnaires revealed the following results: an average "agree" factor not less than 88.24%.

Conclusion

In light of economic upsurge, Kazakhstan's legislation that covered foreign investment and subsoil use activities had been significantly modified during this time, shaping both the investment regime and petroleum production, very differently from how they were first introduced. Thus, the law on foreign investment first adopted in 1994 was estimated to attract foreign investment into the collapsed post-Soviet economy and industry. After amendments in 2003, however, the law changed significantly, now regulating , if not limiting , foreign presence in this strategically important sector. Both the subsoil and the petroleum laws were changed in 2009 from the 1999 laws in almost the same way, thus changing the whole concept of licensing and taxation. The approach changed from being initially valued as investment-favorable (applied from 1999 to 2004), through a so-called mixed transitional approach (applied from 2004 to 2009), to the final approach, evaluated as more regulatory toward foreign participation (in use since 2009).

Comparing the changes discussed above, we can assume that Kazakhstan has been transitioning from a country with a ruined post-Soviet economy to one pretending to host a free market. This transition creates an inevitable demand for the creation of a favorable environment for foreign investment, as well as for guarantees for foreign investors' stable and safe operations in the country in the beginning of such a transition. On the other hand, Kazakhstan has been moving up in the list of the developing nations since the declaration of its independence in 1991, which means that the country has to be concerned about the wealth of its citizens related to benefits from the natural resources. This positive trend creates the demand for future research in terms of analyzing whether the country has been maintaining the balance between providing a favorable investment regime and retaining profits, as well as whether the tools used for shaping investment have had a real impact on financial activities.

Bibliography

Ambalov, V., & Heim, I. (2020). Investments in the digital Silk Road. In I. Heim (Ed.), *Kazakhstan's diversification from the natural resources sector: Strategic and economic opportunities*. London, UK: Palgrave Macmillan.

Baldakhov, U., & Heim, I. (2020). Institutional reform in Kazakhstan. In I. Heim (Ed.), *Kazakhstan's diversification from the natural resources sector: Strategic and economic opportunities*. London, UK: Palgrave Macmillan.

Deloitte. (2017). *From bytes to barrels: The digital transformation in upstream oil and gas*. Retrieved from Deloitte website: https://www2.deloitte.com/content/dam/Deloitte/global/Documents/Energy-and-Resources/gx-online-from-bytes-to-barrels.pdf

Dosmukhamedov, E. (2003). *Foreign direct investment in Kazakhstan: Politico-legal aspects of post-communist transition*. Oxford, UK: Palgrave Macmillan.

Dunning, J. H., and Lundan, S. M. (2008). *Multinational enterprises and the global economy*. 2nd ed. Cheltenham, UK: Edward Elgar Publishing.

Eden, L. (2009). Letter from the editor-in-chief: FDI spillovers and linkages. *Journal of International Business Studies, 40*(7), 1065–1069.

Esembayev, G. A. (2010). Processes of foreign investment in Kazakhstan. *Vestnik KazNU, 2*, 90–96.

Johnston, D. (1994). *International petroleum fiscal systems and production sharing contracts*. Tulsa, OK: PennWell Publishing Company.

Kostova, T., Roth, K., & Dacin, M. T. (2008). Institutional theory in the study of multinational corporations: A critique and new directions. *Academy of management review, 33*(4), 994–1006.

Maulenov, K. (2005). *Petroleum law of the Republic of Kazakhstan and oversees states*. Almaty, Kazakhstan: Zhety Zhargy.

Muminov, A. (2018, June 08). *What hinders direct investment in Kazakhstan*. Capital. Retrieved from: https://kapital.kz/finance/69713/chto-sderzhivaet-pryamye-investicii-v-kazahstan.html

Ospanova, S. (2012). *Policies on local content: Overview of Kazakhstan*. Astana, Kazakhstan: British Embassy.

Rodrick, D. (2003). *Growth Strategies*. Working paper, Department of Economics, Johannes Kepler University of Linz, no. 0317, Johannes Kepler University of Linz, Department of Economics, Linz, Austria.

Sekaran, U. (1992). *Research methods for business*. New York, NY: Wiley.

Sornarajah, M. (2004, 2017). The international law on foreign investment (3rd ed.). Cambridge, UK: Cambridge University Press.
Tharenou, P., Donohue, R., & Cooper, B. (2007). *Management research methods*. Cambridge, UK: Cambridge University Press.
UNCTAD (2017). World Investment Report 2017. Retrieved from: http://unctad.org/en/PublicationsLibrary/wir2017_en.pdf

3

The Effects of Oil Revenues on Kazakhstan's Economy

Irina Heim and Kairat Salimov

Introduction

As was discussed (see Baldakhov & Heim, 2020, and Heim & Romanov, 2020, this volume), in the 1990s, the oil sector quickly became the primary economic sector in Kazakhstan. During the period of the 1990s, as a result of the national privatization program, Kazakhstan transformed its economic structure from a Soviet-era planned economy to an oil-dependent one. Currently, oil sector earnings are responsible for about 35% of total export revenues and further contribute 20% of national budget finances, which translates to around 6.5% of the real GDP (Pomfret, 2005). The government's radical reforms aimed at strengthening the

I. Heim (✉)
Henley Business School, University of Reading, Reading, UK
e-mail: irina.heim@henley.ac.uk

K. Salimov
Ministry of Finance, Nur-Sultan, Kazakhstan

I. Heim (ed.), *Kazakhstan's Diversification from the Natural Resources Sector*, Euro-Asian Studies, https://doi.org/10.1007/978-3-030-37389-4_3

economy by highlighting the effects of its *Modernization 3.0 Program*[1] in shaping the economic landscape to become one of the top 30 countries with a prosperous economy in the coming years (Borghijs, 2017). Among the actions proposed is increased exploitation of the Caspian oil reserves. Despite the challenges of transitioning from a planned to a market-based economy, Kazakhstan sought to attract the most significant share of foreign direct investments (FDI) per capita among Central Asian nations. The increased oil production strongly and positively influenced Kazakhstani economic growth, as well as the volume of its revenue collection. Since 2000, revenues from the oil sector have been responsible for nearly 20% of government expenditure. The cumulative effect of oil income on the general economy is tremendous, taking into account the amount of foreign investments in the form of FDI it has attracted to the country. This chapter discusses the effect of oil revenues (OR)[2] by examining their influence on Kazakhstan's economic development since it declared independence in 1991 after the breakup of the Soviet Union.

Institutional Theory and Sustainable Development of Resource-driven Unbalanced Economies

Institutional theory in economics emerged from two streams of thoughts: first, the idea that state defines the legal framework, which ensures that market economy functions (new institutional economics, or NIE), and, second, transaction cost theory explaining that economic organizations manage by themselves to reduce costs associated with economic transactions which are influenced by the institutions governing the market (old institutionalism). NIE considers the question of why economic institutions emerged the way they did and not otherwise, by explaining the problem of resource allocation and utilization (Vargo & Lusch, 2016).

[1] The third stage of modernization in Kazakhstan. Announced on January 31, 2017, by the former President Nazarbayev. More details about this strategic initiative in the paragraphs below.

[2] The income that a government accrues from taxation and duties (both customs and excise duties) collected for servicing the public expenditure.

Coase addressed the question of economic exchange based on transaction cost (Coase, 1937, 1972). Williamson aimed to explain how organizational forms are grounded in response to the ways in which economic actors minimize transaction costs by managing their exchange activities. According to Williamson, these costs are incurred because the exchange activities of organizations are embedded in the institutional environment (Williamson, 1981).

Institutions can be defined in different ways; in economics, institutions are often defined as the rules of the game in a society or, more formally, the humanly devised constraints that shape human interaction (North, 1990). Institutions matter since without a stable institutional framework, transaction costs may become so high that certain transactions are not undertaken at all (Peng & Meyer, 2016). Institutions develop over time, and institutional transition is a "fundamental and comprehensive change introduced to the formal and informal rules of the game that affect organisations as players" (Peng, 2003: 275). Different economies will have very different performance characteristics because of different informal norms and enforcement. North (1990) also concluded that successful political-economic systems have evolved flexible institutional structures that can survive the shocks and changes that are a part of successful evolution.

Institutional transition in emerging countries moving from central planning to market economy (to this group belong all transitional countries including Russia and Kazakhstan) is often linked with other economic concepts in order to explain certain phenomenon. The overview of selected contributions of the institutional theory in economics is given in Table 3.1.

This chapter will consider the differences in socio-economic development between oil and non-oil regions in Kazakhstan. It will justify the need for oil rent redistribution through the diversification from the extractive sector of the economy, based on the view of oil as a common-pool resource, and the need for sustainable management of such resources suggested by neo-institutional theory.

Table 3.1 Concepts in economics linked with neo-institutional theory

Theory	Focus	Indicative literature
Transaction-cost economics	Rule and governance systems that develop to regulate or manage economic exchange	Coase (1972) Williamson (1981)
Game-theoretic perspective	Institutions are in equilibrium where outcomes depend on the choices made by another player; common-pool resources and sustainability	Ostrom (1990, 2005)
Evolutionary economics	Routines (or capabilities) are made up of conscious and tacit knowledge and skills held by participants who carry out organizational tasks. To survive, a firm must be able to reproduce and modify its routines in the face of changes	Nelson and Winter (1982)
Resource-based theory (RBT)	RBT emphasizes the possibility of organizational actors to strategically manage resources and capabilities under their control. Some resources are not elastic in supply, developing over a long period of time and difficult to reproduce because they are based on tacit knowledge	Penrose (1959), Barney (1991)
Rational choice theory (RCT)	RCT views institutions as governance or rule system which represent deliberate constructions established by individuals seeking to promote or protect their interests	Moe (1984)

Source: Authors, adapted from Scott (2014) and review of the literature

Economic Development in the post-Soviet Period

Kazakhstan is a country located strategically between Europe and Asia; it is often referred to as a Central Asian state. Borghijs (2017) observes that the sparsely populated nation of 18 million inhabitants sits on 2.7 million square kilometers landlocked by China in the east, Russia in the north, and Uzbekistan, Turkmenistan, and Kyrgyzstan in the south. Pomfret (2005) notes that among the nations united under the Union of Soviet Socialist Republics (USSR), Kazakhstan was the last to declare independence. He observes that the country is abundant in oil and natural gas, while also rich in substantial deposits of unmined gold, copper, aluminum, and chrome. Nowadays, Kazakhstan is the world's leading oil producer. However, as Sakal (2015) noted, despite tremendous natural wealth, the policies governing natural resources over the years have failed to improve the living conditions of the majority of Kazakhstan's population.

Firstly, the transition from a Soviet economy to an independent nation state has led to mistrust and conflicts between two major ethnic groups, namely Russian and Kazakh,[3] followed by a mass exodus that further weakened Kazakhstan's economy during the first half of the 1990s. Additionally, the failure of the country to attract foreign investment (FDI) in this period hindered the development of its petroleum and mineral sectors (Pomfret, 2005). Consequently, in the first five years after Kazakhstan attained self-rule, the economy lost 30% of its real GDP value and inflation skyrocketed. The situation changed slightly for the better in the 1996–1997 period before dipping further in 1998.[4] The economic downturn ended in 1999, opening a new era of robust economic development in the country. Overall, the 1990s was a turbulent period for the economy of Kazakhstan. During the economic decline in the 1991–1995 period, the industrial contribution to the GDP dropped to 33% from 45%; the contribution of agriculture to the GDP declined from 27% to 5%; at the same time, the services industries' contribution to the GDP rose to 63% from 29% before independence (Borghijs, 2017).

Pomfret (2005) claims that the poor economic conditions arose because, after declaration of independence, the country's leadership focused on secession politics and internal conflict resolution at the expense of the economic development of the nation. He suggests that the cause of this was former President Nursultan Nazarbayev's[5] economic policy for 1992–1994 period, which was aimed at maintaining close commercial bonds with Russia. He argues that to maintain ties with the largest economy of the breakaway states, Kazakhstan followed Russia's footsteps, which included the radical reforms of price liberation and

[3] Uzbeks, Ukrainians, and Germans are minority groups.

[4] Resulting in default of the Russian State in August 1998.

[5] Former President Nazarbayev served as President of Kazakhstan since the office was established in 1990 (28 years ago). The institution of the presidency plays an important role in the political system of Kazakhstan; that is why the president initially announces all significant initiatives.

privatization of state corporations in 1992. In this endeavor, Kazakhstan's leadership failed to set an agenda for the country's macroeconomic development (Pomfret, 2005). While the country evolved in the shadow of Russia, pluralism flourished in 1994 before leadership bolstered its political authoritarianism, making Kazakhstan less democratic than Russia (Sakal, 2015). He stated that Kazakhstan suspended its economic reforms for close to a decade and that then privatization spiraled during this period. Between 1995 and 1997, Kazakhstan sold all of its treasured state corporations through a process similar to Russia's "voucher scheme." After the depletion of national wealth held in public enterprises, Kazakhstan's leadership turned its attention in the development of its oil sector (Pomfret, 2005). He notes that, against this backdrop, the economy suffered severe adverse external shocks at the end of 1990s, both because of the financial crisis in Russia in August 1998[6] and because of falling oil prices in this period, resulting in Kazakhstan devaluing its currency by a substantial margin. Kazakhstan's economy became predominantly dependent on the energy sector. From independence to the present date, Kazakhstan's oil production tripled, making it among the top oil-producing nations in the world.

O&G Industry Overview

Among resource-rich countries, Kazakhstan occupies a top position, possessing 30 billion barrels of proven crude oil reserves (see Table 3.2) and 4.8 billion cubic meters of natural gas, which altogether account for 2.22% of the world's petroleum reserves, contributing 7% of oil reserves in Eurasia. Kazakhstan also holds the top position among the largest petroleum producers, with an annual oil production of 1.4 million barrels a day and a gas production of 220,000 m^3/d. Estimations show that, at these rates, Kazakhstan will contribute to petroleum production for

[6] Russian financial crisis (Russian Default) hit Russia on 17 August 1998. It resulted in the Russian government devaluing the rouble from about US $6 up to US $24 during several months. The reasons for it were internal, such as declining productivity, high fixed exchange rate, and chronic fiscal deficit in combination with two external chocks—1997 Asian financial crisis and declining oil prices.

Table 3.2 World proven crude oil reserves, top ten countries, 2018

Country	Oil reserves, *m b*
Venezuela	302,809
KSA	266,260
Iran	155,600
Iraq	147,223
Kuwait	101,500
UAE	97,800
Russia	80,000
USA	32,773
Kazakhstan	**30,000**
Qatar	25,244

Source: Authors' own processed data based on OPEC Annual Statistical Bulletin (2018), Available at: https://www.opec.org/opec_web/en/publications/202.htm

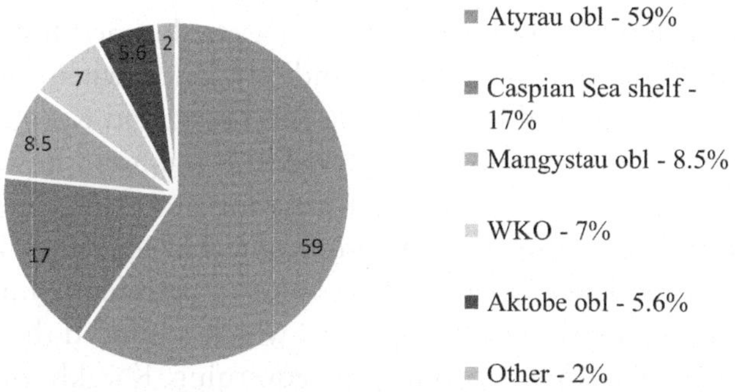

Fig. 3.1 The distribution of hydrocarbon reserves by regions, %. (Source: Authors' own processed data based on KazMunayGas annual report 2016, Available at http://www.kmg.kz/uploads/AnnualReport2016Rus2.pdf)

the next several decades. Major oil and gas fields, also referred as unique fields or megaprojects, and their recoverable oil reserves, according to national statistical data, are Tengiz with 7 billion barrels (1.1 km^3), Karachaganak with 8 billion barrels (1.3 km^3) and 1350 km^3 of natural gas, and Kashagan with 7–9 billion barrels (1.1–1.4 km^3). In 2018, Kazakhstan reached production up to 1.5 million barrels of oil a day (OPEC, 2018), most of which are exported. This development lifted Kazakhstan into the ranks of the world's top oil-producing nations.

Figure 3.1 shows the distribution of hydrocarbon reserves in Kazakhstan by region. There is a curious correlation between the volume of reserves and the regional household income indicators (see Fig. 3.5, this chapter)—the higher the hydrocarbon reserves in the region, the higher the welfare of the people living in the area.

Substantial natural resources deposits fuelled the economic growth. Later, strategic initiatives facilitated the movement of foreign capital into the country through "multi-vector" policies to govern the energy sector. Notable among these efforts is the oil transport network which the state agreed on with its neighbors, Russia and China (Hardin, 2012). Kazakhstan's energy potential became apparent during the Soviet era, precisely five decades ago, although nobody knew with certainty the magnitude of the country's fossil fuel potential (O&G Journal, 1991). The Mangyshlak Peninsula in the western part of the country demonstrated great potential for petroleum production; however, the lack of capital and technical expertise in the Soviet era dimmed hopes of developing these fields until the country's independence, when the American oil giant Chevron moved in to develop the Tengiz and Korolev oil fields. In the Soviet period, oil and gas explored in Kazakhstan flowed through the Orenburg pipeline system into Russia for processing. Processing its petroleum in Russia illustrates a significant challenge that Kazakhstan faced at independence because the country's petroleum infrastructure consisted of old Soviet-era development, which advanced the industry as a one single whole. After becoming self-governing, Kazakhstan needed to develop its expertise and capital to be genuinely sovereign, even as it remained connected to Russia (Sakal, 2015).

Kazakhstan's oil dominance through its petroleum exploration in the Caspian Sea basin was yet to come. After its declaration of independence, Kazakhstan abandoned the rouble as its currency and focused on attracting FDI and international expertise to spur its economic growth, particularly in the energy sector, including both the petroleum and electricity sub-sectors (Pomfret, 2005). The deal between *Chevron* and the local corporation *TengizNeftegaz Production Association* in 1993 gave birth to *TengizChevroil* (TCO). Additionally, to develop the Karachaganak oil field, in 1992 the government engaged both the Italian energy company *ENI* and *British Gas*. Later, they approached *Gazprom*, the owner of the Orenburg oil network. Then, *Gazprom* transferred its stakes to *Lukoil* in 1997. At this time, China, through the *Chinese National Petroleum*

Corporation (CNPC), also tapped into the Kazakhstani energy sector by acquiring a 60% stake in a local natural gas producer—*AktobeMunayGas*. Some European enterprises also entered Kazakhstan to develop its electricity grid, but national leadership later reversed private ownership in the power sub-sector to state control in the name of national security. In 1994, the Kazakhstani government formed an international consortium, in which the state-owned *KazakhstanCaspiyShelf* collaborated with six major international oil companies, including *Total*, *Mobil*, *BP/Statoil*, *Shell*, *Agip* (acquired by *ENI* in 2003), and *BG*. In 1997, Kazakhstan signed production-sharing agreements (PSA), with each company receiving equal stake.

The top export destination for Kazakhstan is China. Kazakhstan's oil exports to China reached 10 billion metric meters in 2015. China's economic growth, however, is currently on a downward turn and with this its demand for oil, affecting Kazakhstan's economy. The publication by Guardian (2017) stated that China, as the leading importer of motor vehicles, plans to ban production of petrol and diesel cars in the near future. British Petroleum Energy Outlook 2019 predicts that China may switch to "low-carbon transport" including bans on sales of all internal-combustion engine cars, increase the share of biofuels, and increase the share of renewables in their energy mix (BP, 2019). Such news is bad for Kazakhstan in terms of having a market for its large output of petroleum. It is likely to affect the flow of oil in the country's pipeline in the southern region. Additionally, Hardin (2012) notes that China's unexploited oil reserves could prove substantial in the future and end up competing with Kazakhstan's oil sector. This chapter, therefore, also explores the alternative avenues of economic growth available for the country, such as the service sector, in order to deter overreliance on ORs to support government expenditure.

Consequently, Hardin (2012) suggests that Kazakhstan ought to continue to pro-actively diversify its economy for stability, as dependence on petroleum alone would be detrimental. There was evidence of this in 2009, when oil prices dropped suddenly. She notes that, currently, ORs account for 35–40% of the state budget and contribute 20% to the country's GDP.[7] She further suggests that the expansion of the energy sector is instrumental in driving growth in the wider economy, particularly in the construction sector. Hardin (2012) argues that Kazakhstan can apply its collaboration in the energy sphere to propagate regional cooperation, which it can extend to enforce peace in the area.

Pomfret (2005) discusses some of the reasons for the dismal performance of the Kazakhstani economy during the first decade of independence. First, although Kazakhstan is rich in fossil fuel reserves and mineral deposits, the government under former President Nazarbayev poorly utilized national resources during the first decade of independence. Kalyuzhnova and Patterson (2016) argue that corruption, government ineffectiveness, weak regulatory frameworks, and anarchy reigned supreme during this period. They note that the country scored poorly on the Index of Economic Freedom (IEF) scale, whose ten components rated government performance in terms of regulatory efficiency, rule of law, open markets, and limited government. Second, the social imbalance between major ethnic groups created a politically unstable nation with an uncertain economy. Third, Kazakhstan embraced democracy in an attempt to open up its political and economic space. According to Pomfret (2005), however, the country's leadership reversed this gain and adopted regressive political tenets, making it less tolerant to divergent political views, even more than the government officials in Russia. Kazakhstan's fortunes changed in 1996, however, when the country turned its attention to developing its oil fields, which amassed riches for its elite. The economic boom came in the new millennium, as oil prices surged, and the country discovered new oil fields with significant oil and gas deposits. This has attracted the attention of scholars of various disciplines to study development in the Caspian state. To this end, there is a significant volume of literature touching on the country's natural resource policies (see next sections), but limited literature discussing the influence of natural resource wealth on the socio-economic dynamics in the region.

[7] GDP is the value of the total goods produced and services delivered in a particular nation for one year.

The Effects of Oil Rents on the Economic Development

Natural gas and oil have been the primary drivers of rapid economic growth in Kazakhstan during the past two decades. Figure 3.2 shows that the country's oil rents[8] more than quadrupled between 1991 and 2011; however, they have recently dropped to 10% of GDP. As a result, during the period of high oil rents, the nation's share in the international oil arena rose from only 0.7% to 1.8%, pushing Kazakhstan into position 18 among the world's oil producers in that year. In some periods, oil and gas accounted for up to 25% of the Kazakhstani GDP and up to two-thirds of the country's exports, making fossil fuels the single most important export commodity.

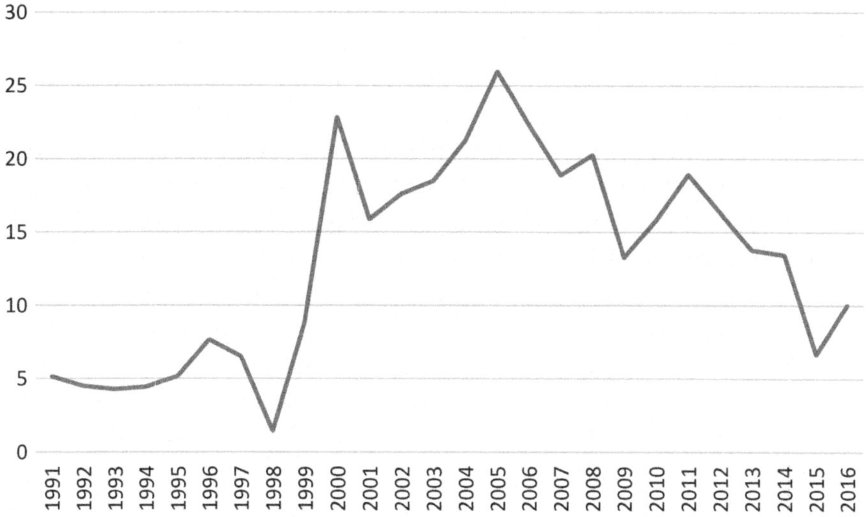

Fig. 3.2 Oil rents in Kazakhstan in 1991–2016, % of GDP. (Source: Authors' own processed data based on WB data)

[8] Oil rents refers to the profit before tax or royalties of oil exploration. Taxes and royalties are paid by oil companies to the state where the oil exploration takes place.

Since the Kazakhstani economy relies heavily on oil, with 60% of the government's revenue from that sector, periods of high oil prices translate into substantial economic performance for the country. On the other hand, price drops result in a slowdown of economic growth. Figure 3.2 illustrates this relationship between oil price fluctuations and the GDP growth of oil-dependent countries such as Kazakhstan, where there was an economic dip in 1998. Similar trends occurred in between 2008 and 2009, and most recently in 2014, when oil prices fell (see Fig. 1.1, Baldakhov & Heim, 2020, this volume). The recent trends also illustrate the inability of an emerging resource-rich country to move out of the middle-income trap.[9]

Recent Economic Development

Research has explored why economic growth in Kazakhstan has slowed significantly. Rahmanov (2016) attributes this decline to the mid-2014 collapse in the price of oil. Additionally, he notes that Kazakhstan's main trading partners, such as Russia and China, are similarly experiencing a slowdown in their economic performance. Accordingly, growth deceleration started in China in 2011, heralding the era of single-digit GDP growth rates. According to Rahmanov (2016), the slowdown in China is the result of the changes in Chinese economic policy from an export-led and investment-driven approach to the more recent domestic consumption-driven framework. This change in economic policy resulted in a sharp drop in the demand for the raw materials and energy that Kazakhstan supplied to China. After that, the double effects of the United Nations' sanctions on Russia and the drop in oil prices took a toll on the country's economic pillars, producing a similar impact in its neighboring country, Kazakhstan. This resulted in a loss of 30% of its export revenues from its two main trading partners, China, and Russia.

[9] Middle-income trap is a term describing the failure of the country to sustain growth and transit from resource-driven growth, based on low-cost labor and capital, to productivity-driven growth (Khakas & Kohli, 2011).

The WB (2017), while giving an overview of the country's economic update, suggests that the Kazakhstani economy continued to suffer from depressed oil prices and weak regional demand for its exports, resulting in a low 1% GDP growth rate in 2016. Consequently, the report notes that the country's budget deficit widened in the wake of reduced oil production, from US $5.5 billion (3% of the real GDP) in 2015 to US $8.2 billion, equivalent to 6.1% of the GDP in 2016. The report, however, suggests that increased FDI inflows, mainly to expand the energy sector, prevented further negative growth. Borghijs (2017) argues that this latest upturn in economic performance allowed the central bank of Kazakhstan, NBK, to restock its foreign exchange reserves, which it had channeled into stabilizing the local currency, the tenge, for the previous two years. Regarding the latter, the IMF (2015) executive board report notes that the fiscal stimulus which the NBK intended to spur economic growth worsened the country's budgetary accounts—the country's fiscal surplus fell from 5% of the GDP in 2013 to just 1.5% in 2014. According to the WB (2017) report, domestic consumption declined considerably in 2016 because of the devaluation of the tenge, resulting in up to 14.6% inflation and denting the purchasing power of local households.

Consequently, the WB suggests that poverty levels, measured by the international rate of US $5 per day, rose to around 20% that year. In phases of lower economic activity, monetary conditions are tight, sharply suppressing lending activity. The report notes, however, that the latest economic trend in Kazakhstan forced the NBK to institute ambitious fiscal reforms aimed at improving the country's monetary policy model and bank operations. The success of the NBK's reforms is evident in the reduced number of non-performing loans in Kazakhstani banks (WB, 2017).

These reforms may lead to future economic growth in Kazakhstan; that growth will likely pick up slowly, but remain below pre-2014 levels, when oil prices were robust. The World Bank projects a GDP growth rate of 3% between 2017 and 2019 as the price of oil recovers gradually to US $55–60 per barrel, and oil output from the Kashagan wells begins to increase to offset any lost production from the mainland oil fields. The WB (2017) report notes that, while Kazakhstani export revenues will rise to support the country's fiscal balance payments and budget deficit, the two balance payments will soon reach a shortfall.

The IMF (2015) report suggests that because of lower oil prices and the dismal economic performance that resulted, Kazakhstan's external position is presently weak. While assessing the value of the tenge based on the Assessing Reserve Adequacy (ARA) framework, the report finds the NBK financial reserves to be below the acceptable adequacy range of 100–150% of the country's composite ARA measurement. The report found that the value of the tenge, hinged on two foreign currencies, the rouble and the US dollar, was overvalued by 4–14%. It also notes, however, that the accumulated value of the oil fund (not considered in the ARA assessment)—standing strong at US $75 billion, 35% of the country's real GDP—cushions the economy in general.

According to Borghijs (2017), the Kazakhstani government instituted a twofold plan to counter the nation's economic downturn. He notes that, first, to counteract the falling domestic consumer demand, the NBK introduced a stimulus package aimed at developing small and medium enterprises (SMEs) and the banking sector, as well as to improve infrastructure. Second, to bridge its budget deficit, the NBK withdrew money from the National Fund for the Republic of Kazakhstan (NFRK), established in 2001 to stabilize the economy. Additionally, the government borrowed US $2 billion from the World Bank and the Asian Development Bank (ADB) to finance its balance payment shortfalls. The IMF (2015) report suggests that in order not to deplete the NFRK too soon, the government had pursued gradual fiscal consolidation over the succeeding few years.

Third, the government embarked on a radical change in its monetary policy. Because of devaluation pressure on the tenge, in the middle of 2005, the NBK opted to unpeg the value of the tenge to foreign currencies. As a result, the tenge depreciated against the US dollar from an exchange rate of 185 tenge to the dollar in 2015 to as much as 390 tenge in 2016, later appreciating slightly to exchange at around 330 tenge to the dollar[10] (see Fig. 3.3). Borghijs (2017) observes that interestingly, the tenge mostly trailed behind the rouble exchange rate against the dollar

[10] Current exchange rate is 390 tenge to US $1 (1 December 2019).

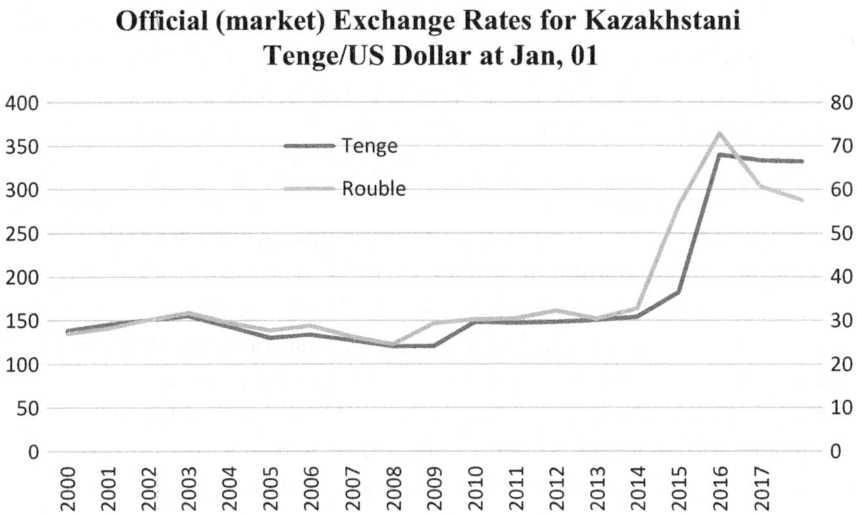

Fig. 3.3 The movement of the dollar exchange rate for the Russian rouble and Kazakhstani tenge. (Source: Authors' calculations based on NBK and CBR data)

during this floatation, as shown in Fig. 3.3. The effect of the depreciation of the tenge was a high inflation rate and even higher prices of imported goods in the wake of diminished demand.

The Effects of OR on Socio-economic Development

Gilpin and Gilpin (2001)argue that under the influence of the order of global markets, statehood appears to lose its distinction. After the end of the Cold War era, international economic scholarship shifted its focus from nations to markets. Consequently, Sakal (2015) observes that Kazakhstan, which liberalized its market to international players after independence, falls in the same category. He suggests that agendas of liberalization and privatization dominated the Kazakhstani political landscape in the 1990s. In this regard, Ostrowski (2010) notes that the country privatized some mining enterprises, transport systems, and oil refineries to foreign corporations throughout this period. Sakal (2015) further suggests that, even currently, the state continues its quest to integrate into the international market by attracting considerable amounts of FDI for the development of its fossil fuel sector, which is a pillar of the country's economic growth and requires massive capital injection.

A number of authors noted that developing and emerging resource-rich economies perform more poorly in terms of economic growth and socio-economic development than those counterparts who lack comparable volumes of natural resources[11] (Sachs & Warner, 1995; Stiglitz, 2007; William, 2011; Crivelli & Gupta, 2014). Scholars have emphasized that Kazakhstan also bears significant risk because of the nation's overreliance on ORs to support its socio-economic development, and suffers from the effects of the *Dutch disease* (Howie & Atakhanova, 2014). Prior research also established a connection between the country's currency exchange rate and volatility in oil prices. For example, Kutan and Wyzan (2005) argued that price volatility of raw materials makes management of natural resource revenues difficult and thereby restricts economic growth. Kalyuzhnova and Patterson (2016) explain that the Dutch Disease is a direct product of an appreciation of a national currency because of a boom accruing from exports of natural resources; in turn, the result is the shrinking of production and the manufacturing sectors in an economy. They assert that the findings from the Jahan-Parvar and Mohammadi (2011) study, as well as the Sachs and Warner (2001) research, demonstrate this principle. The Gylfason (2001) study explains the mechanisms that link natural resource revenues to low economic growth rates, such as low levels of human capital, rent seeking, the Dutch disease, and government mismanagement (Kalyuzhnova & Patterson, 2016).

Some authors consider natural resources to be the engine that propelled economic growth (i.e., Stevens, 2003). They note those additional subsequent studies by scholars such as Lederman and Maloney (2007), Stijns (2005), and earlier research by Maloney (2002), which measured reserves per capita or net resource export by every worker, established the

[11] The O&G industry dominating economy suppresses economic growth and often resource-rich countries are unable to use wealth to develop their economies and have therefore lower economic growth than expected, even lower than natural resource-scarce economies (Sachs & Warner, 1995). This phenomenon has been called a "paradox of plenty" or "resource curse."

positive effect of natural resources on real GDP growth. Nevertheless, among the oil-rich emerging and developing nations examined, only Malaysia, Botswana, Thailand, and Indonesia managed a GDP growth rate of at least 4% along a long-term horizon (Gylfason, 2001). According to Ploeg (2011), the difference between the four oil producers and their underperforming counterparts rested in the economic policies instituted by their governments, particularly in industrialization and economic diversification. Fasano (2000) notes that the United Arab Emirates exemplify an explicit example of an economic diversification policy by using their fossil fuel revenues to improve the living standards of their citizens, especially in social sectors like education, health, and infrastructure improvement.

According to Gylfason (2001), the natural resources sector employs less human capital compared to an industry such as production or manufacturing. He argues that an economy that relies on natural resources for economic growth ought to institute significant diversification policies because the natural wealth becomes increasingly depleted over time. A Director of the Asia and Pacific Department of the IMF suggests (Singh, 2013):

> *for inclusive growth in addition to the wise use of the resources it is imperative that backward and forward linkages are developed between the natural resource sector and the wider economy. Achieving this objective involves financial sector deepening, building infrastructure, enhancing human capital, and promoting the agricultural sector.*

Kalyuzhnova and Patterson (2016) propose that Kazakhstan's government uses its Ministry of Gas and Oil, which manages the fossil fuel sector, to operate the country's energy policy. They note that the basis of the state's energy policy is sustainable economic development, sound environmental practices, promotion of accountability, and adoption of modern technologies to attract maximum FDI.

Successful stories of resource-led economies, such as Finland, Sweden, Norway, Canada, and the UK, can be attributed to strong public institutions and a lower level of corruption. Well-managed government institutions enact sound policies, which help manage natural resource revenues for overall economic development. As a rule, strong institutions are necessary for robust socio-economic performance, but weak public institutions exert an adverse effect on economic growth (Kalyuzhnova & Patterson, 2016).

ORs drained to a centralized institution increase the efficiency of reallocation through economies of scale and stabilize the economy against external shocks (Kendall-Taylor, 2011). Najman et al. (2005) suggested that the distribution system in resource-rich countries can be organized in three ways. First, "official public redistribution" comprises of revenues and taxes that stem from oil exports that the government shares locally, including financial transfers to the NFRK. Second, "company redistribution" includes direct, indirect, and induced incomes, which the oil companies spend or invest locally. This type of revenue is critical in diversifying regional economies. For the OR to benefit more people in the oil-producing regions,[12] it must generate large indirect employment and social programs, since oil companies directly employ only a small number of workers. The third type of OR redistribution, the "unofficial redistribution," reflects two factors at play: informal individual household undertakings created from small businesses and self-employment (usually not declared) and corrupt applications (transacted in secrecy).

Although the inflow of oil incomes accelerated the economic development of the most peripheral regions of Kazakhstan, some regions still experienced little sustainable economic growth (see Fig. 3.4).

Kalyuzhnova and Patterson (2016) noted that the fact that oil-producing western areas remain mainly in poverty is particularly surprising, despite several cycles of oil boom.

The Most Recent Socio-economic Reforms

According to the WB (2017) economic update on Kazakhstan, former President Nazarbayev enacted broad political reforms aimed at creating a balanced political system in the country in the first quarter of 2017. The report notes that through a constitutional amendment, the office of the

[12] Aktobe, Kyzylorda, and the Caspian Sea, later including WKO, Atyrau, and Mangystau.

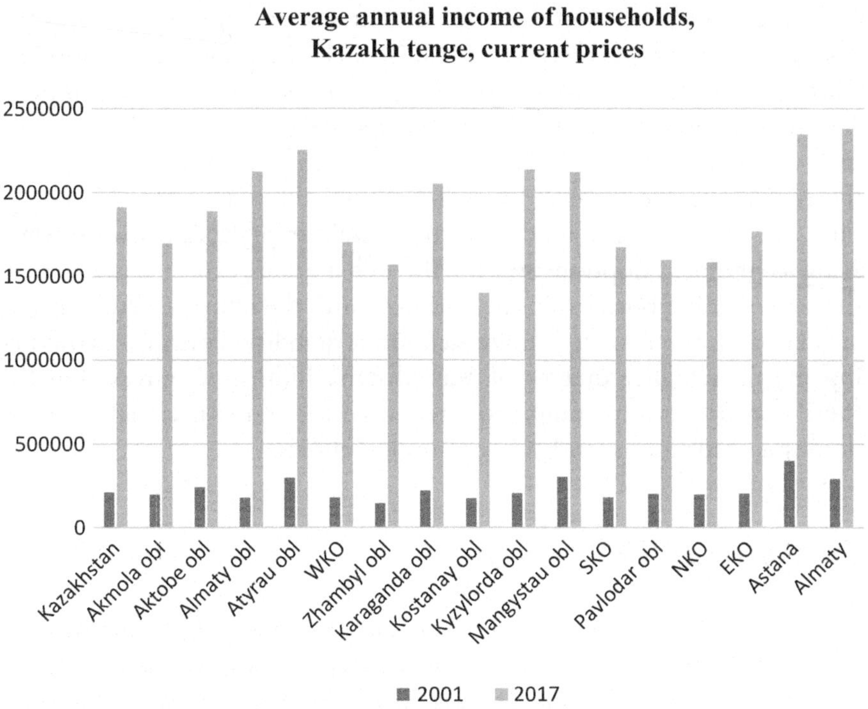

Fig. 3.4 Kazakhstan's regional household income distribution in 2001 and 2017. (Source: Authors, based on Committee on Statistics, Ministry of the national economy of the Republic of Kazakhstan)

president retained most of the critical functions of influencing policy-making decisions, while the office shared part of that power with both parliament and the executive arm of the government. The WB (2017) report notes that the presidency retained its strategic roles, such as commanding security and defense functions, but transferred socio-economic policy management to the other two arms of the government. The report observes that the constitutional amendment also moved the role of creating or dissolving government agencies and approving state programs from the President to the Cabinet. The new changes similarly empowered the lower house of parliament to exercise its powers in the hiring or firing of the cabinet (WB, 2017). The report further suggests that the former president also pledged more authority to local governments.

Termed *Modernization 3.0*, these reforms intended to trigger an economic revolution of Kazakhstan (WB, 2017). According to Borghijs (2017), the sweeping changes were targeted at making the state competitive internationally and place it in the ranks of the top 30 leading economies of the world by 2050. He suggests that economic agenda prioritized five critical areas in its push for economic transformation of the country. First, the plan aimed to modernize the Kazakhstani economy by accelerating technology adoption. Second, these changes are expected to improve the ease of doing business in the nation. Third, the reforms were targeted at increasing the country's macroeconomic stability. Fourth, restructuring meant a higher quality of Kazakhstan's human resources. Finally, these transformations sought to strengthen the state's national security, domestic institutions, and anti-corruption efforts.

Strategy 2050

The WB (2017) report indicates that Kazakhstan is overcoming its economic challenges in the short term. The report, however, also suggests that the state faces a daunting task in the long run in diversifying its economy beyond dependency on fossil fuel revenues. To achieve the goal of becoming one of the top 30 most advanced economies of the world, diversification of the economy is necessary. From this perspective, recent key initiatives in Kazakhstan, namely *Strategy 2050*, as well as the country's *Nurly Zhol* and the *One Hundred Concrete Steps*, aimed at modernizing Kazakhstan, are of particular interest.

Borghijs (2017) argues that Kazakhstani leadership knows of the ominous challenge the country faces in its quest for radical economic growth. He suggests that this understanding drove the country to develop its *Strategy 2050* Program in 2012. The implementation of this plan is a crucial measure of success in the wake of the economic downturn in the state. He suggests that some of the areas of focus in this strategy could include the expansion of sectors driven by high local demand, such as building and construction, machinery assembling, development of pharmaceutical industries, production of construction materials, and promoting industries that bring foreign exchange, including tourism, light industries, and agribusiness. Additionally, the strategy aims to encourage innovation in such vital industries as information technology, communication, clean energy technologies, and biotechnology (Borghijs, 2017).

Nurly Zhol

According to the WB (2017) report, this modernization program, which is intended to compliment the country's long-term strategy, consists of an infrastructure improvement undertaking at the cost of the US $15 billion between 2015 and 2020 periods. The report suggests the infrastructure investments aimed at improving connectivity in this landlocked state are not only in the transport sector but further cover other areas, such as logistics, energy, industry, and utilities (i.e., heating and water systems). Additionally, the report observes that investments also include those oriented toward the growth of the SME sub-sector.

Chin (2016) argues that the ADB study on meeting the infrastructural development needs of the Asian continent forms the basis of the *Nurly Zhol* initiative. He notes that the ADB study estimated infrastructure requirements for central Asian countries in the 2016–2030 period is 7% of the real national GDP, which translates to about US $500 billion. Borghijs (2017) observes that for Central Asia to meet this goal, individual states must make substantial investments in their infrastructure improvement. Consequently, he suggests that Kazakhstan needs to collaborate with various international financial institutions, including the ADB, to raise necessary capital to finance its long-term goals. In this regard, from 1994 to date, Kazakhstan's borrowed amount from the ADB stands at US $4.4 billion. Chin (2016) notes that the nation uses the ADB loans to finance various infrastructure developments, such as transport route networks, boosting national energy security, supporting the growth of the private sector, and supplementing social security.

The *One Hundred Concrete Steps* Concept

Launched in 2015, the *One Hundred Concrete Steps* concept encompasses a wide-ranging set of institutional reforms that includes promoting a professional civil service, strengthening the country's regulatory structure, promoting accountability, transparent government financial management, and improving the administration of public enterprises. The Kazakhstani government is now expected to play a regulatory role in setting targets for the privatization of state-owned businesses between 2016 and 2020. The aim is to promote private sector participation in the economy, enhance efficiency, and reduce state contributions to just 15% of the GDP by transferring its stake into 65 large public enterprises that encompass the postal service, railway network, airports, and Air Astana. The state also took bold steps to promote a business-friendly environment in the nation by making it easier to get electricity, start a business, trade across borders, acquire construction permits, resolve insolvency, and increase protection for small and medium investors. These steps have led to Kazakhstan's ranking increasing to 35 in 2017 from 51 in 2016, as per the *Ease of Doing Business Report* by the WB.

Conclusion

Since the 1990s, oil production in Kazakhstan has increased tremendously, turning oil into the most critical commodity to support the growth of the country's economy. However, this study finds that Kazakhstan's quest to be among the top 10 oil-exporting countries has yet to bear fruit, as the state currently occupies the 12th position among the leading oil exporters in the world (OPEC, 2018). After its declaration of independence and starting the process of privatization of public enterprises, Kazakhstan redesigned its economic structure from a Soviet-era industrial style. In this process, it became a booming economy in terms of oil. Currently, the oil sector contributes about 35% of Kazakhstan's export income and up to 20% of the country's budget expenses. These numbers translate into almost 6.5% of the real national GDP. To this extent, Kazakhstan's government seeks to strengthen the oil sector's role in the economy in the next few decades, as established through its radical reforms. As a result, the government tripled the nation's oil production within a span of twenty years, from 475 thousand barrels a day in 1998 to more than 1.5 million barrels a day in 2018. The country is further increasing its oil output by developing the Caspian wells.

FDI inflows into Kazakhstan rose significantly in the new millennium to support the growth of the oil and energy sectors; however, though the oil sector generates substantial revenues, it contributes less to employment opportunities. This brings us to the role of the policies concerning the redistribution of ORs and how the energy sector in Kazakhstan is governed. The government's *Modernization 3.0* policy strategy intends to initiate an economic insurgency by aiming to turn Kazakhstan into an internationally competitive economy. Through this initiative, Kazakhstani leadership hopes that by 2050, their state will be among the top 30 economies of the world. The current transformative economic agenda targets five strategic areas. The first strategy aims to modernize the national economy through fast-tracking technological acceptance. The second policy expects to create a business-friendly environment to promote the growth of the private sector. The third plan targets increasing the stability of the macroeconomic environment to attract more FDI inflows into Kazakhstan. The fourth strategy, on the other hand, aims to restructure the quality of Kazakhstan's human resources by promoting education for all. Finally, the recent policy change has the aim to transform the state's institutions to encourage accountability, good governance, national security, and anti-corruption measures. To this end, Kazakhstan still needs to put more effort into diversifying its economy and bringing market forces into play.

Bibliography

Baldakhov, U., & Heim, I. (2020). Institutional reform in Kazakhstan. In I. Heim (Ed.), *Kazakhstan's diversification from the natural resources sector: Strategic and economic opportunities*. London, UK: Palgrave Macmillan.

Barney, J. (1991). Firm resources and sustained competitive advantage. *Journal of Management, 17*(1), 99–120.

Borghijs, A. (2017). *Kazakhstan aiming for the top 30.* Retrieved from: https://www.jbic.go.jp/wp-content/uploads/reference_en/2017/03/54472/20170323_seriesMacroKAZ.pdf

British Petroleum (BP). (2019). *Energy outlook.* Retrieved from BP web-site: https://www.bp.com/content/dam/bp/business-sites/en/global/corporate/pdfs/energy-economics/energy-outlook/bp-energy-outlook-2019.pdf

Chin, G. T. (2016). Asian Infrastructure Investment Bank: governance innovation and prospects. *Global Governance: A Review of Multilateralism and International Organizations, 22*(1), 11–25.

Coase, R. H. (1937). The nature of the firm. *Economica, 4*(16), 386–405.

Coase, R. H. (1972). *The firm, the market and the law.* Chicago, IL: University of Chicago Press.

Crivelli, E. & Gupta, S. (2014). *Resource blessing, revenue curse?* Domestic revenue effort in resource-rich countries. IMF Working Paper. Retrieved from IMF web-site http://citeseerx.ist.psu.edu/viewdoc/download?doi=10.1.1.434.7256&rep=rep1&type=pdf

Fasano, U. (2000). *Review of the experience with oil stabilization and saving funds in selected countries.* IMF working paper. Washington: International Monetary Fund, pp. 3–19. Retrieved from https://www.imf.org/external/pubs/ft/wp/2000/wp00112.pdf

Gilpin, R., & Gilpin, J. (2001). *Global political economy – Understanding the international economic order.* Princeton, NJ: Princeton University Press.

Gylfason, T. (2001). *Natural resources and economic growth: What is the connection?* CESifo working paper. Retrieved from: http://hdl.handle.net/10419/75741

Hardin, K. (2012). *Kazakhstan's energy sector since independence: Two decades of growth and challenges ahead?* Retrieved from: https://www.files.ethz.ch/isn/136798/012712_ACUS_Eurasia_Hardin.pdf

Heim, I., & Romanov, M. (2020). The oil and gas industry in Kazakhstan's investment regimes. In I. Heim (Ed.), *Kazakhstan's diversification from the natural resources sector: Strategic and economic opportunities.* London, UK: Palgrave Macmillan.

Howie, P., & Atakhanova, Z. (2014). Resource boom and inequality: Kazakhstan as a case study. *Resources Policy, 39*, 71–79.

IMF. (2015). *Republic of Kazakhstan – 2015 Article IV consultation – Press release; staff report for the republic of Kazakhstan*. Retrieved from IMF web-site: https://www.imf.org/external/pubs/ft/scr/2015/cr15241.pdf

Jahan-Parvar, M., & Mohammadi, H. (2011). Oil prices and real exchange rates in oil-exporting countries: A bounds testing approach. *The Journal of Developing Areas, 45*(1), 309–318.

Kalyuzhnova, Y., & Patterson, K. (2016). Kazakhstan: Long-term economic growth and the role of the oil sector. *Comparative Economic Studies, 58*(1), 93–118.

Kendall-Taylor, A. (2011). Instability and oil: How political time horizons affect oil revenue management. *Studies in Comparative International Development, 46*(3), 321–348.

Khakas, H., & Kohli, H. (2011). What is the middle-income trap, why do countries fall into it, and how can it be avoided? *Global Journal of Emerging Market Economies, 3*(3), 281–289.

Kutan, A., & Wyzan, M. (2005). Explaining the real exchange rate in Kazakhstan, 1996–2003: Is Kazakhstan vulnerable to the Dutch disease? *Economic Systems, 29*(2), 242–255.

Lederman, D., & Maloney, W. (2007). *Natural resources, neither curse nor destiny*. Palo Alto, CA: Stanford University Press.

Maloney, W. (2002). Missed opportunities: innovation and resource-based growth in Latin America. *Economia, 3*(1), 111–167.

Moe, T. M. (1984). The new economics of organization. *American Journal of Political Science, 28*(4), 739–777.

Najman, B., Pomfret, R., Raballand, G., & Sourdin, P. (2005). *How are oil revenues redistributed in an oil economy? The case of Kazakhstan*. Adelaide, SA: University of Adelaide, School of Economics. Retrieved from http://www.economics.adelaide.edu.au/research/papers/doc/wp2005-18.pdf

Nelson, R. R., & Winter, S. G. (1982). The Schumpeterian trade-off revisited. *American Economic Review, 72*(1), 114–132.

North, D. C. (1990). *Institutions, institutional change and economic performance*. Cambridge, UK: Cambridge University Press.

North, D. C. (1994). Economic performance through time. *American Economic Review, 84*(3), 359–368.

O&G Journal. (1991). *First Tengiz oil well placed on production*. June 03, 1991. Retrieved from https://www.ogj.com/articles/print/volume-89/issue-22/in-this-issue/general-interest/first-tengiz-oil-well-placed-on-production.html

OPEC (2018). OPEC Bulletin 2018. Retrieved from https://www.opec.org/opec_web/en/publications/202.htm

Ostrom, E. (1990). *Governing the commons*. New York, UK: Cambridge University Press.

Ostrom, E. (2005). *Understanding institutional diversity*. Princeton, NJ: Princeton University Press.

Ostrowski, W. (2010). *Politics and oil in Kazakhstan*. London, UK: Routledge.

Peng, M. M. (2003). Institutional transitions and strategic choices. *Academy of Management Review, 28*(2), 275–296.

Peng, M. M., & Meyer, K. E. (2016). *International business*. London, UK: Sengage Learning.

Penrose, E. T. (1959). *The theory of the growth of the firm*. Oxford, UK: Basil Blackwell.

Ploeg, F. (2011). Natural resources: Curse or blessing? *Journal of Economic Literature, 49*(2), 366–420.

Pomfret, R. (2005). Kazakhstan's economy since independence: Does the oil boom offer a second chance for sustainable development? *Europe-Asia Studies, 57*(6), 859–876.

Rahmanov, R. (2016). Permanent and temporary oil price shocks, macroeconomic policy, and tradable non-oil sector: Case of Azerbaijan, Kazakhstan, and Russia. In *Proceedings of annual conference of the Bilateral Assistance and Capacity Building for Central Banks (BCC)* (pp. 1–21). Central Bank of the Republic of Azerbaijan. Retrieved from: https://www.cbar.az/assets/4321/WP-series-09_2016.pdf

Sachs, J., & Warner, A. (2001). Natural resources and economic development – The curse of natural resources. *European Economic Review, 45*(1), 827–838.

Sachs, J., & Warner, A. M. (1995a). *Natural resource abundance and economic growth*. NBER working paper series. Working paper 5398. Cambridge, UK: National Bureau of Economic Research.

Sakal, H. B. (2015). Natural resource policies and standard of living in Kazakhstan. *Central Asian Survey, 34*(2), 237–254.

Scott, W. R. (2014). *Institutions and organizations*. Thousand Oaks, CA: Sage.

Singh, A. (2013). Harnessing natural resource wealth for inclusive growth and economic development. In *Conference on harnessing natural resource wealth for inclusive growth and economic development*. International Monetary Fund.

Stevens, P. (2003). Resource impact-curse or blessing? *Investment Policy, 22*, 5–6.

Stiglitz, J. E. (2007). In M. Humphreys, J. Sachs, & J. E. Stiglitz (Eds.), *Escaping the resource curse* (pp. 23–52). New York, NY: Columbia University Press.

Stijns, J.-P. C. (2005). Natural resource abundance and economic growth revisited. *Resources Policy, 30*(2), 107–130.
The Guardian. (2017). *China to ban production of petrol and diesel cars in the near future.* Retrieved from: https://www.theguardian.com/world/2017/sep/11/china-to-ban-production-of-petrol-and-diesel-cars-in-the-near-future
Vargo, S. L., & Lusch, R. F. (2016). Institutions and axioms: an extension and update of service-dominant logic. *Journal of the Academy of Marketing Science, 44*(1), 5–23.
WB. (2005). *Republic of Kazakhstan – Getting competitive, staying competitive: The challenge of managing Kazakhstan's oil boom.* Retrieved from the WB website http://siteresources.worldbank.org/INTKAZAKHSTAN/Resources/CEMengApril27.pdf
WB. (2017). *Kazakhstan – The economy has bottomed out: What is next?* Country economic update. Retrieved from WB web-site: http://documents.worldbank.org/curated/en/585891494402103086/pdf/114856-9-5-2017-20-39-19-KAZCEUclearedforpublication.pdf
William, A. (2011). Shining a light on the resource curse: an empirical analysis of the relationship between natural resources, transparency, and economic growth. *World Development, 39*(4), 490–505.
Williamson, O. E. (1981). The Economics of Organization: the transaction cost approach. *The American Journal of Sociology, 87*(3), 548–577.
Williamson, O. E. (2000). The new institutional economics: taking stock, looking ahead. *Journal of Economic Literature, 38*(3), 595–613.

Part II

Kazakhstan: Strategic Opportunities

The authors of the chapters in this section discuss the advantages of geopolitical positioning of Kazakhstan on the way from China to Europe. Chapter 4 by Ribberink and Schubert changes the focus of discussion from national development initiatives to international, introducing the Belt and Road Initiative (BRI) of the Chinese Government to invest in transportation and digital infrastructure in the Central Asian countries, mainly Kazakhstan, which become a new transportation hub in the region. Ambalov and Heim investigate digital connectiveness alongside the New Silk Road—the second important focus of BRI.

4

Infrastructure Investment and Development Alongside the Belt and Road Initiative

Natalia Ribberink and Lisa Schubert

Introduction

Infrastructure is a key factor for achieving sustainable development goals such as economic growth, human development, and poverty reduction (Miyamoto & Chiofalo, 2015). To prevent under-provision or non-provision of infrastructure, infrastructure policies are introduced by governments or supranational bodies (Égert, Koźluk, & Sutherland, 2009; Estache & Wren-Lewis, 2012). These policies are said to drive investment in infrastructure, which in turn should benefit the economic growth of the recipient economy (Fleischer, 2003). Along with subsidies, allocation of funds to problematic regions and tax incentives, infrastructure investments in the context of BRI should be evaluated in the context of institutional theory on economic geography, focusing hereby on regional development and policy instruments with institutional

N. Ribberink (✉) • L. Schubert
Department of Business, Hamburg University of Applied Science, Hamburg, Germany
e-mail: natalia.ribberink@haw-hamburg.de

I. Heim (ed.), *Kazakhstan's Diversification from the Natural Resources Sector*, Euro-Asian Studies, https://doi.org/10.1007/978-3-030-37389-4_4

dimensions (Kušar, 2011). The BRI may potentially provide evidence to revisit the theoretical institutional concepts of untraded interdependencies (Storper, 1997) and institutional space (Martin, 2005), which currently are investigated on the basis of successful and mainly homogeneous economic regions (Kušar, 2011).

Recently, to benefit from the effects of infrastructure, a number of countries are increasingly involving in the Belt and Road Initiative (BRI), a large-scale infrastructure project introduced by China (Liu, 2016; Vangeli, 2017). Kazakhstan will become a logistical linchpin in the BRI, as discussed later (see Selmier, 2020, this volume). This chapter analyzes the BRI and a special focus is placed on the criterion of private sector involvement opportunities. The analysis is based on the BRI website screenings and accompanied by additional literature-based insights. Here, the Belt and Road website established by the Hong Kong Trade Development Council (HKTDC) and the Business Opportunities' section of the Asian Infrastructure Investment Bank (AIIB) are screened. The HKTDC is a statutory body aiming at promoting and creating opportunities for Hong Kong businesses with a global network of 40 offices (HKTDC, 2018a). Under their website's Belt and Road section, they provide a database of investment projects from major economies along the Belt and Road that are open to cooperation (HKTDC, n.d.). The AIIB is a multilateral development bank, initiated by China, which focuses on the provision of financial support for the development of infrastructure (Zou, 2018).

Infrastructure and Large-scale Infrastructure Investment Policy

The term infrastructure can be defined in different ways, economic infrastructure, which comprises assets that enable the society and the economy to function, such as transport, telecommunications, electricity and water. The term also relates to social infrastructure, which comprises assets to support the provision of public services, such as schools, hospitals and social housing, human capital and institutional infrastructure (International Transport Forum, 2018; World Economic Forum and

Boston Consulting Group, 2014). Infrastructure is also characterized by the need for investment, meaning the need to set up and develop transport, energy, and telecommunication networks. Further, it is also characterized by long-term usage and capital commitment, as well as high capital requirements. Infrastructure is of the utmost importance for every country: it enlarges markets for labor and goods, as well as increasing output and productivity of an economy (Delmon, 2017). Therefore, poor infrastructure may impede economic growth and international competitiveness (ibid.).

Infrastructure policies are all public or governmental measures aiming at the supply and improvement of infrastructure in a country or across a region (Gabler, 2014). An adequate infrastructure is the base for potential economic growth as well as competitiveness, so therefore essential (Revoltella, Brutscher, Tsiotras, & Weiss, 2016). However, it is not only governments that may introduce infrastructure policy; it can also stem from supranational bodies. In this latter case, there are several options. The first may be centralized harmonization, meaning that a supranational body can make policy decisions that are binding to all member states. The second option is decentralized harmonization, which implies that the regulatory body has no power to affect the policy but may increase and facilitate information exchange between the member states. The third option would provide the supranational body with the power to introduce binding policies, where the exact implementation is responsibility of each member state (Estache & Wren-Lewis, 2012).

Different reasons for the introduction of infrastructure policies can also be identified. Generally, governments involve themselves in infrastructure sectors through policy introduction in order to prevent under-provision or non-provision of infrastructure. The reason for government involvement in the infrastructure sector and policy intervention may evolve from *market failure* (see Baldakhov & Heim, 2020, this volume). For example, in the case of the existence of a natural monopoly, private suppliers can exercise their market power by providing a service below the required level, but at a higher price, which needs to be regulated by the government. Furthermore, the policy could be a reaction to network externalities and distributional concerns, such as environmental concerns, and the aim of providing infrastructure services at affordable prices. There can also be specific cases where the provision of infrastructure by the private sector is restrained by the costs of a project or its technical feasibility, in cases when infrastructure would not otherwise be if the government did not intervene (Égert et al., 2009).

Regardless of the issuing body, infrastructure policies can be seen as the drivers of infrastructure investment, in turn, a driving force of an economy (Fleischer, 2003). An infrastructure policy may be considered large-scale if it aims at improving infrastructure through increasing investment in more than one country. These policies are designed to ensure that infrastructure meets social needs, that the most appropriate providers are involved and that related investment is efficient (Égert et al., 2009). In order to achieve this, infrastructure policies can involve the public and private sector to different extents (ibid.).

Infrastructure Investment

Infrastructure investment can be classified as a key feature of governmental policy in both developed and developing countries (Chatterjee, Posch, & Wesselbaum, 2017). Such an infrastructure policy may influence provision and ownership of infrastructure, whereby different actors can be involved in the investment. Public policies may focus on public provision and ownership or private provision and ownership, as well as a mixture of both variants. The mix of public and private involvement in infrastructure investment and establishment could be in the form of public-private partnerships (PPPs) (Directorate-General for Internal Policies of the Union, 2010; Égert et al., 2009). A PPP can be understood as an agreement between a government authority and a private firm, having the delivery of a public infrastructure project and service under a long-term contract as its subject (McGuinn et al., 2016). These partnerships can accelerate infrastructure development, as the private sector's financial resources are incorporated in the investment and its skills in designing, building and operating infrastructure may be used (World Economic Forum and Boston Consulting Group, 2013). Recently, PPPs have become increasingly relevant for public infrastructure investment, especially in the transport sector, as they serve as an alternative to spending by governments (Égert et al., 2009; Inderst, 2016). This form of infrastructure financing can be especially interesting if governments wish to reduce their fiscal deficit (Klein, 2012).

Considering investments in transport infrastructure, the term infrastructure investment covers all spending on new transport construction as well as the improvement of existing networks (OECD, 2018). At times, investment in infrastructure is classified as a foreign direct investment (FDI), where the investor invests in infrastructure assets abroad. These assets usually comprise gas, oil, petrochemicals, electricity utilities, transportation, mining, telecommunication and other tangible assets (Sawant, 2010). Yet, there is no unified definition of the term FDI, which means the term can be conceptualized differently and will not always be used in the matter of infrastructure investment. The most common concept of FDI is "the commitment by one country or firm or individual … to put substantial resources in another country … for the purpose of running a business in one sector or other of the recipient country" (Bodomo, 2017, p. 8). As indicated by the definition, the infrastructure investment would need to be on a larger scale, meaning across countries.

Investment in infrastructure has several effects on the host economy. If the investment is performed thoughtfully, it has the potential to increase an economy's productive potential in the long-term perspective (Rhodes, 2018). This may be enabled through enhanced connectivity of transport infrastructure and through decreasing transportation costs (Bhattacharyay & Bhattacharyay, 2017). Since high logistical costs are seen as a factor negatively affecting trade volumes, a decrease in transportation costs would allow companies to increase the volume of traded goods and utilize the advantage of economies of scale (Celbis, Nijkamp, & Poot, 2014; Rhodes, 2018). Further, infrastructure investment can enable improvement of economic efficiency, as the newly established or improved infrastructure may allow people to move or commute easier and follow employment opportunities in accordance with their skills (Rhodes, 2018). Through these effects, infrastructure may increase economic growth (Bhattacharyay & Bhattacharyay, 2017); however, the actual effect of infrastructure investment on growth is largely country-specific (Égert et al., 2009).

The Belt and Road Initiative

The Belt and Road Initiative, which was first proposed by President Xi Jinping in October 2013, may be understood as a systematic approach to jointly build the Silk Road Economic Belt (SREB), and the twenty-first-century Maritime Silk Road (MSR), often also simply referred to as Belt and Road (State Council of the People's Republic of China, 2015) and evolved from China's *Going Global* strategy (Liu, 2016). The initiative targets are, to a great extent, overseas investments in infrastructure projects, such as roads, railways and seaports, but also in information and communication technology as well as in energy (EY, 2015; Larçon & Barré, 2017), with a focus on improving transport connectivity along the targeted regions (Steer Davies Gleave, 2018).

However, the objective of the BRI is not limited to infrastructure establishment. According to the State Council of the People's Republic of China (2015) the initiative aims at "[…] promoting orderly and free flow of economic factors, highly efficient allocation of resources and deep integration of markets; encouraging the countries along the Belt and Road to achieve economic policy coordination and carry out broader and more in-depth regional cooperation of higher standards; and jointly creating an open, inclusive and balanced regional economic cooperation architecture that benefits all". Geographically and economically, the initiative is said to cover, or rather involve, about 65 countries across Asia, Africa and Europe (Li & Tang, 2017), jointly comprising 30% of the world's population and around 60% of global GDP (Steer Davies Gleave, 2018).

The BRI as a large-scale initiative identifies several overland corridors (Derudder, Liu, & Kunaka, 2018), but it does not yet provide a clearly defined development plan nor a clear list of projects to be concluded under the BRI (Steer Davies Gleave, 2018). One underlying reason for this may be the intention of China to present the initiative as an open and nonexclusive program (Grimmel & Li, 2018). The only available description of BRI projects can be found in the *Vision and Actions on Jointly Building a Silk Road Economic Belt and 21st-Century Maritime Silk Road*, published by the Chinese National Development and Reform Commission, Ministry of Foreign Affairs and Ministry of Commerce of the People's Republic of China (2015), which states that the initiative covers the area of the ancient Silk Road but does not limit its scope to this area. Projects under the BRI are not only limited to investment in transport infrastructure but also cover other areas such as telecommunication and electricity as well as "other projects conducive to the improvement of people's living standard along the Silk Road" (Bank of China, 2017). Concerning the definition of transport infrastructure under the BRI, there is no official document stating what is to be included under the broad definition of transport infrastructure. However, transport infrastructure, which is planned to be established under the BRI, will include, among others, railways, roads and seaports (Larçon & Barré, 2017).

An additional reason for the lack of clear definition of projects or a list of projects might be the evolving character of the BRI, as it is continuously reshaped and developing through engagement between third countries and China and the fact that the BRI may not be seen as a program of specific investments (Steer Davies Gleave, 2018). Besides, the initiative does not have a clearly defined timeline as to when the projects pursuing the development of all related corridors are to be completed. However, the initiative is believed to be in place until 2049, which will be the year of the 100th anniversary of the People's Republic of China (Hillman, 2018a). Besides the nature of the BRI, which seemingly does not provide an exact definition of a BRI project, it appears that there is no single branch of the Chinese government reporting and responsible for projects, which leads to the lack of a database enabling the identification of BRI projects (Steer Davies Gleave, 2018). Based on the findings, the BRI may allow any project to be part of the initiative as long as it falls into the geographical scope of the initiative.

Regional Participation

Considering the geographical scope of the project, the BRI covers a wide area and includes many countries. Until now, most of the engagement, and thereby most of the investment in infrastructure under the BRI, has come from China or Chinese enterprises (Baker McKenzie, 2017; Deloitte, 2018). However, the BRI is inviting countries to join the construction process of the SREB and the MSR (National Development and Reform Commission, 2015) and should not be understood as an investment plan exclusively led by China (Zou, 2018). The BRI is said to be open and inclusive, allowing any country or economy interested in participating, supporting and benefiting from the BRI to do so (ibid.). However, due to the heterogeneity of countries along the SREB and MSR as well as the fact that several countries covered by the BRI are classified as developing countries or regions, it is said to be more difficult to achieve regional integration (Grimmel & Li, 2018), and promoting participation in the implementation provides a greater challenge.

To accomplish regional participation, apart from the introduction of policies for domestic construction and development, the Chinese government attaches great importance to international bilateral and multilateral cooperation since the implementation of the initiative, and thereby the establishment of the Belt and Road greatly depends on the joint efforts of countries along the different routes as well as on the enterprises located within those countries (Donghong & Lingling, 2017). While striving for international bilateral and multilateral cooperation, the BRI also emphasizes policy coordination between target regions. This means that countries along the Belt and Road are asked to jointly formulate development plans and measures for advancing cross-national or regional cooperation, to function as support for practical cooperation in order to enable the implementation of large-scale projects (HKTDC, 2018b).

From September 2013 onward, China has repeatedly included the BRI on its diplomatic agenda, promoting the BRI on diversified platforms and made it a frequently mentioned term during official visits within all important countries and regional organizations along the Belt and Road, with the aim of deepening the understanding of target regions and increasing their willingness to participate (Zou, 2018). So far, China has pursued several agreements and memoranda of understandings (MoUs) with foreign countries. The main aim of these agreements and MoUs is to achieve policy coordination, and many of them aim to align national or regional development plans of the BRI targeted regions with the plans to establish the SREB and the MSR (Pauls & Gottwald, 2018). By the end of 2017, China had signed 100 agreements to jointly build the Belt and Road with 86 countries and international organizations (Zou, 2018). However, since the BRI has only been introduced in 2013, the levels of regional participation, the mechanisms used to achieve it as well as a general commitment to regional integration and cooperation among foreign countries are not yet defined (Pauls & Gottwald, 2018).

In the case of Kazakhstan, some domestic efforts demonstrating the potential of interconnectedness and correspondence with the BRI objectives can already be reported. In 2015 the state program of infrastructure development *Nurly Zhol* for 2015–2019 was launched and approved by the President of the Republic of Kazakhstan through the Decree of April 6, 2015, No. 1030 (Ministry of Foreign Affairs Kazakhstan, 2018). The program aims at the integration of the main domestic regions in Kazakhstan through establishing an effective infrastructure by means of the hub approach. These efforts are expected to lead to the formation of an interlinked domestic market, with increased efficiency and long-term economic growth of the Kazakh economy. While initially designed for domestic needs, this program is eligible to complement the infrastructural development alongside the BRI campaign, through the integration of newly established domestic routes and nodes on the BRI grid.

Private Sector Involvement Opportunities Under the BRI

Private sector involvement is an objective that has been recognized under the BRI; although the BRI is promoted by the Chinese government, it is the enterprises that play the primary role in BRI construction (Zou, 2018, p. 161). So far, Chinese state-owned enterprises have, to a great extent, been the beneficiaries of the BRI project construction (Deloitte, 2018), which would imply little involvement of private-owned companies or international companies. However, this is likely to change as the BRI is said to be not only for the benefit of Chinese state-owned enterprises (Zou, 2018) but also for the increasing number of MNEs obtaining deals for BRI project, both of which continue growing (Deloitte, 2018).

To increase private sector involvement, the problem of transparency, which seems to persist and may be a hurdle to an increased involvement of enterprises, including foreign enterprises, needs to be solved (ibid.). Deloitte (2018) suggests partnering with national, provincial or local government agencies such as the National Development and Reform Commission, Chinese state-owned and private-owned companies as well as other MNEs and professional institutions. This suggestion indicates a wide variety of options for partnering, again underlining the problem of the lack of a single Chinese government body responsible for BRI projects, while it also begs the question of how this process can be structured openly. Nevertheless, two institutions list opportunities for private sector involvement, namely the HKTDC and the AIIB, but these two institutions may not be the sole providers of information on participation opportunities.

The Belt and Road website established by the HKTDC provides a section that lists investment projects from major countries along the Belt and Road. The website aims to assist businesses by providing them with a database of opportunities. Most projects included in the database are said to be infrastructure related. However, they may also belong to other areas and the website allows for filtering by sector and region as well as a form of cooperation. A further opportunity for private sector involvement is provided by the AIIB; the AIIB serves its purpose as a support platform for building the Belt and Road, as it has been established by several countries and therefore also provides a platform for joint participation and consulting (Zhu, 2015). The website of the AIIB provides a section labeled "Business Opportunities", under which project procurement opportunities can be found. These opportunities comprise AIIB-financed projects that are open for tender, and participation is open to suppliers, contractors, and consultants worldwide (Asian Infrastructure Investment Bank, n.d.).

Similar to the database provided by the HKTDC, the AIIB only serves as a platform for information on open opportunities but does not provide a platform where the actual tendering takes place. Therefore, it is unclear how exactly the process should take place. Although there are seemingly different platforms in place that allow for private sector involvement, the actual procedure of such involvement is nontransparent. Overall, Chinese projects are less open to local and international participation. Out of all contractors involved in Chinese-funded projects, 89% are Chinese companies, followed by a minority of local and foreign companies (Hillman, 2018b.).

Investment Volume, Funding, and Financing

The determination of the investment volume under the BRI is somewhat limited. This may be explained by a lack of clearly defined projects as well as lack of set plans for development and implementation of infrastructure along with the targeted and participating countries (Hillman, 2018a; Steer Davies Gleave, 2018). Therefore, numbers on investment volumes are only available for some countries; additionally, these numbers may include projects not directly related to the BRI or may not differentiate between the kinds of infrastructure to be established under the BRI.

The BRI may be the largest overseas investment program launched by a single country, and as a result, financing of the initiative is complex (Rizzi & Tettamanti, 2018). Currently, China has the highest financial commitment, through the involvement of different financial institutions but also the state itself. Different banks and funds are involved, of which the majority are Chinese or Chinese funded (Rizzi & Tettamanti, 2018; Steer Davies Gleave, 2018). The private sector is also regarded as an important funding channel, though the involvement has so far been minor (Tettamanti, 2018). However, this may change as the initiative aims to attract private capital, among others, in the form of public-private partnerships (Jianxun, 2017). Due to many different stakeholders, a complex structure of funds and financing options under the BRI framework is evolving. Some major financing and funding sources, which do not reflect all supporting institutions and mechanisms, are illustrated in Fig. 4.1.

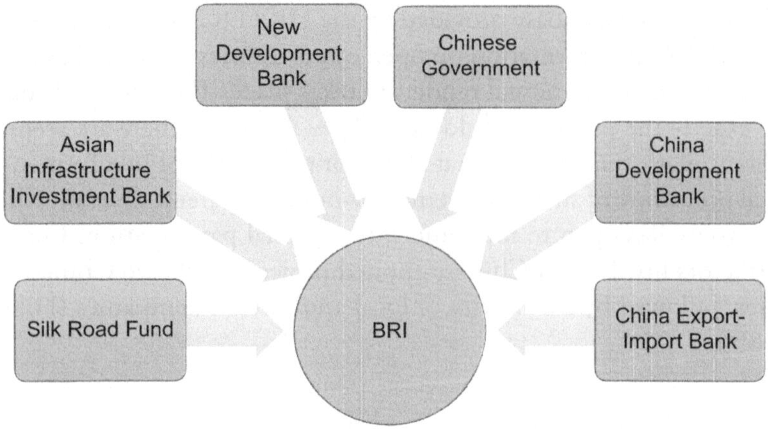

Fig. 4.1 Major financing and funding sources of the BRI. (Source: Authors' own graphic based on Baker McKenzie (2017), EY (2015) and Steer Davies Gleave (2018))

So far, the majority of investments into infrastructure has come from China or Chinese enterprises. Chinese policy banks, for example the China Development Bank (CDB) and the Export-Import Bank of China (EIBC), are especially active (Baker McKenzie, 2017; Steer Davies Gleave, 2018). The CDB is a financial institution set up by the Chinese government with a development-oriented focus, mainly supporting infrastructure development, construction and the development of basic and pillar industries. The EIBC is a Chinese governmental policy financial institution, which focuses on the financial support of electrical and mechanical equipment, high-tech product import and export as well as foreign project contracting and foreign investment. Both policy banks not only provide financing to Chinese companies engaged in infrastructure development along the Belt and Road but also contribute to the Silk Road Fund (SRF) (EY, 2015). So far, the China Development Bank (CDB) has pledged US $38 billion as support for cooperation in the financing, infrastructure and industrial capacity, while the EIBC has pledged US $20 billion for the same purpose (Steer Davies Gleave, 2018). Although China's commitment has been prevailing, this imbalance is expected to change over time, as the BRI grows in scale and size, and Chinese policy banks have no intention of fully funding the BRI projects

(Baker McKenzie, 2017). This is underlined by the fact that the CDB has signed a memorandum with Deutsche Bank which seeks cooperation under the BRI (Rizzi & Tettamanti, 2018). In addition to policy banks as major financiers of the BRI, the Chinese government has pledged US $8 billion to support countries as well as international organizations participating in the BRI.

In 2014, as an additional support, the Silk Road Fund (SRF) was established (Larçon & Barré, 2017), providing a capital of US $40 billion and 100 billion renminbi (RMB), contributed by multiple Chinese agencies: the State Administration of Foreign Exchange contributed 65%, the China Investment Corporation 15%, the CDB 5% and the EIBC 15% to the overall capital (Silk Road Fund, n.d.-a, n.d.-b). The fund, which has been established as a long-term development fund, aims at promoting social and economic development, as well as interconnection along the Belt and Road (EY, 2015).

The focus of the BRI lies in Central Asia, including Kazakhstan (Pauls & Gottwald, 2018). The fund is positioned to provide equity investment, including direct investment, debt investment such as loans and bonds as well as investment in funds, meaning that the fund may create sub-funds. With US $2 billion of investment volume dedicated to Kazakhstan, the fund aims to provide equity predominantly for projects with the potential of successful implementation which would otherwise have too high a debt ratio, if financed with debt (Silk Road Fund, n.d.-a, n.d.-b). Investment is said to follow four principles, which are integration, profit, cooperation and openness. The principal of integration means that investments should be in line with national development strategies and the planning of involved countries. The principle of profit implies that investments should only be directed to profitable projects. The third principle demands cooperation with domestic and foreign enterprises as well as financial institutions. Lastly, the principle of openness describes an inclusive approach, referring to the openness to the involvement of any country that is interested in participating (Zou, 2018). Although these principles touch upon a clearer description of eligibility, they do not state in detail how financial support decisions are made or which exact variables are taken into account.

In addition to the Silk Road Fund, the AIIB, which was established in 2015, further aims to partially finance the large investment needed for projects across Asia and other target regions of the initiative. This multilateral financial institution has been founded by 57 countries (HKTDC, 2018b), of which 37 are regional, i.e. Asian, countries and 20 are non-regional countries (Pauls & Gottwald, 2018). Meanwhile, the number of shareholder countries in the AIIB has increased to 87, while the largest shareholders are China, Russia, Germany, France, India, Australia and Korea. The focus of the AIIB is on improvement of Asia's infrastructure (Asian Infrastructure Investment Bank, 2016b). Nevertheless, Article 11 (1) of the Articles of Agreement of the bank states that funding may be provided to all members, regional or non-regional, including any agency, instrumentality or political subdivision of members, as well as any entity or enterprise operating within any member's territory; this funding may also be extended to nonmembers, if support serves the objectives and interests of the bank (Asian Infrastructure Investment Bank, n.d.). Although financing is therefore not regionally limited, the actual financial support provided by the AIIB to non-regional members is limited. The current limit for the financing of non-regional members, set for 2018, amounts to 15% of the total approved financing by the bank (Asian Infrastructure Investment Bank, n.d.). The AIIB set three thematic priorities for its activities, namely the support of cross-border projects, the introduction of instruments improving private capital mobilization and the support of sustainable or green infrastructure. Funding provided by the AIIB will be in the form of sovereign-backed and non-sovereign-backed loans and equity participation as well as guarantees (Asian Infrastructure Investment Bank, 2016b). Regarding the loan provision of the bank, the projects submitted will be assessed across several criteria, taking into account the project's development objectives, scope and design, and the soundness of technology used. It will include other technical variables, as well as economic soundness, including an analysis of the project's costs, risks and financial soundness, as well as environmental and social variables. The other variables to be taken into account are integrity and financial management, legal concerns and procurement (Asian Infrastructure Investment Bank, 2016a, b). Non-sovereign-backed loans will only cover 35% of any project's value but may be higher, if no other form of co-financing is available (Asian Infrastructure Investment Bank, 2016a, b).

With the aim of funding projects in developing countries, the BRICS New Development Bank was established in July 2014. This is an international multilateral financial institution and the initial capital of US $100 billion was provided evenly by member state signatory to the establishment of the bank (EY, 2015). The BRICS countries are Brazil, Russia, India, China, and South Africa (Wulf, 2015). Although the name may indicate a sole focus on the BRICS countries, the bank focuses not only on those five countries but also on other emerging and developing economies (Carrai, 2018; Zou, 2018). Furthermore, even though the BRICS New Development Bank is frequently mentioned under the light of the BRI, the bank is not directly linked to it, as it will fund infrastructure-related projects across the world and is not limited to or aiming at financing BRI projects only, and has, so far, not financed any project directly linked to the BRI (Carrai, 2018; Rizzi & Tettamanti, 2018). Therefore, the findings on the BRICS New Development Bank stand in contrast to the claim that the bank is a major financer of the BRI.

Besides the main financial supporters illustrated above, other funds such as the China-Eurasia Economic Cooperation Fund, the China-CEE Investment Cooperation Fund and the China-ASEAN Maritime Cooperation Fund, as well as multilateral financial organizations such as the World Bank and the Asian Development Bank, are involved in the establishment of the SREB and the MSR by way of financing their establishment (Jianxun, 2017).

Overall, several options for financing are given; however, financial support available under the BRI is most likely not to cover the cost of a whole project in participating countries and is mainly focused on Asia. These financial options could potentially open up further project and partnership opportunities for Kazakhstan.

Conclusion

Large-scale infrastructure investment policies are introduced by governments or supranational bodies to cope with under-provision or even non-provision of infrastructure; these policies target a greater geographical region and the infrastructure can take many different forms, including economic and social infrastructure. The introduction of infrastructure investment policy aims at increasing investment in the provision or improvement of infrastructure, while the actors involved in the provision may be public, private or a combination of both, for example through public-private projects. The investment in infrastructure boosts economic growth, reduces trade costs, and increases competitiveness, while the actual effects on any individual economy may vary.

The BRI—being a representative and current example of a large-scale infrastructure investment policy—creates various opportunities for the Kazakh economy to catch up in terms of economic development, international trade and global value chain participation, assuming a sophisticated and sustainable integration of related projects and their proper implementation at the national level in correspondence with long-term domestic development goals.

Bibliography

Asian Infrastructure Investment Bank. (2016a). *Operational policy on financing.* Retrieved from https://www.aiib.org/en/policies-strategies/operational-policies/operational-policy-financing.html

Asian Infrastructure Investment Bank. (2016b). *Procurement policy.* Retrieved from https://www.aiib.org/en/opportunities/business/.content/index/_download/20160226051326635.pdf.

Asian Infrastructure Investment Bank. (n.d.). *Business opportunities.* Retrieved from https://www.aiib.org/en/opportunities/business/index.html?business=investment.

Balázs, P., Bodewig, K., Brinkhorst, L. J., Cox, P., Grosch, M., Peijs, K., Secchi, C., Simpson, B., Trautmann, C., Vinck, K., & Wojciechowski, P. (2017).

Joint declaration of the European coordinators on the future of TEN-T & CEF. Brussels, Belgium: European Commission.

Baldakhov, U., & Heim, I. (2020). Institutional reform in Kazakhstan. In I. Heim (Ed.), *Kazakhstan's diversification from the natural resources sector: Strategic and economic opportunities*. London, UK: Palgrave Macmillan.

Bank of China. (2017). *BoC economic review monthly*. Hong Kong, China: Bank of China.

Bhattacharyay, B. N., & Bhattacharyay, M. (2017). *Institutional architecture for financing Pan-Asian infrastructure connectivity*. Munich, Germany: Center for Economic Studies and Ifo Institute (CESifo).

Bodewig, K. (2018). *Baltic Adriatic – Third work plan of the European coordinator*. Brussels, Belgium: European Commission.

Bodewig, K., & Secchi, C. (2014). *Attracting investment – towards transport infrastructure – potential lines for action*. Brussels, Belgium: European Commission.

Bodomo, A. (2017). *The globalization of foreign investment in Africa – The role of Europe, China and India*. Bingley, UK: Emerald Publishing Limited.

Brinkhorst, L. J. (2018). *Mediterranean – Third work plan of the European coordinator*. Brussels, Belgium: European Commission.

Caesar, B., Heilmann, M., Saalbach, J., & Schreiner, W. (2018). Grenzüberschreitender Öffentlicher Verkehr: Immer noch Barrieren trotz EU. In K. M. Pallagst, A. Hartz, & B. Caesar (Eds.), *Border Futures – zukunft Grenze – Avenir Frontière: Zukunftsfähigkeit grenzüberschreitender Zusammenarbeit* (pp. 207–2031). Hannover, Germany: Akademie für Raumforschung und Landesplanung.

Carrai, M. A. (2018). It is not the end of history: The financing institutions of the belt and road initiative and the Bretton Woods system. In J. Chaisse & J. Górski (Eds.), *The belt and road initiative – Law, economics, and politics* (pp. 107–145). Leiden, Netherlands: Brill Nijhoff.

Celbis, G., Nijkamp, P., & Poot, J. (2014). Infrastructure and trade: A meta-analysis. *Region: The Journal of ERSA, 1*(1), 25–62.

Chatterjee, S., Posch, O., & Wesselbaum, D. (2017). *Delays in public goods* (Economics discussion papers, no. 1702). University of Otago.

PwC China. (2017). *China and belt & road infrastructure – CEE transport infrastructure*. n.p.: PwC.

Council of the European Union (CUN). (2018). *Multiannual financial framework: Shaping EU expenditure*. Retrieved from CUN webpage https://www.consilium.europa.eu/en/policies/multiannual-financial-framework/

Decision No 1692/96/EC of the European Parliament and of the Council of 23 July 1996 on Community guidelines for the development of the trans-European transport network. (1996). *OJ L 228, 9.9.1996*, 1–103.
Delmon, J. (2017). *Public-private partnership projects in infrastructure – an essential guide for policy makers*. New York, NY: Cambridge University Press.
Deloitte. (2018). *Embracing the BRI ecosystem in 2018 – Navigating pitfalls and seizing opportunities*. Retrieved from https://www2.deloitte.com/content/dam/insights/us/articles/4406_Belt-and-road-initiative/4406_Embracing-the-BRI-ecosystem.pdf.
Derudder, B., Liu, X., & Kunaka, C. (2018). *Connectivity along overland corridors of the belt and road initiative* (MTI discussion paper, 6). Washington, DC: World Bank Group.
Directive 2014/15/EU of the European Parliament and of the Council of 26 February 2014 on procurement by entities operating in the water, energy, transport and postal services sectors and repealing Directive 2004/17/EC. (2014). *OJ L 94, 28.03.2014*, 243–374.
Directive 2014/24/EU of the European Parliament and the Council of 26 February 2014 on public procurement and repealing Directive 2004/18/EC. (2014). *OJ L 28.03.2014*, 65–242.
Directorate-General for Budget. (2017). *A guide to EU funding*. Retrieved from http://publications.europa.eu/resource/cellar/7d72330a-7020-11e7-b2f2-01aa75ed71a1.0001.02/DOC_1
Directorate-General for Internal Policies of the Union. (2010). *New financing instruments for European transport infrastructure and services TEN-budget, loans, loan guarantee fund, PPP: How shall they be applied and combined to achieve an optimal result?* Brussels, Belgium: European Parliament.
Directorate-General for Regional and Urban Policy. (2015). *European structural and investment funds 2014–2020: Official texts and documentaries*. Brussels, Belgium: European Commission.
Donghong, L., & Lingling, T. (2017). China's "belt and road" and business perspectives. In J.-P. Larçon (Ed.), *The new silk road – China meets Europe in the Baltic Sea region* (pp. 21–41). Hackensack, NJ: World Scientific.
Égert, B., Koźluk, T., & Sutherland, D. (2009). *Infrastructure investment: Links to growth and the role of public policies*. Economic department working paper, no. 686. Paris: OECD.
Estache, A., & Wren-Lewis, L. (2012). *Supranational infrastructure regulation: Institutional opportunities and challenges*. ECARES working paper, 2012–025. Brussels, Belgium: ECARES.

European Commission (EC). (2018a). *EU budget for the future – The connecting Europe facility.* Retrieved from https://ec.europa.eu/energy/en/content/connect-europe-facility-factsheet-06062018

European Commission (EC). (2018b). *Corridors*. Retrieved from https://ec.europa.eu/transport/node/2443

European Commission (EC). (2018c). *Quality of railroad infrastructure.* Retrieved from https://ec.europa.eu/transport/facts-fundings/scoreboard/compare/investments-infrastructure/quality-rail-infrastructure_en

European Commission (EC). (2018d). *Quality of roads*. Retrieved from https://ec.europa.eu/transport/facts-fundings/scoreboard/compare/investments-infrastructure/quality-roads_en

European Commission (EC). (2018e). *Quality of port infrastructure*. Retrieved from https://ec.europa.eu/transport/facts-fundings/scoreboard/compare/investments-infrastructure/quality-port-infrastructure_en

European Commission (EC). (2018f). *Quality of Air transport infrastructure.* Retrieved from https://ec.europa.eu/transport/facts-fundings/scoreboard/compare/investments-infrastructure/quality-airports-infrastructure_en

European Commission (EC). (2018g). *Connecting Europe Facility*. Retrieved from https://ec.europa.eu/transport/themes/infrastructure/ten-t-guidelines/project-funding/cef_en

European Commission (EC). (2018h). *Calls for tender*. Retrieved from EC web-site https://ec.europa.eu/transport/facts-fundings/tenders_en

European External Action Service. (2014). *Facts and figures on EU-China trade.* Retrieved from EC web-site https://eeas.europa.eu/sites/eeas/files/tradoc_144591.pdf

European Investment Bank (EIB). (2009a). *EIB financing of the trans-European networks*. Luxembourg, Luxembourg: European Investment Bank.

European Investment Bank (EIB). (2009b). *Europe's leading public financial institutions launch "Marguerite", the 2020 European fund for energy, climate change and infrastructure*. Retrieved from http://www.eib.org/en/infocentre/press/releases/all/2009/2009-242-europes-leading-public-financial-institutions-launch-marguerite-the-2020-european-fund-for-energy-climate-change-and-infrastructure

European Investment Bank (EIB). (2011). *EIB transport lending policy.* Luxembourg, Luxembourg: European Investment Bank.

European Investment Bank (EIB). (2012). *An outline to project bonds credit enhancement and the project bond initiative*. Luxembourg, Luxembourg: European Investment Bank.

European Investment Bank (EIB). (2018a). *Trans-European networks*. Retrieved from http://www.eib.org/en/projects/sectors/tens/index.htm

European Investment Bank (EIB). (2018b). *The European fund for strategic investment: From crisis response to lasting impact*. Luxembourg, Luxembourg: European Investment Bank.

European Investment Bank (EIB). (2018c). *Evaluation of the European Fund for Strategic Investment*. Luxembourg, Luxembourg: European Investment Bank.

European Investment Bank and European Commission. (2008). *The loan guarantee instrument for trans-European transport network projects – Fact sheet*. Luxembourg, Luxembourg: European Investment Bank and European Commission.

EY. (2015). *Navigating the belt and road – Financial sector paves the way for infrastructure*. Retrieved from https://www.ey.com/cn/en/services/specialty-services/china-overseas-investment-network/ey-navigating-the-belt-and-road-financial-sector-help-pave-the-way-for-overseas-expansion

Federal Ministry of Transport and Digital Infrastructure. (2018). *An overview of the trans-European transport network (TEN-T)*. Retrieved from https://www.bmvi.de/SharedDocs/EN/Articles/G/an-overview-of-the-trans-european-transport-network-ten-t.html

Fleischer, T. (2003). *Infrastructure networks in Central Europe and EU enlargement*. Budapest, Hungary: Institute for World Economics – Hungarian Academy of Science.

Gabler. (2014). Infrastrukturpolitik. In E. Winter (Ed.), *Gabler Wirtschaftslexikon* (pp. 1574–1575). Wiesbaden, Germany: Springer Fachmedien Wiesbaden.

Gajewska, A., & Abadie, R. (2017). *The road ahead – CEE transport infrastructure dynamics*. Retrieved from https://www.pwc.pl/en/publikacje/2017/the-road-ahead-cee-transport-infrastructure-dynamics.html

Gelderman, C. J., Ghijsen, P. W., & Brugman, M. J. (2006). Public procurement and EU tendering directives – explaining non-compliance. *International Journal of Public Sector Management, 19*(7), 702–714.

Gleave, S. D. (2018). *Research for TRAN committee: The new silk route – opportunities and challenges for EU transport*. Brussels, Belgium: European Parliament, Policy Department for Structural and Cohesion Policies.

Góralczyk, B. (2017). China's interests in central and Eastern Europe: Enter the dragon. *European View, 16*(1), 1–10.

Grimmel, A., & Li, Y. (2018). *The belt road initiative: A hybrid model of regionalism*. Working papers on East Asian studies (122/2018).

Grosch, M. (2018). *Orient east med – third work plan of the European coordinator*. Brussels, Belgium: European Commission.
Halvarsson, A., Rydell, I., Holström, M., Blagoeva, T., & Bain, R. (2014). *Ex-post evaluation of the loan guarantee instrument for trans-European transport network projects (LGTT)*. Brussels, Belgium: European Commission.
Heyman, E. (2013). *Project bond initiative*. Frankfurt, Germany: Deutsche Bank.
Hillman, J. E. (2018a, April 3). *How big is China's belt and road?* Retrieved from https://www.csis.org/analysis/how-big-chinas-belt-and-road.
Hillman, J. E. (2018b). *China's belt and road initiative: Five years later*. Retrieved from https://www.csis.org/analysis/chinas-belt-and-road-initiative-five-years-later-0
HKTDC. (2018a). *Annual report 2017–2018*. Hong Kong: HKTDC.
HKTDC. (2018b). *The belt and road initiative*. Retrieved from http://china-trade-research.hktdc.com/business-news/article/The-Belt-and-Road-Initiative/The-Belt-and-Road-Initiative/obor/en/1/1X3CGF6L/1X0A36B7.htm
HKTDC. (2018c). The belt road initiative. Retrieved from http://china-trade-research.hktdc.com/business-news/article/The-Belt-and-Road-Initiative/The-Belt-and-Road-Initiative/obor/en/1/1X000000/1X0A36B7.htm
HKTDC. (n.d.). *Project database*. Retrieved from https://beltandroad.hktdc.com/en/project-database
Holzner, M., Heimberger, P., & Kochnev, A. (2018). *A European silk road*. Vienna, Austria: Vienna Institute for International Economic Studies.
Inderst, G. (2016). *Infrastructure investment, private finance, and institutional investors: Asia from a global perspective*. ADBI working papers, no. 555.
International Transport Forum. (2018). *Private investment in transport infrastructure – Dealing with uncertainty in contracts*. Paris: International Transport Forum.
Jianxun, S. (2017). Financing China's "belt and road" Initiative. In J.-P. Larçon (Ed.), *The new silk road – China meets Europe in the Baltic Sea region* (pp. 157–182). Hackensack, New Jersey: World Scientific.
Johnson, D., & Turner, C. (1997). *Trans-European networks – The political economy of integrating Europe's infrastructure*. London: Macmillan Press LTD..
Klein, M. (2012). *Infrastructure policy – basic design options*. Policy research working paper (6274). The World Bank.
Kowalski, B. (2017). China's foreign policy towards central and Eastern Europe: The "16+1" format in the South – South cooperation perspective. Cases of the Czech Republic and Hungary. *Cambridge Journal of Eurasian Studies 1*, 1–16. https://doi.org/10.22261/7R65ZH.

Kušar, S. (2011). The institutional approach in economic geography: An applicative view. *Hrvatski geografski glasnik, 73*(1), 39–49.
Larçon, J.-P., & Barré, G. (2017). China meets Europe by the Baltic Sea. In J.-P. Larçon (Ed.), *The new silk road: China meets Europe in the Baltic Sea region* (pp. 1–20). Hackensack, NJ: World Scientific.
Li, D., & Tang, L. (2017). China's "belt and road" and business perspectives. In J.-P. Larçon (Ed.), *The new silk road: China meets Europe in the Baltic Sea region* (pp. 21–42). Hackensack, NJ: World Scientific.
Liu, Z. (2016). "The 16+1 cooperation" in the context of "the belt and road initiative". In D. Dimitrijević (Ed.), *Danube in the function of the new silk road* (pp. 155–179). Belgrade, Serbia: Institute of International Politics and Economics.
Martin, R. (2005). Institutional approaches in economic geography. In E. Sheppard & T. J. Barnes (Eds.), *A companion to economic geography* (pp. 77–94). Oxford, UK: Blackwell Publishing.
McGuinn, J., O'Brien, S., Moreira, G., Oulès, L., van den Bogaerde, S., & Vansina, F. (2016). *Study on permitting and facilitating the preparation of TEN-T core network projects*. Bruxelles, Belgium: Milieu Ltd..
Baker McKenzie. (2017). *Belt & road: Opportunity & risk – the prospects and perils of building China's new silk road*. Retrieved from https://www.bakermckenzie.com/-/media/files/insight/publications/2017/10/belt-road/baker_mckenzie_belt_road_report_2017.pdf?la=en.
McKinsey & Company. (2016). *One belt and one road: connecting China and the world*. Retrieved from https://www.mckinsey.com/industries/capital-projects-and-infrastructure/our-insights/one-belt-and-one-road-connecting-china-and-the-world
Miyamoto, K., & Chiofalo, E. (2015). *Official development finance for infrastructure: Support by multilateral and bilateral development partners*. OECD development co-operation working papers, no. 25. Paris: OECD Publishing.
National Development and Reform Commission, Ministry of Foreign Affairs, Ministry of Commerce of the People's Republic of China. (2015). *Visions and actions on jointly building silk road economic belt and 21st-century maritime silk road*. Retrieved from http://en.ndrc.gov.cn/newsrelease/201503/t20150330_669367.html
OECD. (2018). *Infrastructure investment (indicator)*. Retrieved from https://data.oecd.org/transport/infrastructure-investment.htm
Office of the Commissioner of the Ministry of Foreign Affairs of the People's Republic of China in Macao Special Administrative Region. (n.d.). *Five-*

year outcome list of cooperation between China and Central and Eastern European Countries. Retrieved from http://www.fmcoprc.gov.mo/eng/news/t1514538.htm.

Pauls, R., & Gottwald, J.-C. (2018). Origins and dimensions of the belt and road initiative: Experimental patch work or grand strategy? In R. Taylor & J. Jaussaud (Eds.), *China's global political economy – managerial perspectives* (pp. 31–54). London, UK: Routledge.

Peijs, K. (2018). *Rhine Danube – third work plan of the European coordinator*. Brussels, Belgium: European Commission.

Ping, H., & Zuokui, L. (2017). *The cooperation between China and Central & Eastern European Countries (16+1): 2012–2017*. Beijing, China: Social Science Academic Press (China).

Italian Presidency. (n.d.). *Building infrastructure to strengthen Europe's economy*. Retrieved from European Commission web-site: https://ec.europa.eu/transport/themes/infrastructure/ten-t-guidelines_en

Press and Information team of the Delegation to China. (2016, May). *China and the EU*. Retrieved from https://eeas.europa.eu/topics/external-investment-plan/15394/china-and-eu_en

Press and information team of the Delegation to China. (2017). *Chronology of EU-China Relations*. Retrieved from https://eeas.europa.eu/topics/external-investment-plan/18537/chronology-eu-china-relations_en

PwC & London Economics & ECORYS. (2013). Public procurement in Europe – cost and effectiveness.. European Commission.

PwC; London Economics; ECORYS. (2013). *Public procurement in Europe – Cost and effectiveness – Annex: Detailed methodology and data*. n.p.: European Commission.

Regulation (EU). (2013). No 1316/2013 of the European Parliament and of the Council of 11 December 2013 establishing the Connecting Europe Facility. *OJ L 348, 20.12.2013*, 129–171.

Regulation (EU). (2015). No 2015/1017 of the European Parliament and the Council of 25 June 2015 on the European Fund for Strategic INvestments, the European Investment Advisory Hub and the European Investment Project Portal. *OJ L 169, 1.7.2015*, 1–38.

Regulation (EU) No 1300/2013 of the European Parliament and of the Council of 17 December 2013 on the Cohesion Fund and repealing Council Regulation (EC) No 1084/2006. (2013). *OJ L 347, 20.12.2013*, 281–288.

Regulation (EU) No 1301/2013 of the European Parliament and of the Council of 17 December 2013 on the European Regional Development Fund and on

specific provisions concerning the Investment for growth and jobs goal and repealing Regulation (EC) No 1080/2006. (2013). *OJ L 347, 20.12.2013*, 289–302.
Regulation (EU) No 1315/2013 of 11 December 2013 on Union guidelines for the development of the trans-European transport network. (2013). *OJ L 348, 20.12.2013*, 1–168.
Revoltella, D., Brutscher, P.-B., Tsiotras, A., & Weiss, C. (2016). *Infrastructure Investment in Europe and international competitiveness.* EIB working papers, no 2016/01.
Rhodes, C. (2018). *Infrastructure policies and investment* (Briefing paper (6594)). London, UK: House of Commons Library.
Rizzi, C., & Tettamanti, M. (2018). The first pillar of the B&R initiative funding: The institutional funding. In X. Yu, C. T. Rizzi, F. E. Ziccardi, & L. Guo (Eds.), *China's belt and road – The initiative and its financial focus* (pp. 89–118). Singapore: World Scientific.
Sawant, R. J. (2010). The economics of large-scale infrastructure FDI: The case of project finance. *Journal of International Business Studies, 41*, 1036–1055.
Selmier, W. T., II. (2020). Kazakhstan as logistics linchpin in the belt and road initiative. In I. Heim (Ed.), *Kazakhstan's diversification from the natural resources sector: Strategic and economic opportunities.* London, UK: Palgrave Macmillan.
Silk Road Fund. (n.d.-a). *Silk road fund.* Retrieved from http://www.silkroadfund.com.cn/enweb/23775/23767/index.html
Silk Road Fund. (n.d.-b). *Types of investment.* Retrieved from http://www.silkroadfund.com.cn/enweb/23798/23803/index.html
Stanzel, A., Kratz, A., Szczudlik, J., & Pavlićević, D. (2016). *China's investment in influence: The future of 16 + 1 cooperation.* London, UK: The European Council of Foreign Relations.
State Council of the People's Republic of China. (2015). *Full text: Action plan on the belt and road initiative.* Retrieved from http://english.gov.cn/archive/publications/2015/03/30/content_281475080249035.htm
Steinicke, M. (2012). Public procurement. In B. Iversen, P. Wegener Jessen, B. O. Gram Mortensen, M. Steinicke, & E. Sørensen (Eds.), *Regulating competition in the EU* (pp. 701–754). Copenhagen, Denmark: DJØF Publishing.
Storper, M. (1997). *The regional world: Territorial development in a global economy.* New York, NY/London, UK: Guilford Press.
Tettamanti, M. (2018). The second pillar of the B&R Initiative Funding: The private sector. In X. Yu, C. Rizzi, M. Tettamanti, F. E. Ziccardi, & L. Guo

(Eds.), *China's belt and road – The initiative and its financial focus* (pp. 119–162). Singapore: World Scientific.

The Treaty on the Functioning of the European Union (Consolidated Version). (2012). *OJ C 326, 26.10.2012*, 1–390.

Trautmann, C. (2018). *North Sea Baltic – Third work plan of the European coordinator*. Brussels, Belgium: European Commission.

Tuszyńska, B., & Gouadères, F. (2018). *Trans-European Networks- guideline*. Retrieved from http://www.europarl.europa.eu/factsheets/en/sheet/135/trans-european-networks-guidelines

Van der Putten, F.-P., Seaman, J., Huotari, M. E., & Otero-Iglesias, M. (2016). *Europe and China's new silk roads*. European Think-tank Network on China.

Vangeli, A. (2017). China's engagement with the sixteen countries of central, east and Southeast Europe under the belt and road initiative. *China & World Economy, 25*(5), 101–124.

World Economic Forum and Boston Consulting Group. (2013). *Strategic infrastructure: Steps to prepare and accelerate public-private partnerships*. Cologny/Geneva: World Economic Forum.

World Economic Forum and Boston Consulting Group. (2014). *Strategic infrastructure – steps to operate and maintain infrastructure efficiently and effectively*. Cologny/Geneva, Switzerland: World Economic Forum.

World Economic Forum and Boston Consulting Group. (2015). *Africa strategic infrastructure initiative: A principled approach to infrastructure project preparation facilities*. Cologne/Geneva, Switzerland: World Economic Forum.

Wulf, H. (2015). *BRICS. Realistische alternative für globale reformen? Global governance spotlight, 6*. Bonn, Germany: SEF.

Zhu, L. (2015). The construction model of "one belt and one road": Mechanisms an platforms. In R. Wang & C. Zhu (Eds.), *Annual report on the development of the Indian Ocean region* (pp. 111–127). Singapore: Springer Singapore.

Zou, L. (2018). *The political economy of China's belt and road initiative*. Hackensack, NJ: World Scientific.

5

Investments in the Digital Silk Road

Vitaly Ambalov and Irina Heim

Introduction

In the past 25 years, Kazakhstan has succeeded in attracting direct investments, predominantly in the natural resource sector, worth about US $149 billion (UNCTAD, 2018), and established effective cooperation with major transnational corporations, catalyzed through implementation of institutional reform and democratic transformation (see Baldakhov & Heim, 2020, this volume). Government initiatives have demonstrated commitment to structural reforms and are intended to improve the economy's resistance to external shocks, while digitalization is recognized as a critical factor in ensuring the sustainable development of the country.

The original version of this chapter was revised: Reference was corrected in the chapter. The erratum to this chapter is available at https://doi.org/10.1007/978-3-030-37389-4_11

V. Ambalov
Republican Confederation of Entrepreneurship, Minsk, Belarus

I. Heim (✉)
Henley Business School, University of Reading, Reading, UK
e-mail: irina.heim@henley.ac.uk

I. Heim (ed.), *Kazakhstan's Diversification from the Natural Resources Sector*, Euro-Asian Studies, https://doi.org/10.1007/978-3-030-37389-4_5

Digital Kazakhstan, a state program ratified in 2017, forecasts that one-third of the GDP growth of 6% will be directly related to the development of information and communication technology (ICT). To implement the program *Digital Kazakhstan*, the state has planned for digitalization of centers for each state body or institution, including governmental agencies. The program is essential for the country as the world is entering the era of the new digital economy (NDE)[1] where co-creation of value[2] invades every process, from product design and engineering, over-manufacturing and logistics to services, and thus digital information is the top priority. This means that analysts now need to be more concerned with network effects while planning investment projects, in detail as well as in general, with transactions, modes and fixed nodes, acquisition, and greenfield investments (Buckley, 2016).

Despite the possibilities of modern ICT, it cannot solve all the problems associated with managing network interactions due to the eclectic behavior of value chain actors, which increasingly are not firms, but complex and unstable nodal structures. These chains become fragmented into specialized tasks, which are geographically dispersed across the nodes of global value chains.[3] In Kazakhstan, there is an understanding of this problem and actions are being taken to integrate local enterprises into global value creation hubs. An example of such a node is the Karachaganak Petroleum Operating B.V. (KPO).[4] Recently, the consortium created has implemented a long-term digitalization program (Karachaganak news, 2018). However, most companies in Kazakhstan are still on their path of realization that in NDE they will have to turn to business process re-engineering again so as not only to improve performance processes but also to re-establish an organizational interface between such activities (Bodrožić & Adler, 2018). With the growing popularity of business

[1] The new digital economy (NDE) is emerging from a combination of technologies, mainly from the ICT space, that are becoming pervasive across mechanical systems, communications, infrastructure, and built environment (UNCTAD, 2017).

[2] Co-creation puts the spotlight squarely on consumer-company interaction as the locus of value creation (Prahalad & Ramaswamy, 2004).

[3] Dispersed business networks that are organized and coordinated by global firms as a common project of independent suppliers, which has its certain time frame and sequence of actions (Smorodinskaya & Katukov, 2017).

[4] The Karachaganak project brings expertise and knowledge from five oil & gas companies—ENI, Royal Dutch Shell, Chevron, Lukoil, and KazMunayGas.

process re-engineering in the 1990s, business actors grasped the role of intra-corporate networks and the necessity of reducing vertical (strong) links and enhancing horizontal (weak) ones, which has led to an emergency of matrix organizational structures. By the third decade of the twenty-first century, the global economy will have come to the need for such re-engineering throughout, at every level from an individual business process to the national and global economy. A feature of re-engineering in the NDE environment is the inclusion of all countries, firms, and processes in global value chains—a direct consequence of the widespread adoption of ICT, especially the internet and cloud technologies.

Digitalization is usually considered as a means of ensuring the growth and productivity of the economy and the well-being of citizens, but, like any other technology, it also exhibits features that limit the advantages and may even undermine developing countries' economic performance. New technologies can present a double negative impact to low-income countries: the benefits from the production of labor-intensive products are reduced and the ability to compensate for the technological disadvantages of an unskilled labor is reduced (Rodrik, 2018). The growth of investments, which is currently a driver of economic growth, contributes to the reduction of the impact of this technological shock on the Kazakhstani economy as new MNE market entries create new opportunities for local enterprises. In the settings of NDE the role of modern MNEs changes to become a "meta-integrator", able to leverage knowledge within and between the different constituent affiliates of its international network, which requires efficient internal markets and well-structured cross-border hierarchies (Narula, 2016). This creates an indigenous labor force with a suitable level of training and skills, to be able to participate in this *meta-integration* with the least transaction costs and disruption to the lives of ordinary people (Dunning & Lundan, 2008). New role needs in management methods based on value co-creation and the appropriate country institutions (see Baldakhov & Heim, 2020, this volume). At the same time, the R&D community can advise on economic theory adaptation to the reality of a new digital service economy.

Kazakhstan eagerly explores opportunities of the NDE in parallel with other advantages embedded within the processes of globalization. WTO accession, expansion in cooperation with MNEs, and changes in the regulatory and legal environment create incentives for foreign investors, while new local industry development institutes promote local companies to play a more important role in the infrastructure projects implemented in the country. Prompt incentives provided to improve the national education system, and the foundation of new universities (including private) like the public International Information Technology University established in Almaty in close cooperation with the Carnegie Mellon University (USA) or public Kazakh-British Technical University[5] in Almaty, mitigated the shortage in ICT professionals. Nevertheless, the R&D environment is not yet developed enough to exploit the full potential of the educational system, which needs a flow of duly funded research projects. The level of R&D expenditure is still shallow, accounting for approximately 0.2% of GDP (see below), which might constrain implementation of economic development programs, including scientific programs of digitalization and the application of ICT.

From the theoretical perspective, the promotion of digital economy investments will require adaptation of management theories since studies so far have focused on the digital transformation of single industries (Kretschmer & Claussen, 2016). Business system architecture also needs to be compatible with ICT architecture, so that a respective computer cluster node reflects every business system component or every business cluster node is reflected in a respective ICT cluster node.

In this chapter, we use the model of NDE in resource-rich countries (Heim, 2019) to study diversification of the ICT cluster by linking it with the O&G cluster, integrating this poll with national clusters of other countries, thus making use of the mutually beneficial cooperation within the international cluster system. This approach can be used to interpret the BRI, an initiative in understanding what this means for frontier states as receivers of action, investment, and infrastructure. Countries-receivers of BRI are exposed to direct (physical, economic) and ancillary (social, environmental, political) benefits and costs (Sternberg, Ahearn, & McConnell, 2017). Assessment of such advantages and disadvantages in a cluster node model may be useful for BRI projects.

[5] An idea to establish KBTU belongs to the former President of the RK, Nursultan Nazarbayev, who had a number of meetings with official representatives of the UK. This activity resulted in the Memorandum of Understanding signed by the two states in November 2000. British Prime Minister Tony Blair and Nursultan Nazarbayev became patrons of the university.

New Digital Economy Institutions

As the overview of the literature on institutional theory has revealed, the targets of the institutional theory analysis are an organization and an economy, both approached from the point of view of utility maximization. Therefore, classical institutional theory does not consider networks of different actors and value as a purpose of economic exchange. Of particular interest in understanding the role of institutions in a multiple-stakeholders' environment is the implication of institutional theory for political science, particularly as seen in the works of Ostrom (1990, 2005) on the governance of common-pool resources. She studies the role of institutions in the complex and interrelated resource integration and service exchange collaborative management of natural ecosystems organized around shared purposes (as cited in Vargo & Lusch, 2016). This is a similar point of view on institutions to that which was adopted by the theory of value co-creation. The purpose of institutions from the value co-creation perspective is to enable cooperation and coordination in ecosystems, as well as to reconcile conflict in the increasingly complex and interrelated integration of resources (Vargo & Lusch, 2016). These institutional structures can be viewed at various levels of aggregation such as micro-, meso-, and macro-levels (Lusch & Vargo, 2014). In these structures value flows from one actor to another and is created through multiple levels of interactions which are not fixed and evolve over time (Vargo, Wieland & Akaka, 2015).

Institutional theory itself cannot explain all aspects of emergency of digital and tertiary sector of the economy, including effects of government policies in countries. Therefore, institutional theory needs to be linked to other theories in order to explain more recent trends in the global economy. In the next paragraphs of this chapter we will discuss the main trends in the economic development of Kazakhstan to make the reader familiar with institutional development in the country.

Information and communication technology advancement causes changes not only in production processes but also in the architecture of economic systems, affecting processes of internationalization, direct foreign investments, and industrial policies.[6] A critical issue here is the interoperability[7] of economic actors that act within global networks, and distributed production systems that extensively use outsourcing within their national industrial clusters and readily cross borders in search of assets, markets, and efficiency. ICT has contributed significantly to creative destruction[8] through the emergence of some new firms and industries and the decline of others. It impacts industrial organizational structures and has obvious implications for employment. Directly and indirectly, ICT can also reduce market friction and transaction costs and affect competitive positioning, with resulting impact on productivity improvement and economic growth (OECD, 2011). However, in the academic literature we do not find strong evidence that ICT helps reduce transaction costs. On the contrary, in the NDE era, due to the growth in volumes of data and information, transaction costs increase according to the amount of costs associated with cybersecurity, information costs, cost of digital transformations, and so on.

NDE holds considerable promise for businesses able to take advantage of new technology and mitigate risk. Large and small companies that rely on the new tools of the NDE, in both developed and developing countries alike, can make their organizations more efficient, as well as serve customers more effectively, and push through innovative business transformations. While large companies might have access to more comprehensive data than higher-level platform owners or end users, access to all the world's relevant data by the end user is not required to speed up innovation or carve new market space within NDE (UNCTAD, 2017).

Research suggests the structure of the digital economy in resource-rich countries (Heim, 2019). This model demonstrates the intersection of the

[6] Industrial policy can be defined as strategic efforts of a government to encourage structural changes and development leading to fostering competitiveness via growth in manufacturing and the related services sector (Aiginger, 2007; Altenburg, 2011).

[7] Interoperability is the ability of entities of an organization to work together that covers aspects ranging from the technical to the business level (Li & Liu, 2018).

[8] Creative destruction as a process of industrial change that increasingly revolutionizes the economic structure from within, destroying the old one and creating a new structure (Schumpeter, 1934)

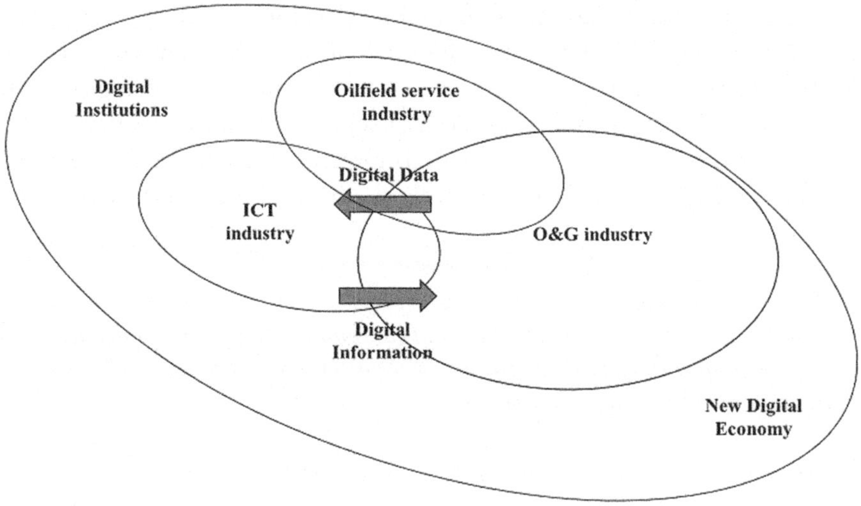

Fig. 5.1 NDE in resource-rich countries. (Source: Heim, 2019)

three cluster nodes involved in the extraction of natural resources: the O&G industry, the oilfield service industry, and the ICT industry (see Fig. 5.1). Moreover, the activities of actors are carried out in the field of the NDE, where the behavior of actors is influenced by other digital institutions. Through the ICT industry, the data produced by the O&G industry and the oilfield service industry can be converted into information necessary for process control, which indicates the mutual interest of the parties in aligning the technological level of the collaborating cluster nodes.

ICT is relatively undeveloped in Kazakhstan, especially in SMEs, in which the level of adoption is very low. The main gaps are lack of financial resources for investments in ICT equipment and services, which leads to a lack of modern technologies, as well as skills gaps. The reason why SMEs often cannot access financial resources is their inability to provide evidence of long-term financial stability and to pay the loan back (Heim, Kalyuzhnova, Li & Liu, 2018). Kazakh companies are attempting to participate in the digital economy, but knowledge and financial resources are available to big players only, usually state-owned. That is why digital technologies[9] are now mainly developed with state support. For instance, KazMunayGas, a national oil and gas company (NOC KMG), started an ambitious project of transformation and digitization of business processes. A shared services center (SSC), one of the first in Kazakhstan, has recently been created. Dmitry Basisty, Deputy General Director, KMG Global Solutions B.V., in the interview with Irina Heim said:

> *The key point of such organizational structure is dedication of certain auxiliary business functions of the national oil and gas company to separate companies to have manufacturing facilities free to focus on the core activities—oil and gas exploration, production, transportation, refining, etc.*

Some of the companies in the O&G industry are advanced from the ICT development standpoint; however, there are others in which ICT does not exist, companies with only basic technologies. In Kazakhstan, there is an intensive activity of *meta-integrators*, such as, for example, MNEs taking part in a joint KPO project. International O&G giants—ENI, Royal Dutch Shell plc, Chevron, Lukoil, and KazMunayGas (national oil company of Kazakhstan)—managed to put their efforts to invest in this project with $22 bill. KPO, in cooperation with operator companies, identified several digitalization initiatives that are important for the project in Kazakhstan, as well as for parent companies. Digitalization is an important initiative for KPO, as well as for its employees and subcontractors but also for the development of local businesses and creation of conditions for new business.[10]

Institutional theory is a reliable tool for filling in this knowledge gap, since NDE, and any of its actors, is a complex system for which survival

[9] Digital technologies include (1) advanced production equipment, robotics, and factory automation, (2) new sources of data from mobile and ubiquitous Internet connectivity, (3) cloud computing, (4) big data analytics, and (5) artificial intelligence. These technologies and processes are based, in one way or another, on advanced ICT, so that the driver of the NDE is the continued improvement in ICT (UNCTAD, 2017).

[10] Karachaganak news (2018). Available at: http://www.kpo.kz/fileadmin/user_upload/karachaganak_news_2018/NOVOSTI_SENTJABR__2018.pdf

is the main goal, and in order to ensure their survival, organizations must comply with rationalized and institutionalized expectations of their environment and adopt the expected structures and management practices (Geppert, Matten, & Walgenbach, 2006). Since Chinese internet firms see the digital Silk Road as an opportunity to seek government support (Shen, 2018), this is one of the reasons why an institutional view is useful (Ramamurti & Hillemann, 2018).

Technological Digital Divide

NDE has its roots in microelectronics industry. In the mid-1960s Gordon Moore, a founder of Fairchild Semiconductor, observing evolution of semiconductor technology, predicted that the number of the components (transistors, resistors, diodes, or capacitors) in an integrated circuit would double approximately every two years, which turned out to be one of the most successful predictions in modern history (Mack, 2011). Over the last 50 years, the increase in the density of transistors and their number on a single chip has become a drive for the exponential growth of processor performance, and the use of economies of scale has made it possible to quickly reduce the cost associated with their performance. The demand for chips ensured steady growth of the sectors of the economy related to microelectronics: precision engineering, optical instrument production, production of ultrapure materials, and other aspects of it. The expanded capabilities of electronics promote R&D in new digital technologies. Simultaneously gross revenues of ICT-dedicated industries as well as a number of the ICT applications grow exponentially, and investing opportunities emerge respectively. It is worth noting that costs and energy consumption by the ongoing ICT race grow at a roughly equal pace. Microelectronics is becoming an important industry as NDE is based on the continued exponential improvement in the cost performance of ICT, mainly microelectronics (UNCTAD, 2017).

The growing complexity of the chips entails a growing digital divide between developing and developed countries in terms of participation in high value-added activities. The cost of the most advanced semiconductor factories now exceeds US $10 billion, with individual tools approaching $100 million. This rocketing cost of entry means that now only four companies in the world have the capacity to make semiconductor chips based on leading-edge technology: Intel (USA), Samsung (Korea), TSMC (Taiwan), and USA-Singapore based GlobalFoundries (Jones, 2017). Developing and transition economies, including Kazakhstan, are not ICT importers for this reason; the digitalization paradigm makes the task to eliminate the so-called technological digital divide[11] more challenging and requires governments to amend economic policy with particular emphasis on intensified investments in digital infrastructure and R&D.

Peter Drucker stipulated that it is technology import-export balance, not the national trade balance, that determines the national welfare at a particular life stage of a nation (Drucker, 1992). In the NDE era, the conclusion can also be extended to the export-import balance of ICT. Countries unable to create and export assets with a significant ICT component will need to spend a notable part of their incomes on the imports. Historically uneven distribution of technology creation centers and under-developed R&D in developing and emerging countries are the main reasons for digital inequality. Research into the role of ICT in development (ICT4D) is often based on the concept of the "digital divide" which can be defined as "lack of technological access or ownership existing between individuals, households, companies and regions" (Dey & Ali, 2016; OECD, 2001). The digital divide has long been a significant concern of governments, the international community, and researchers (UNCTAD, 2010). Most of the research has focused on reasons for the digital divide, for example infrastructural bottleneck (Rao, 2005), gender (Cooper, 2006), socioeconomic development (Çilan, Bolat, & Coşkun, 2009), or skills and interests (Min, 2010). However, ICT can also help companies in emerging countries to better compete in the global economy (Salnikova, 2013). For instance, Rimmel and Diedrich (2000) claimed that in business-to-business operations, companies use internet technologies to integrate their value chains, where the largest impact can be achieved by SMEs. Levy and Powell (2003) studied

[11] Digital divide between technological levels of domestic and foreign enterprises.

internet adoption strategies of SMEs in the UK Midlands and found little evidence that SMEs do more than develop websites and adopt email. Ntwoku, Negash, and Meso (2017) studied personal computers and internet diffusion by SMEs in Cameroon and the environmental factors that negatively affect institutionalization of e-commerce in Tanzania (Kabanda & Brown, 2017). Previous research also included studies of the determinants of ICT adoption by SMEs within transition economies of Czech-Polish region (Hanclova, Rozehnal, Ministr, & Tvrdikova, 2015), business performance monitoring software for SMEs in Chile (Lind, Sepúlveda, & Nuñez, 2000), as well as impact of initiatives to pursue a higher degree of ICT and e-technology adaptation by SMEs (Milis, 2008).

According to Qureshi (2015), the effect of ICT on development can be studied at the individual, organization, country, region, and world level. Investments in R&D, including ICT-related, are important for overcoming the digital divide but also for economic development (Fraumeni & Okubo, 2005). Global statistics show that lack of R&D funding is specific not only to Kazakhstan but to most emerging and transition economies. Figures 5.2 and 5.3 show the dynamic diagrams of R&D expenditure measured in a percentage of GDP for the period from 2005 to 2015 and the current account balance measured in a percentage of GDP for the period from 2005 to 2017, respectively, for six countries with low, medium, and high R&D expenditures. The period selected for interpretation is remarkable for signs of the global financial crisis of 2008 in the middle, accompanied by the drop in prices of natural resources, and the high volatility of many currencies.

Research suggests that there is a positive and significant relationship between volatility, R&D intensity, and the various patent-related measures—especially when the innovation measures are filtered to distinguish the very innovative firms from the less innovate ones (Mazzucato & Tancioni, 2012). To reduce the technological digital divide through innovations and improve overall economic development, policy in Kazakhstan should be focused on diversification from the O&G sector, supporting domestic companies and research in ICT-related sectors, encouraging export-oriented projects, and pushing such companies to join international initiatives (see Han & Ghobadian, 2020 and Selmier, 2020, this volume). Without involvement in international R&D

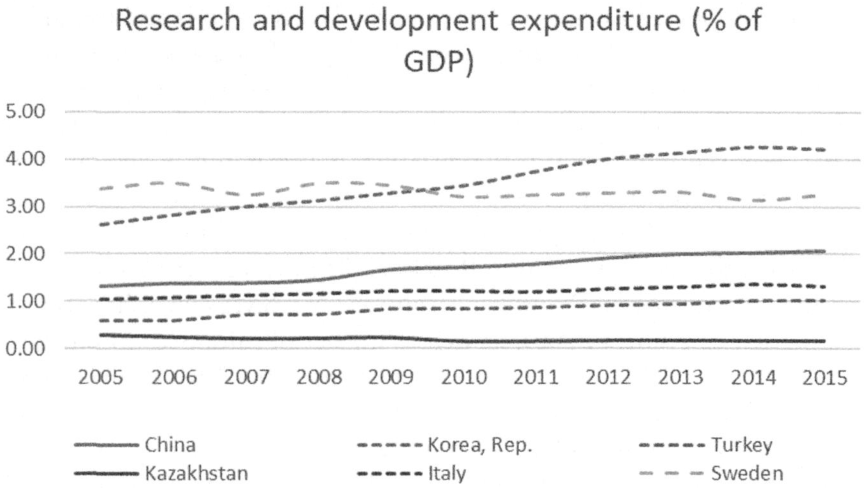

Fig. 5.2 Research and development expenditures for selected countries, percentage of GDP. (Source: Authors, own processed data based on World Bank (2018))

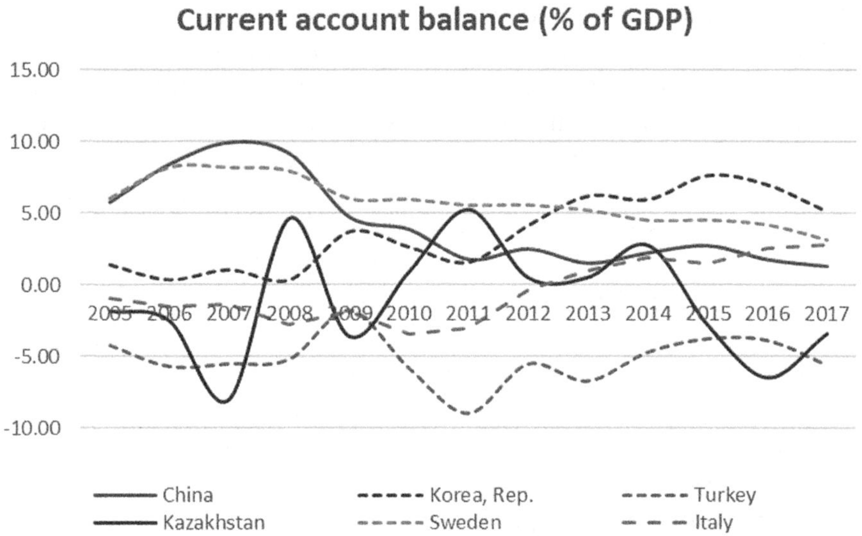

Fig. 5.3 Current account balance for selected countries, percentage of GDP. (Source: Authors, own processed data based on World Bank (2018))

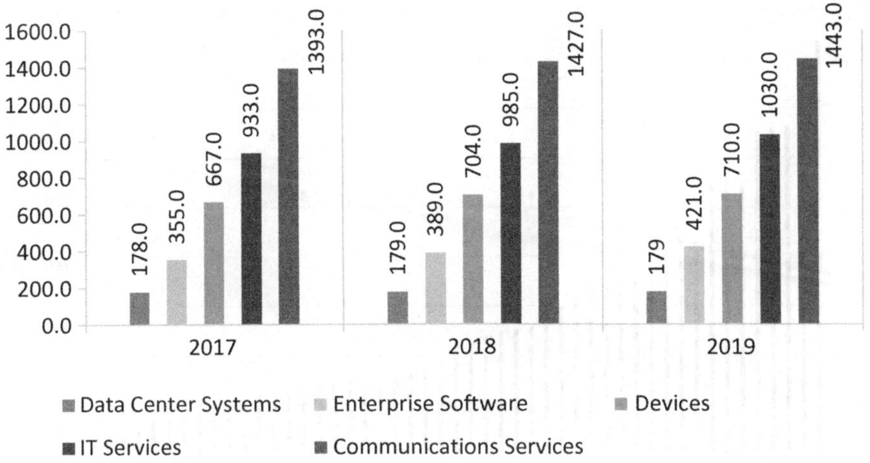

Fig. 5.4 Worldwide ICT spending forecast, Bln US dollars. (Source: Authors, own processed data based on Gartner)

projects, no emerging economy can implement the strategy to minimize the economic discontinuities between developed and developing economies due to the unavoidable increase of ICT expenditure which follows an upward trend (Fig. 5.4).

In previous decades companies and states were able to achieve positive growth with limited application of ICT components for the selective automation of key individual processes. During digital transformation, almost every nation and company needs to apply ICT technologies. For instance, in the O&G industry, critical to the economy of Kazakhstan, the next generation of ICT technologies applied by O&G companies could reduce cost by approximately 20%, at an oil price of about US $70 per barrel (Choudhry, Mohammad, Tan & Ward, 2016). Provided this is the case, the forecast is that digitalization of the O&G industry could lead to the reduction of capital expenditures by approximately 20%. Taking into consideration the capital-intensive character of the O&G industry, there is a great motivation to make the most of the digital transformation (Verdu, 2017).

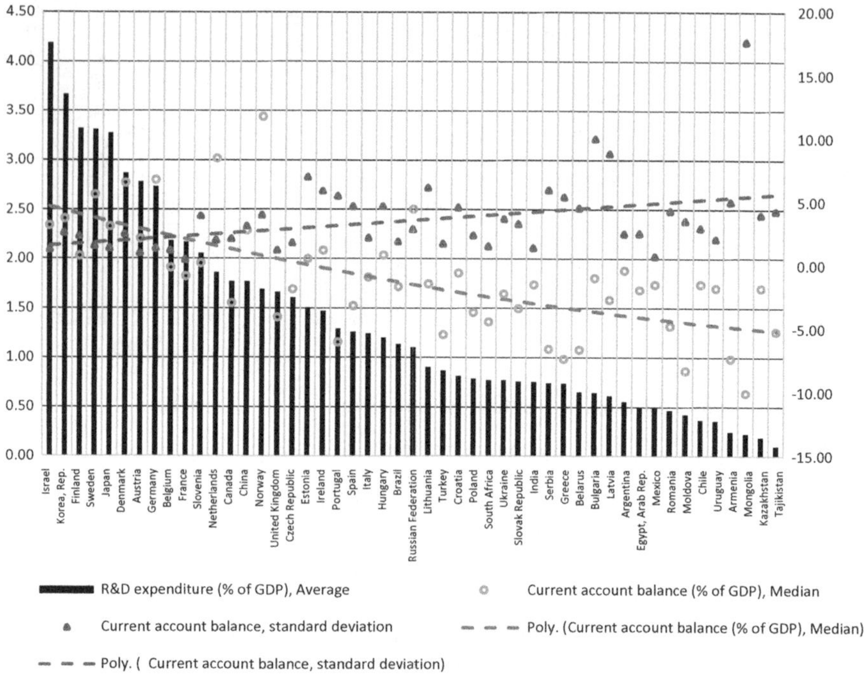

Fig. 5.5 Research and development expenditures and the sustainability of the economy for countries. (Source: Authors, own processed data based on World Bank (2018))

The sample of 49 countries, including Kazakhstan, with R&D expenditure over 0.5% of GDP, except for the USA, is provided in Fig. 5.5. The average R&D expenditure as a percentage of GDP, the median of a current account balance as a percentage of GDP, and the median and standard deviation of the current account balance were calculated for each country.

As illustrated by the diagrams above, the current account balance dynamic shows a correlation between total R&D expenditure and current account fluctuations. For countries with median R&D expenditure less than the world average (about 2% of GDP) in the period between 1996 and 2015, the average current account balance, usually, has greater volatility or was negative.

It can be concluded that Kazakhstan needs to increase investments in R&D, including ICT and especially its digital component, as digital technology is interesting not only as an information- and communication-related process but as an element of innovation activity cycle. This cycle requires a whole host of other technologies, as well as infrastructure, and physical and intellectual assets; it should be considered in terms of interaction among all concurrent technological, institutional, and social change (Grübler, 2003). Investment in new technologies with predominantly digital components will decrease the technological digital divide.

Since the emerging outline of the NDE is still unclear, digital inequality (being the difference between those involved in the digital world and those uninvolved) sharpens the inequality between countries that still stay behind the cutting edge of digital transformation. Although it is still uncertain what advantages NDE will give to average users, those who are capable of accumulating, accessing, and analyzing big data would accrue greater advantages (UNCTAD, 2017). Developing, transition and small countries, having no such capabilities, stand on very unfavorable grounds. Digital technology implementation inequality is evident even in Europe, which explores only 12% of its digital potential: the UK operates at 17% of its digital capacity, while Germany at just 10%. The recognized leader in digitalization, USA, explores about 18% of its potential illustrated as a digital threshold. The Netherlands and some other countries are European net digital service exporters,[12] while Italy is a net importer. In general, Europe's digital capability is far beyond that of the USA, while much of Europe relies on the import of the US technology for its own digital development (McKinsey, 2016).

Digital ICT invasion in every NDE aspect and influence on institutional structures and local content policy (LCP) in resource-rich countries such as Kazakhstan puts new requirements on economic cluster structure analysis methods and the examination of MNE performance as the principal FDI source. MNEs entering a market affect every business actor, through its technology, including ICT, and governmental bodies

[12] A net exporter is a sector that contributes to the growth of the economy via the trade balance and therefore should provide more employment and business opportunities (McKinsey, 2016).

and agencies in emerging markets have to take measures to enhance the competitiveness of local companies. For this reason, Kazakhstan was the first post-Soviet state to promote the competitiveness of local industry through the National Agency for Development of Local Content (NADLoC),[13] an industrial subcontracting node and quality improvement accelerator for the local ICT-focused companies (see Sabirov & Shakulikova, 2020, this volume).

The Digital Silk Road

ICT is a broad area affecting every aspect of human activity. However, the NDE it provoked is far from a revolutionary form of economic structure, and digitalization is now not a fundamentally new phenomenon. Information had not changed its role principally since the age of the Great Silk Road when goods and knowledge moved alongside the routes crossing Central Asia and the territory of modern Kazakhstan. The information used within the exchange of goods was crucial for the trade itself and the key decision-making of governors. But only electronic computers "made us understand that information is a form of energy, like electricity, and a source of energy for intellectual labor" (Drucker, 1992). The Great Silk Road gave birth to the intensive use of digital information, too. Musa Al-Khwarizmi, a scholar from Central Asia who lived in the ninth century modified Indian digits and transformed them into Arabic numerals. Further, he invented algorithms and algebra and these inventions spread across Asia and to many other countries (Arger, 2015). A few centuries later the decimal number system spread across Europe also and achieved the current status.

The beginning of the Digital Era as we see it today can be identified as of July 1948, when the *Bell System Technical Journal* published *A Mathematical Theory of Communication* written by Claude Shannon (1948). In the article, Shannon presented the modern concept of information and showed how to measure the indefinite phenomenon of

[13] Since 2018—Qazaqstan Industry and Export Center JSC or QAZINDUSTRY.

information quantitatively, with absolute accuracy. He demonstrated the essential unity of all information media, pointing out that text, telephone signals, radio waves, pictures, film, and every other mode of communication could be encoded in the universal language of binary digits, presenting the idea that information can be transmitted without any error once it becomes digital.[14] The proof of possibility to measure information and its entropy made it possible to combine advances of many sciences that resulted in digital information and communication systems. Therefore, speaking about digitalization, we should remember that digitized information always contains some entropy as understood by Shannon, one of those "who changed the world so that the old one after transformation is neglected" (Gleick, 2011).

Kazakhstan entered the Digital Age in the year of Shannon's article publication (1948) when the Sector of Mathematics and Mechanics was established to join the development of mathematical methods of data processing and transmission. Later, the Sector matured into the Institute of Mathematics and Mechanics, Kazakhstan National Academy of Sciences, and made a fair contribution to the global science and IT progress. The work of world-famous institute members Amerbayev and Akushsky and many others laid the foundation for a computer that was the first to reach the speed of 1 million operations per second in the early 1960s (Malinovsky, 1998). Afterward, the academic and industry research institutes developed computer modeling in high-energy physics, geophysics, economic management, and so on, but the research activities had shrunk in the early 1990s from funding shortages. Consequently, imported ICT products conquered the emerging ICT market. Programs which provided necessary automation solutions with minimum adjustment became most popular in Kazakhstan (Pak, 2012).

Nonetheless, the Kazakhstan countrywide innovation system demonstrates its ability to create projects that meet international standards. An example of such a project is the development of digital technology used to model and optimize oil pumping practices in a pipeline section, by integrating the SmartTrans software and the SCADA system (see Table 5.1).

[14]Waldrop, M.M. (2001), Claude Shannon: Reluctant Father of the Digital Age. Available at: https://www.technologyreview.com/s/401112/claude-shannon-reluctant-father-of-the-digital-age/

Table 5.1 The convergence of technologies in the O&G industry

Technology	Current adoption
Communication: third-party data transfer devices, hard-wired connected equipment, radio, wireless, satellites	In the upstream sector, telecommunication infrastructure is extremely limited or absent In the downstream sector, communications are negatively impacted by large metal constructions
Central data and control systems: supervisory control and data acquisition systems (SCADA)	Central data and control system at plants Old technology with many technical barriers still dominates
Historian systems	Transfer cross-functional data into a single centralized location. Built on outdated databases, dependent on the quality of data from other outdated systems
Industrial internet	Companies are replacing older equipment by IoT-enabled smart sensors. This gives O&G companies, much like any other industry, the potential to perform greater analytics and obtain business insights
Security infrastructure and industrial control systems	As the industrial internet becomes more and more embedded in the O&G technology ecosystem, the demand for security infrastructure will grow Security concerns are related to possible impact scenarios in the interconnected ecosystem
Asset management systems	Nowadays, O&G companies have the opportunity to implement better asset management systems Limitations of these systems can include integration between procurement systems and asset maintenance data, still widely using Excel files stored on individual computers; no integration of this information is available With the installation of IoT-enabled sensors, analytics can help to improve asset performance

Source: Author, adapted from Industrial Internet Consortium (2015)

Case Study: Smart Oil Transportation Program

KazTransOil, an operator of the main pipelines in Kazakhstan in cooperation with leading Kazakh Universities research centers and Kazakhstan National Academy of Science, has used digital technology to model and optimize oil pumping practices in a pipeline section by integrating the SmartTrans software and the SCADA. This system will help the operator to digitize transportation systems in order to solve energy efficiency problems while transporting oil. The program uses real-time data to control and manage oil streams in the pipelines. It is integrated with SCADA and ACEM—another important ICT technology for the O&G industry. The program also uses real-time operational data (process equipment operation modes, oil pumping volumes and parameters, etc.) from SCADA. In addition to KazTransOil, the consumers of the technology are supposed to be the Caspian Pipeline Consortium, the Kazakhstan-China Oil Pipeline, the North-Western Pipeline Company Munaitas, and the Karachaganak Petroleum Operating B.V. (Astana Times, May 2018). Kazakhstani researchers developed digital technology to optimize "hot" oil pumping, that is the movement of heat transfer oils under high temperature conditions. They have constructed an algorithm for solving the problem of changing temperatures and throughput. For this purpose, the dynamic programming method has been used to find a minimum cost for energy consumed. The "hot" oil pumping process has been investigated by determining the optimal operating conditions for pumps and preheaters (Beysembetov, Bekibaev, Zhapbasbaev, Makhmotov, & Sayakhov, 2017).

Such initiatives between the research universities and O&G sectors can become an important part of the New Silk Road project, boosting development of the O&G infrastructure in the Central Asian region. Development of the energy infrastructure in Eurasia meets China's interests in diversification of routes of energy supplies (IENE, n.d.).

Private initiatives in a framework of public action encourage restructuring, diversification, and technological dynamism beyond what market forces on their own would generate (Rodrik, 2007). Through appropriate industrial policy, Kazakhstan has made good progress in the development of communication and technologies related to data acquisition, storage, and application. The telecommunication services market has been growing on average 8% annually since 2010; the offer of special telecommunication services, like satellite tracking, satellite terminal control, and internet access, has also been expanding. Gross investments peaking at US $2 billion in 2012 had shrunk for four years thereafter but have been following an upward trend since 2016 due to growing demand for communication services and the need to replace outdated equipment (Shinkeeva, 2018). More than 82% of households have access to the internet. Yet, the technological gap between local and foreign companies is substantial. Figure 5.6 shows fluctuations of the Kazakh ICT market. However, large areas and potential capabilities of the country make us believe in the recovery of the market and renewed interest of investors in the future.

Global ICT giants are optimistic about the digital future of Kazakhstan which is illustrated by Inspur,[15] China, intending to create a supercomputer and cloud cluster, as well as training and study centers and laboratories established by Hewlett Packard, Cisco, Intel, Konica Minolta, and Microsoft (KazNU, 2018).

Digitalization in the financial sector is the key trend worldwide. It will change the ways in which financial institutions operate and will give

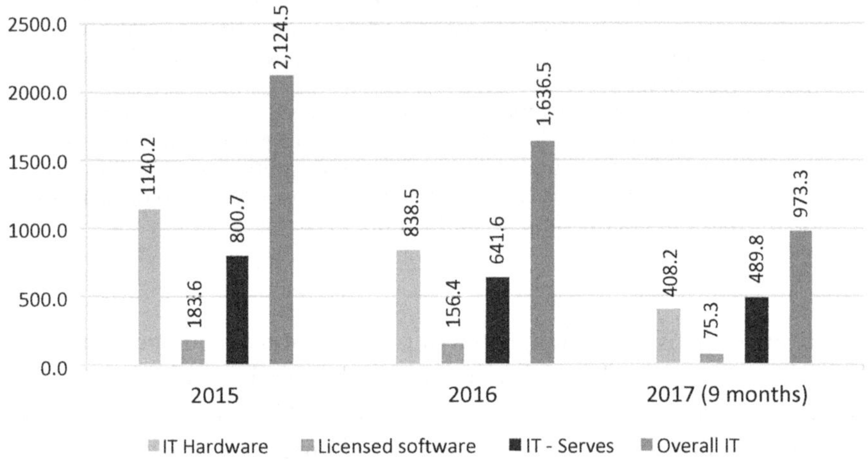

Fig. 5.6 ICT expenditures in Kazakhstan, 2015–2017, million US dollars. (Source: Authors, own processed data based on ITK)

[15] Inspur is a leading global data center and cloud computing solutions provider. Among the world's top three server providers, they deliver and deploy robust, performance-optimized, purpose-built solutions to major data centers around the globe to address important emerging fields and applications. Source: https://www.inspursystems.com

more opportunities for cross-border cooperation. Far beyond the internet application, fintech companies such as the big data technologies, artificial intelligence, and blockchain are increasingly used in bank, insurance, and other financial institutions. Some experts predict that Kazakhstan's e-commerce market will double to US $2 billion by 2020. There are three

Case Study: Fintech and E-commerce

On April 24, 2018, China CITIC Bank[16] Corporation Limited and Shuangwei Investment Co. Ltd.[17] bought 60% of the share capital of Altyn Bank JSC from Halyk Bank[18] of Kazakhstan JSC, CITIC Bank acquired 50.1% of the shares and Shuangwei had 9.9%. At the same time, the Kazakhstan shareholder continues to own 40% of Altyn Bank's shares and reserves certain rights in accordance with the shareholder agreement signed between the parties.

The China CITIC Bank ranks 7th in terms of assets in China and is represented in 130 countries. Altyn Bank, formerly known as subsidiary of HSBC Bank Kazakhstan, has been operating in the banking market of Kazakhstan since 1998, was acquired and has been fully owned by the Halyk Bank since November 2014. Altyn Bank, a licensed corporate and retail bank, has branches in Almaty, Astana, Atyrau, Aktau, and AIFC. It also ranks 13th in terms of assets and has the highest credit rating among commercial banks in Kazakhstan.

This transaction allows Halyk Bank to play a key role in implementing initiatives in the building of the Silk Road Economic Belt. It will promote financial cooperation as well as digitalization. The CITIC Bank paid particular attention to fintech area and launched a series of platforms, for exam-

(continued)

[16] CITIC Bank Corporation Ltd., founded in 1987, ranks 7th in terms of assets in China and is represented in 130 countries. It offers various banking products and services to large corporate clients and individuals, both in China and abroad. The Bank's total assets have reached US $900 billion. The ratings of the bank: BBB from Fitch and Baa2 from Moody's.

[17] China Shuangwei Investment Co. Ltd. is a limited liability company wholly owned by China Tobacco Corporation. The company is responsible for managing and investing in a number of key strategic projects in the fields of energy, real estate, agriculture, education, medical services, logistics, infrastructure, culture, network information, financial products, energy saving, supporting projects in the tobacco industry, and related advisory business services.

[18] Halyk Bank of Kazakhstan is the leading financial group in Kazakhstan operating in various segments including retail, SMEs and corporate banking services, insurance, leasing, brokerage, and asset management. The bank has been listed in the Kazakhstan Stock Exchange since 1998 and in London Stock Exchange since 2006.

(continued)

ple, the digital bank and risk control system based on big data and cloud platform. The CITIC Bank has also built China's first blockchain-based Letter of Credit System online.

There are three important parts in Altyn Bank digital promotions. Firstly, the Altyn Bank launched the first full-scale digital bank, the Altyn-I, in Kazakhstan, with a full range of financial services for individuals. All products and processes are transferred online, from accounts and issuing a debit cards, to international currency transfers or receiving an unsecured loan. The Altyn-i MasterCard credit or debit card can be linked to the Apple Pay service using the preinstalled wallet application in iPhone or other Apple devices. Secondly, the strategic alliance between the largest banks of Kazakhstan and China will help the Altyn Bank to expand opportunities in banking technologies, cross-selling, trade finance, treasury operations, and payments in RMB and will also attract key Chinese clients working in Kazakhstan.

The Altyn Bank has joined the Chinese Cross-Border Interbank Payment System (CIPS) as an indirect participant. The system is designed for international settlements in Chinese yuan and allows foreign market participants to make payments in yuan directly to Chinese partners. Major shareholder of the bank, China CITIC Bank Corporation Ltd., being a direct participant of CIPS, provides the indirect participation for Altyn Bank.

Thirdly, combining with its own fintech framework, CITIC Bank will strengthen the sharing of matured technologies such as the payment tools, mobile banking, and big data application and will support the Altyn Bank to expand the business as well as to build the platform. These steps allow the bank to introduce to their customers in Kazakhstan the financial services similar to those offered by China CITIC Bank to its clients in China.

China and Kazakhstan signed the *Memorandum of Understanding on E-commerce Cooperation* between the Ministry of Commerce of the People's Republic of China and the Ministry of National Economy of the Republic of Kazakhstan in 2018. In line with this memorandum, China and Kazakhstan will build up an e-commerce cooperation mechanism in the innovative regulation of customers, preferential tax policy, and construction of the infrastructure. The two countries will also jointly boost the cooperation of Silk Road e-commerce, strengthen experience sharing, carry out personnel training, and promote the dialogue between government and enterprises. They will support further cooperation of enterprises between the two countries in the e-commerce area and expand cross-border trade of featured products by e-commerce in particular, so as to offer more development opportunities and spaces to SMEs of the two countries, as well as continuously improve trade facilitation and cooperation levels, and further

(*continued*)

(continued)

boost sustainable and steady development of bilateral economic and trade relationships. An example of cooperation in this area is a framework agreement on strategic cooperation signed between KTZ Express, a subsidiary of Kazakhstan Railways, and the Chinese companies Huawei and Ili Baitexing Commercial Trading (Sha, 2019). The pact is aimed at the development of cross-border e-commerce using the capabilities of Kazakhstan's logistics infrastructure. It will be based on using the capabilities of the logistics infrastructure of *KTZ Express*, dry port *Altynkol*, SEZ *Khorgos*, port Aktau, transport and logistics centers, and airports.

KTZ Express plans to serve the transit flows arising from China and the EU's courier services, which are expected to attract more than 1 million tons of cargo per year. The transport of commercial packages in transit will be carried out by *KTZ Express*. The two parties also discussed the organization of between four and ten container trains per month.

reasons for the high-speed development of e-commerce in Kazakhstan: the rise of internet penetration, convenient payment tool and a lower cost for the goods delivery infrastructure. The key point for cross-border e-commerce cooperation between China and Kazakhstan is the high demand for consumer goods in Kazakhstan which boosts demand for imports from China. The high-tech products, household goods, and light industrial products mostly come from the USA, Germany, Japan, Russia, China, and other countries. The related statistics show that clothing, footwear, sporting goods, and household goods from Russia account for 3-4% of the national e-commerce market, while Kazakhstan accounts for less than 1%.

Policies to improve digital connectivity between the countries in Central Asia have led to Digital Silk Road initiative, first announced in March 2015 in the news release issued by the National Development and Reform Commission and later in July 2015 at the China-EU Digital Cooperation Roundtable in Brussels. Among the proposed plans was the establishment of an internet community that would facilitate cross-border e-commerce and internet banking through the development of software infrastructure. However, this is one of the less-discussed aspects of the New Silk Road, perhaps because investments in the hardware infrastructure have so far dominated

According to Ren Xianliang, Vice Minister of the Cyberspace Administration of China, the Digital Silk Road should be undertaken in addition to implementing the *Internet Plus* plan, whereby everything will be connected to a superfast broadband network (Huanxin, 2015). The Digital Silk Road is meant to give Chinese telecommunication companies access to new markets along the Silk Road. By improving the infrastructure in Central Asia, the initiative offers "mutual benefits" while showcasing Beijing's green economic model (Wu, 2017). In addition to commercial motivations, the new fiber-optic Silk Road could also have geopolitical and strategic implications. For landlocked countries such as Kazakhstan, this could mean greater access to international data networks, at a cost averaging a tenth that of satellite communications and with a bandwidth significantly enhanced by fiber-optic technology (Rolland, 2015).

Initiatives of the New Silk Road, including the Digital Silk Road, will open new opportunities for international cooperation, including the development of digital technologies. BRI intends to promote global economic growth and has already fueled discussions on globalization and prospective aid in mitigating economic development inequality between emerging and mature economies (ACCA, 2017).

Digitalization of the O&G Industry

After the oil price plunge in 2014, the global O&G industry faced the tendency of a long-term low-price environment, with organizations looking beyond short-term tactics and taking a more proactive and strategic approach, for example digitalization. Now, organizations face a new disruption—new technologies disrupt the existing industry value chains and entirely change the way companies operate in many industries, including O&G. Technological innovation—including the adoption of NDE—along with macroeconomic trends and changing consumer behavior is transforming the way resources are consumed and produced (McKinsey, 2017). Harnessing new technologies is essential in enhancing the operational excellence of the companies in the new O&G market dynamics. They now have opportunities to achieve further efficiencies through adopting new technologies. According to the Cisco report *A New Reality for Oil & Gas* (2015), "integration IT-OT technologies[19] and business processes has become imperative to boost operational effectiveness and ensure survival".

According to the Industrial Internet Consortium (2015), currently the O&G industry is beginning to experience the convergence of new emerging technologies such as big data, analytics, and intelligence systems, cloud computing and mobile technology, as well as social media (see Table 5.1). As a result, the industry is demonstrating higher levels of performance, and optimization that results in a higher return on investments for the O&G companies, leveraging these new technologies. Digitalization has been driven primarily by the emergence of NDE, latest data available for analysis that were previously not possible to capture real-time data. O&G companies created remote operation centers where transactions with primarily large investments are analyzed, but old technologies still dominate in the O&G ICT architecture.

According to an Accenture survey (2013), O&G companies struggled for complete and timely assessment of the impact of operational decisions on corporate performance. They have started to invest in the new technologies to achieve a higher return on investments, but still much more needs to be done to realize these outcomes. These technology trends are internet of things, mobility, cloud computing, and big data analytics. The examples where analytical technologies can potentially drive better business outcomes are summarized in Table 5.2.

To conclude, ICT is a tool that not only constitutes an industry in its own right but also permeates all sectors of the economy, where it acts to integrate and enable technologies. ICT has a profound impact on society, and its production and use have essential effects on the development of economic, social, and environmental areas (Caperna, 2010). The next section will give an overview of the ICT developmental programs in Kazakhstan.

[19] Operational technology (OT)—technology, which is used in specific operational processes, such as supply chain, manufacturing, and transportation. In the O&G, operational technology is also referred to as industrial control systems (Cisco, 2015).

Table 5.2 The points where analytics can potentially drive better business outcomes in the O&G value chain

Upstream operations	Downstream operations	Corporate operations
Forecast and production commitment	Optimize integrated value chain	Optimize cash flow to meet planned capital expenditure commitments effectively
Efficiently deliver unconventional plays	Configure the supply chain to enable cost reduction	Enable management of contingent labor
Improve working standards		Measure and manage market risk at a commercial level
Manage equipment supply chain	Measure and manage market risk at commercial and logistics levels	Improve working standards
Execute capital projects to time, budget, and scope	Improve working standards	Execute capital projects to time, budget, and scope

Source: Author, adapted from Accenture (2013)

Local ICT Industry Development

So, what are the limitations of local companies' development in Kazakhstan? According to the "Local content management framework" (2004)—an Agip Kazakhstan North Caspian Operating Company NV or Agip KCO (since January 2009—North Caspian Operating Company BV or NCOC) an internal document—managers of the company have seen a number of potential barriers related to local development that can be applied to both, the ICT and the O&G industries. First of all, weak domestic skills and/or supplier base—low domestic capacity levels—are insufficient to meet business needs.

The ICT sector in Kazakhstan is currently underdeveloped in comparison with some other emerging economies (see Table 5.3). As a result, the demand for ICT goods is mostly covered by imports, and the share of the LC is exceptionally low for IT equipment. As discussed above, this

Table 5.3 The share of ICT goods as percentage of total merchandise trade annual in 2012–2018

Country/year	2012	2013	2014	2015	2016	2017	2018
Czech Republic	14.53	13.11	13.42	13.54	12.72	13.33	15.10
Hungary	17.45	14.77	11.92	11.62	11.38	11.18	11.34
Kazakhstan	0.44	0.33	0.84	0.19	0.16	0.13	0.11
Russian Federation	0.31	0.42	0.80	0.81	0.60	0.63	0.47
Ukraine	1.10	0.93	0.96	0.82	0.95	0.93	0.98
China	27.06	27.42	25.94	26.56	26.50	27.07	27.31

Source: Authors, adapted from UNCTAD statistics

Table 5.4 Local goods share in ICT technologies in Kazakhstan

Indicators	2009	2014
Share of Kazakhstani content in overall IT market	7%	Not less than 32%
Share of Kazakhstani content in IT services	30%	80%

Source: Author, compiled from Government of Kazakhstan (2010), the Program for Development of Information and Communication Technologies in the Republic of Kazakhstan 2010–2014

means future comparative disadvantage for the country when the natural resources will be exhausted. For IT services, often considered to be more local, the share of LC was only 30% (Government of Kazakhstan, 2010). In the program, the government had set ambitious targets: to achieve a share of LC of 10% in equipment and 80% in services by 2014. Reaching these targets required developing the infrastructure, as well as a number of policy changes, including improving the business environment and fostering skills development.

This also assumes development of local ICT capabilities (see Table 5.4). The barriers for local industry development are listed below:

- Lack of appropriate technical skills base in labor force
- Inadequate or outdated equipment
- Weak technology base, that is limited IT infrastructure
- Lack of understanding of international tender processes
- Insufficient awareness or poor practice on health, safety, and environment (HSE)

- Inadequate knowledge of international commercial practices on HSE
- Inadequate knowledge of international commercial practices, for example financing
- Import laws

This demonstrates that lack of ICT can be a barrier not only in local IT companies develoment but also in the competitiveness of Kazakhstan's O&G companies and the whole energy sector. This raises the question as to how the level of ICT adoption in the energy sector can be effectively increased. The Government of Kazakhstan has recognized the importance of technological change disrupting the economy, launching a *Program for Development of Information and Communication Technologies in the Republic of Kazakhstan in 2010–2014* and a *Program Information Kazakhstan—2020 for 2013–2017 years*. At the end of year 2017 it also launched a *Program Digital Kazakhstan*, which aims to accelerate industrial development in Kazakhstan and, more specifically, the transition of the Republic of Kazakhstan to an information and innovative economy with the formation of a competitive export-oriented national ICT sector.

Calculations of LC in ICT procurement can be seen in Table 5.5.

To implement an integrated state policy in ICT and state management of information and communication infrastructure, a joint stock company called *National ICT Holding Zerde* was established in 2008. According to the information at *Holding Zerde* website, the implementation of the state *Program Digital Kazakhstan* will be in four key areas:

Table 5.5 Plan of ICT procurement for NOC KMG

Year	Goods, thousands tenge	LC, %	Services[a], thousands tenge	LC, %	IT programs, thousands tenge	LC, %
2015	309,906	1	1,581,034	96	117,354	0
2014	2,189,805	0	1,904,774	93	575,960	0
2013	157,314	0	963,468	84	314,730	0
2012	103,679	1	1,668,169	83	2,260,453	12

Source: Heim (2019)
[a]Prices are not available for all positions

- creating a *Digital Silk Road* including the development of reliable, affordable, high-speed, secure digital infrastructure;
- shaping a *creative society*, including the development of competencies and skills for the digital economy, an upgrading of digital literacy, and training of ICT specialists for industries;
- digital transformation in the economy assuming the widespread introduction of digital technology to enhance the competitiveness of various branches of the economy;
- the formation of *proactive digital government*, including improvement of electronic and mobile government platforms, with optimization of the public services supply sphere.

However, launching all these programs does not in any way guarantee the success of development; time has to pass for results to be visible.

The program requires enhancing skills through the public-private partnership in information technologies (OECD, 2013). As of December 2017, the list of investment programs of the Holding Zerde (2017b) accounted for eight projects including:

- central provision of the IT services for state bodies;
- data processing centers (data centers) in 14 regional centers and in Almaty to provide a set of information services for all government agencies;
- unified notary information system;
- unified service monitoring system;
- a consolidated computing platform for civil defense;
- an information system for technical inspection of motor vehicles;
- single contact center of state bodies of Kazakhstan;
- unified e-mail system of state bodies of Kazakhstan.

The list of public-private partnerships the Holding Zerde has taken part as of December 2017 (Zerde, 2017a) includes five projects:

- automation of crop production traceability;
- automation of monitoring of fish and fish products turnover;
- intelligent transport system;

- automation of traceability of farm animals and livestock products;
- smart city.

In September 2017 the Government of Kazakhstan presented the state-initiated program *Digital Kazakhstan*, and in December 2017 the government developed and presented a detailed plan of the program to the President of Kazakhstan (KazInform, 2017a, b).

ICT procurement also comprises a part of procurement in the O&G industry and therefore is the subject of local LC regulation in the O&G sector. However, these two policies are not synchronized, as LCP in the ICT industry is focused on this sector only and investments and public-private projects target mostly ICT in the public services domain. However, according to Adewuyi and Oyejide (2012), knowledge-intensive sub-sectors control systems and the ICT sector, feeding into the O&G industry, can also serve other sectors and neighboring countries, creating backward linkages and providing a potential for spillovers. Backward linkages between a company and its suppliers, including the ICT supplier, are generally relatively labor intensive and thus an attractive source of diversification for governments. These linkages may also increase GDP, and therefore governments may actively target linkages in their IP in the hope that complementary development of the national system of innovation may result in a competitive, diversified economy in the future (Morris, Kaplinsky & Kaplan, 2011).

Conclusion and Future Research

The New Silk Road concept was recently mentioned by the Chairman of the Security Council of Kazakhstan and former President Nazarbayev in his speech as one of the historical advancements of the country and a platform for the future development of the global exchange of goods and intellectual cooperation between nations (Nazarbayev, 2018, 2019). Kassym-Jomart Tokayev took office as President of Kazakhstan on March 19, 2019, succeeding Nursultan Nazarbayev, who resigned, after 29 years in office. The new president admits that the modern technologies play an important role in the world economy and development of Kazakhstan. In

September 2019 he met the founder of the Alibaba Group in China. According to Akorda (2019), the official site of the President of Kazakhstan, he said the following: "I appreciate your desire to support Kazakhstan. We have a strategic agreement that cooperation between China and Kazakhstan in the digital economy will be developing further, and we are interested in your engagement."

The digital economy is a key driver of growth and development; it can boost competitiveness across all sectors, new opportunities for business and entrepreneurial activity, and new avenues for accessing overseas markets and participating in global e-value chains. NDE also provides new tools for tackling persistent development problems. Yet, NDE comes with a host of challenges for policymakers, including the need to bridge the digital divide, minimize potential negative social and development impacts, and deal with complex internet-specific regulatory issues (UNCTAD, 2017). Thus, the role of economic policies in information-based economies will by no means become less critical in terms of NDE. It is "even more urgently pressing scholars to study all aspects of the way and method people apply to handle information dedicated to improving information systems" (Li & Liu, 2018). For academia it raises the question: do current management conceptual frameworks hold true in the new economy and what needs to be researched? How the combined effects of digital technologies transform organizations, industries, and institutions? From the strategic perspective how do firms achieve and sustain a competitive advantage in new market conditions? How does the use of digital technology as strategy or complementary resources change the way value is created and extracted?

From the innovation perspective, will digital technologies depend more on open-sourced innovations? While innovations become more global, regulation and institutions still remain local. This also raises the question: how will different digital institutions affect new business models? What will be the role of institutions such as regulations, antitrust, and the local legal frameworks in a digital world? Do institutions face new challenges due to the spread of digital technologies? What are the consequences of digitalization for organizational knowledge and learning taking into consideration increasing connectivity and sharing of information and knowledge? How do employees adapt to the new digital business processes? In relation to Central Asia, digitalization comes to the New Silk Road, and considering Kazakhstan's development rate and endowment factors, investments in *Digital Kazakhstan* have the potential to become as attractive as the development of the natural resources sector of the economy.

Bibliography

ACCA. (2017). *The Belt and Road Initiative: Reshaping the global value chain*. Shanghai, China: Association of Chartered Certified Accountants.

Accenture. (2013). *Is the energy industry drowning in data?*. Retrieved from https://www.accenture.com/in-en/~/media/Accenture/Conversion-Assets/DotCom/Documents/Global/PDF/Technology_8/Accenture-Digitizing-Energy-Industry-Drowning-Data.pdf

Adewuyi, A. O. & Oyejide, T. A. (2012). Determinants of backward linkages of oil and gas industry in Nigerian economy. *Resource Policy, 37*(4), 452–460.

Aiginger, K. (2007). Industrial policy: A dying breed or a re-emerging phoenix. *Journal of Industry, Competition and Trade, 7*(3–4), 297–323.

Akorda (2019, September 12). Kassym-Jomart Tokayev held a meeting with the founder of Alibaba Group Jack Ma. Retrieved from https://www.akorda.kz.

Altenburg, T. (2011). *Industrial policy in developing countries: Overview and lessons from seven country cases*. Bonn: DIE (Discussion paper 4/2011).

Ambalov, V., & Heim, I. (2018). Cluster nodes as a unit for value co-creation: The role of information technologies in competitiveness of the oil and gas industry. In W. Liu, K. Nakata, W. Li, & C. Baranauskas (Eds.), *Proceedings of 18th IFIP WG 8.1 international conference on informatics and semiotics in Organisations, ICISO 2018* (pp. 155–163). Reading, UK: Springer.

Amighini, A. (2017). *China's belt and road: A game changer?* Milan, Italy: ISPI.

Arger, A. (2015). *The Silk Road and its impact on globalization*. Washington, DC: Washington State University.

Astana Times. (2018). *Kazakhstan develops smart oil transportation programme*. Retrieved from https://astanatimes.com/2018/05/kazakhstan-develops-smart-oil-transportation-programme/

Baldakhov, U., & Heim, I. (2020). Institutional reform in Kazakhstan. In I. Heim (Ed.), *Kazakhstan's diversification from the natural resources sector: Strategic and economic opportunities*. London, UK: Palgrave Macmillan.

Beysembetov, I. K., Bekibaev, T. T., Zhapbasbaev, U. K., Makhmotov, E. S., & Sayakhov, B. K. (2017). The use of digital technology to optimize oil pipeline transportation. *Pipeline Science & Technology, 1*(3), 219–232.

Bodrožić, Z., & Adler, P. S. (2018). The evolution of management models: A neo-Schumpeterian theory. *Administrative Science Quarterly, 63*(1), 85–129.

Buckley, N. (2017, April 12). *Financial Times*. Retrieved from https://www.ft.com/content/900d96ee-1ade-11e7-a266-12672483791a

Buckley, P. J. (2016). The contribution of internalisation theory to international business: New realities and unanswered questions. *Journal of World Business, 51*(1), 74–82.

Caperna, A. (2010). Integrating ICT into sustainable local policies. In Silva, C.N. (Ed.), *Handbook of research on E-Planning: ICTs for urban development and monitoring* (pp. 340–364). Hershey, PA: IGI Global.

Choudhry, H., Mohammad, A., Tan, K. T, & Ward, R. (2016). *The next frontier for digital technologies in oil and gas*. Retrieved from https://www.mckinsey.com/industries/oil-and-gas/our-insights/the-next-frontier-for-digital-technologies-in-oil-and-gas

Çilan, Ç. A., Bolat, B. A., & Coşkun, E. (2009). Analyzing digital divide within and between member and candidate countries of European Union. *Government Information Quarterly, 26*(1), 98–105.

Cisco. (2015). *A new reality for oil & gas*. Retrieved from https://connectedfutures.cisco.com/report/a-new-reality-for-oil-gas/

Cooper, J. (2006). The digital divide: The special case of gender. *Journal of Computer Assisted Learning, 22*(5), 320–334.

Dey, B., & Ali, F. (2016). A critical review of the ICT for development research. In B. Dey, K. Sorour, & R. Filiery (Eds.), *ICTs in developing countries* (pp. 3–23). London, UK: Palgrave Macmillan.

Drucker, P. F. (1992). *The age of discontinuity: Guidelines to our changing society*. New Brunswick, USA/London, UK: Transaction Publishers.

Dunning, J. H. (1980). Toward an eclectic theory of international production: Some empirical tests. *Journal of International Business Studies, 11*(1), 9–31.

Dunning, J. H. (1995). Reappraising the eclectic paradigm in an age of alliance capitalism. *Journal of International Business Studies, 26*(3), 461–491.

Dunning, J. H., & Lundan, S. M. (2008). *Multinational enterprises and the global economy* (2nd ed.). Cheltenham, UK: Edward Elgar.

Fraumeni, B. M., & Okubo, S. (2005). R&D in the national income and product accounts: A first look at its effect on GDP. In C. Corrado, J. Haltiwanger, & D. Sichel (Eds.), *Measuring capital in the new economy* (pp. 275–322). Chicago, IL: University of Chicago Press.

Geppert, M., Matten, D., & Walgenbach, P. (2006). Transnational institution building and the multinational corporation: An emerging field of research. *Human Relations, 59*(11), 1451–1465.

Gleick, J. (2011). *The information*. New York, NY: Panteon Books.

Grübler, A. (2003). *Technology and global change*. Cambridge, UK: Cambridge University Press.

Han, T. & Ghobadian, A. (2020). Chinese investments across the New Silk Road. In I. Heim (Ed.), *Kazakhstan's Diversification from the Natural Resource Sector: Strategic and Economic Opportunities*. London, UK: Palgrave Macmillan.

Hanclova, J., Rozehnal, P., Ministr, J., & Tvrdikova, M. (2015). The determinants of IT adoption in SMEs in the Czech-Polish border areas. *Information Technology for Development, 21*(3), 426–444.

Heim, I. (2019). *Local content policy and value co-creation: Adopting information technologies in the oil and gas industry*. Unpublished PhD dissertation.

Heim, I., Kalyuzhnova, Y., Li, W., & Liu, K. (2018). Value co-creation between foreign firms and indigenous SMEs in Kazakhstan's oil and gas industry: The role of information technology spillovers. *Thunderbird International Business Review, 61*, 911. https://doi.org/10.1002/tie.22067

Huanxin, Z. (2015). *Digital Silk Road linked to 'net plus'*. Retrieved from the website of the State Council of the People Republic of China http://english.www.gov.cn/news/top_news/2015/12/24/content_281475259901640.htm

Industrial Internet Consortium (IIC). (2015). *Beyond digitalisation: The convergence of big data, analytics and intelligent systems in oil & gas*. Retrieved from https://futurerobotics.files.wordpress.com/2015/09/beyond_digitization_an_iic_energy_task_group_white_paper.pdf

Institute of Energy for South-East Europe (IENE). (n.d.). *New Silk Road to Boost Asian oil and gas development*. Retrieved from https://www.iene.eu/new-silk-road-to-boost-asian-oil-and-gas-development-p1759.html

Jones, R. (2017). *Economics after Moore's Law*. Retrieved from http://www.softmachines.org/wordpress/?p=2097

Kabanda, S., & Brown, I. (2017). Interrogating the effect of environmental factors on e-commerce institutionalization in Tanzania: A test and validation of small and medium enterprise claims. *Information Technology for Development, 23*(1), 59–85.

Karachaganak News. (2018). Retrieved from http://www.kpo.kz/en/newsroom/company-news/company-news/article/kpo-held-an-international-digitalization-forum-in-uralsk.html

KazInform. (2017a). The Prime Minister announced priorities of Digital Kazakhstan program. Retrieved from http://lenta.inform.kz/en/pm-announced-priorities-of-digitalkazakhstan-program_a3064476.

KazInform. (2017b). Digital Kazakhstan program to be submitted to Head of State for approval. Retrieved from http://www.inform.kz/en/digital-kazakhstan-program-to-besubmitted-to-head-of-state-for-approval_a3092695.

KazNU (2018). *Vectors of digitalization*. Retrieved from http://www.kaznu.kz/en/3/news/one/12390/

Kretschmer, T., & Claussen, J. (2016). Generational transitions in platform markets—The role of backward compatibility. *Strategy Science, 1*(2), 90–104.

Levy, M., & Powell, P. (2003). Exploring SME internet adoption: Towards a contingent model. *Electronic Markets, 13*(2), 173–181.

Li, Q., & Liu, K. (2018). An abductive process of developing interactive data visualization: A case study of market attractiveness analysis. In W. Liu, K. Nakata, W. Li, & C. Baranauskas (Eds.), *Proceedings of 18th IFIP WG 8.1 international conference on informatics and semiotics in organisations, ICISO 2018* (pp. 289–298). Reading, UK: Springer.

Lind, P., Sepúlveda, E., & Nuñez, J. (2000). On the applicability of a computer model for business performance analysis in SMEs: A case study from Chile. *Information Technology for Development, 9*(1), 33–44.

Lusch, R. F., & Vargo, S. L. (2014). *Service-dominant logic: premises, perspectives, possibilities*. New York, NY: Cambridge University Press.

Mack, C. A. (2011). Fifty years of Moore's law. *IEEE Transaction on Semiconduction Manufacturing, 24*(2), 202–206.

Malinovsky, B. (1998). *Essays on history of computer science and technology in Ukraine*. Kyiv, Ukraine: Feniks.

Mazzucato, M., & Tancioni, M. (2012). R&D, patents and stock return volatility. *Journal of Evolutionary Economics, 22*(4), 811–832.

McKinsey. (2016). *Digital Europe: Pushing the frontier, capturing the benefits*. McKinsey Global Institute. Retrieved from https://www.mckinsey.com/~/media/McKinsey/Business%20Functions/McKinsey%20Digital/Our%20Insights/Digital%20Europe%20Pushing%20the%20frontier%20capturing%20the%20benefits/Digital-Europe-Full-report-June-2016.ashx

McKinsey. (2017). *Beyond the super-cycle: How technology is reshaping resources*. McKinsey Global Institute. Retrieved from https://www.mckinsey.com/~/media/McKinsey/Business%20Functions/Sustainability/Our%20Insights/How%20technology%20is%20reshaping%20supply%20and%20demand%20for%20natural%20resources/MGI-Beyond-the-Supercycle-Executive-summary.ashx

Milis, K. (2008). Critical analysis of policy measures for the advancement of the level of computerization of SMEs. *Information Technology for Development, 14*(3), 253–258.

Min, S.-J. (2010). From the digital divide to the democratic divide: Internet skills, political interest, and the second-level digital divide in political internet use. *Journal of Information Technology & Politics, 7*(1), 22–35.

Morris, M., Kaplinsky, R., & Kaplan, D. (2011). Commodities and linkages: industrialisation in Sub Saharan Africa. MMCP discussion paper; no. 13.

Narula, R. (2016). *The Modern MNE as an efficient meta-integrator: emerging market MNEs need to foster internal embeddedness to succeed.* Discussion paper N JHD-2016-02. Reading, UK: Henley Business School, University of Reading.

National Bank of Kazakhstan. (2018). *Direct investments statistic according to the directional principle.* Astana: National Bank of Kazakhstan.

National Development and Reform Commission (NDRC). (2015). *Vision and actions on jointly building silk road economic belt and 21st-century maritime silk road.* Retrieved from http://en.ndrc.gov.cn/newsrelease/201503/t20150330_669367.html

Nazarbayev, N. (2018). *Seven facets of the Great Steppe.* Retrieved from https://www.akorda.kz

Nazarbayev, N. (2019). Interview: BRI a great idea with perspective. *Xinhua Net.* Retrieved from: http://www.xinhuanet.com/english/2019-04/27/c_138014919.htm

Ntwoku, H., Negash, S., & Meso, P. (2017). ICT adoption in Cameroon SME: Application of bass diffusion model. *Information Technology for Development, 23*(2), 296–317.

OECD. (2001). *Understanding the digital divide.* Paris, France: OECD Publishing.

OECD. (2011). *OECD guide to measuring the information society.* Paris, France: OECD Publishing.

OECD. (2013). Enhancing Skills through Public-Private Partnerships in Kazakhstan's Information Technology Sector. Retrieved from https://www.oecd.org/countries/kazakhstan/Enhancing%20Skills%20though%20Public-Private%20Partnerships%20in%20Kazakhstan's%20Information%20Technology%20Sector.pdf

Ostrom, E. (1990). *Governing the commons.* New York, UK: Cambridge University Press.

Ostrom, E. (2005). *Understanding institutional diversity.* Princeton, NJ: Princeton University Press.

Pak, I. T. (2012). *From the history of the development of computer science in Kazakhstan*. Almaty, Kazakhstan: Ministry of Education and Science of the Republic of Kazakhstan.

Prahalad, C. K., & Ramaswamy, V. (2004). Co-creation experiences: The next practice in value creation. *Journal of Interactive Marketing, 18*(3), 5–14.

Qureshi, S. (2015). Are we making a better world with information and communication technology for development (ICT4D) research? Findings from the field and theory building. *Information Technology for Development, 21*(4), 511–522.

Ramamurti, R., & Hillemann, J. (2018). What is "Chinese" about Chinese multinationals? *Journal of International Business Studies, 49*(1), 34–48.

Rao, S. S. (2005). Bridging digital divide: Efforts in India. *Telematics and Informatics, 22*(4), 361–375.

Rimmel, G., & Diedrich, A. (2000). Exploring the logic of E-business and the new economy. In *Proceedings of 2nd SNEE conference on economic integration in Europe*. Mölle, Sweden.

Rodrik, D. (2007). *One economics, many recipes: Globalization, institutions, and economic*. Princeton, NJ: Princeton University Press.

Rodrik, D. (2018). *New technologies, global value chains, and developing economies*. No. w25164. National Bureau of Economic Research.

Rolland, N. (2015). *A fiber-optic silk road*. Retrieved from https://thediplomat.com/2015/04/a-fiber-optic-silk-road/

Sabirov, B., & Shakulikova, G. (2020). Diversification and local industry development. In I. Heim (Ed.), *Kazakhstan's diversification from the natural resources sector: Strategic and economic opportunities*. London, UK: Palgrave Macmillan.

Salnikova, O. V. (2013). Small business development based on the information and communication technologies. *American Journal of Economics and Control Systems Management, 1*, 10–14.

Schumpeter, J. (1934). *The Theory of Economic Development*. Cambridge, MA: Harvard University Press.

Selmier, W. T., II. (2020). Kazakhstan as a logistic linchpin in the Belt and Road Initiative. In I. Heim. (Ed.), *Kazakhstan's Diversification from the Natural Resource Sector: Strategic and Economic Opportunities*. London, UK: Palgrave Macmillan.

Sha, N. (2019, July 12). *SF Airlines launches route links China, Kazakhstan*. Caspian Policy Center. Retrieved from https://www.caspianpolicy.org/sf-airlines-launches-route-links-china-kazakhstan/

Shannon, C. E. (1948). A mathematical theory of communication. *Bell System Technical Journal, 27*(3), 379–423.

Shen, H. (2018). Building a digital silk road? Situating the internet in China's belt and road initiative. *International Journal of Communication, 12*, 2683–2701.

Shinkeeva, G. (2018). *Telecommunication sector of Kazakhstan: Results of 2016*. Almaty, Kazakhstan: Rating Agency RFCA.

SJTU. (2015) Federico Musto of Arduino: Our real boss is. *SJTU ParisTech Review*. Retrieved from http://parisinnovationreview.cn/en/2015/11/11/federico-musto-arduino-community/.

Smorodinskaya, N. V., & Katukov, D. D. (2017). Dispersed model of production and smart agenda of National Economic Strategies. *Economic Policy, 6*, 72–101.

Sternberg, T., Ahearn, A., & McConnell, F. (2017). Central Asian 'characteristics' on China's new silk road: The role of landscape and the politics of infrastructure. *Land, 6*(3), 1–16.

UNCTAD. (2010). *Creating business linkages: A policy perspective*. New York, NY/Geneva, Switzerland: UN/UNCTAD.

UNCTAD. (2017). *The 'new' digital economy and development*. New York, NY: UN/UNICTAD.

UNCTAD. (2018). Statistics Data Center. Retrieved from: https://unctad.org.

Van Alstyne, M. W., Parker, G. G., & Choudary, S. P. (2016). Pipelines, platforms, and the new rules of strategy. *Harvard Business Review, 94*(4), 54–62.

Vargo, S. L. & Lusch, R. F. (2016). Institutions and axioms: an extension and update of service-dominant logic. *Journal of the Academy of Marketing Science, 44*(1), 5–23.

Vargo, S. L., Wieland, H., and Akaka, M. A. (2015). Innovation through institutionalization: A service ecosystems perspective. *Industrial Marketing Management, 44*(1), 63–72.

Verdu, M. (2017). *The IoT will enable the gas and oil industry to cut production costs by UP to &30 per barrel*. Barcelona: IoT Solutions World Congress.

World Bank. (2018). *Research and development expenditure (% of GDP)*. The World Bank. Retrieved from https://data.worldbank.org/indicator/GB.XPD.RSDV.GD.ZS

Wu, W. (2017). China's digital silk road: Pitfalls among high hopes. Retrieved from https://thediplomat.com/2017/11/chinas-digital-silk-road-pitfalls-among-high-hopes/

Yensebayev, R. (2018, December). Digital Kazakhstan: Transforming through modern technology. *Astana Times*. Retrieved from https://astanatimes.com/2018/02/digital-kazakhstan-transforming-through-modern-technology/

Zerde (2017a). "Digital Kazakhstan" State Program. Retrieved from https://zerde.gov.kz/en/activity/program-control/digital-kazakhstan/#hcq=4K3MWCq.

Zerde (2017b). Holding activities. Investment projects. Retrieved from https://zerde.gov.kz/en/activity/investment-projects/Common-notarial-informationalsystem-Project/.

Part III

China and Regional Development

The authors of the chapters in this section explore the role of Chinese investments in the economy of Kazakhstan and the Central-Asian region. Han and Ghobadian gives an overview of Chinese investments in Kazakhstan as a trade hub in Eurasia. Selmier discusses Kazakhstan's strategic position on the New Silk Road, between China and Russia, East Asia and Europe. It catalyzes the development and promotion of a regional headquarters hub and integration. The chapter argues that sophisticated planning and development is necessary, and this will require integration and coordination between Kazakhstan and China.

6

Chinese Investments Across the New Silk Road

Tian Han and Abby Ghobadian

Introduction

The rise of China is arguably one of the most prominent events in the twenty-first century. With its economic might gained from its growth lasting decades, the incoming superpower is determined to play a leading role in the modernization of Middle Asia. Riding the tide, Kazakhstan is actively embracing the opportunity to reform its economy and evoke its geographical advantage as a trade hub in Eurasia.

Kazakhstan and China share common ground on which to collaborate and cooperate, which fits the national interests of both countries. The benefits to Kazakhstan are evident—investment from China partially releases the financial constraints to reform its economy. As a long-standing foreign investor to Kazakhstan, China has already massively invested in exploring natural resources in the last decade. The ambitious Belt and

T. Han (✉) • A. Ghobadian
Henley Business School, University of Reading, Reading, UK
e-mail: tian.han@pgr.reading.ac.uk

I. Heim (ed.), *Kazakhstan's Diversification from the Natural Resources Sector*, Euro-Asian Studies, https://doi.org/10.1007/978-3-030-37389-4_6

Road Initiate (BRI) marks a milestone shift of investment interests from pouring money into the oil and gas (O&G) industry only into exporting infrastructure industry in Kazakhstan. With the establishment of the Asian Infrastructure Investment Bank (AIIB), China fills the vacuum left by the incumbent international financial institutions—the World Bank and IMF—by providing not only funds but also knowledge and expertise in upgrading the infrastructure in relatively underdeveloped areas. This is in line with the objectives set by the Kazakhstan government in the *Kazakhstan 2050 Initiative*. In return, by funding the infrastructure projects in Kazakhstan, China opens up the gate to Europe and henceforth the gate to expanding the economic influence from the east to the west.

Given the profound influence of Chinese investment in Kazakhstan, in this chapter, we will discuss the topic in the context of BRI, particularly the New Silk Road, from which we could infer the motivation behind Chinese investment, and its outlook for the future.

An Overview of Chinese Investment in Kazakhstan

Kazakhstan is one of the founding members of the Shanghai Cooperation Organization (SCO) established in 2001, since when it has kept a close trade and economic relationship with China. Statistical data collected from the National Bank of Kazakhstan (NBK) suggests that FDI from China has rapidly increased since 2000. Prior to 2000, China's total gross FDI was around US $500 million. From 2002 to 2012, China's FDI had increased from US $0.0647 billion to US $2.414 billion, with an average annual growth rate of 38.9%. After 2012, China has invested US $7.793 billion in Kazakhstan, promoting it as the second largest investor just behind the Netherlands. From 2013 to 2015, however, affected by the dramatic depreciation of the Kazakhstani tenge (KZT), the investment from China and other countries has shrunk greatly. In 2013, 2014 and 2015, compared with the same period of previous years, the gross FDI from China decreased by 7.51%, 20.67% and 121.99%, respectively (see Fig. 6.1).

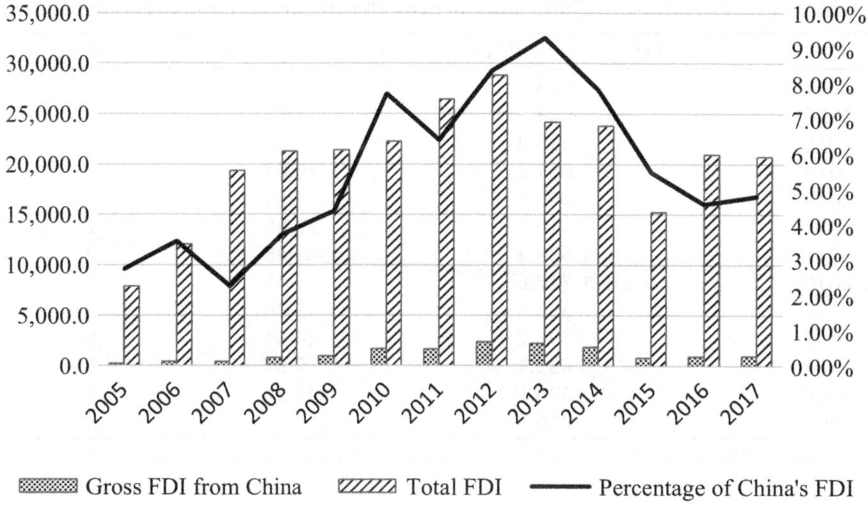

Fig. 6.1 FDI capital inflows from China and the world, and the percentage of China's FDI in the world (2005–2017). (Source: Authors' own processed data based on National Bank of Kazakhstan)

Despite the decline, China is still one of the most important investors to Kazakhstan. As it shows in Table 6.1, since 2006, it has never dropped out of the top six investors club. From 2010 to 2014, it topped as second on the list. By taking the sum of gross FDI from 2005 to 2017, it can be seen that China is the fourth biggest investor in Kazakhstan (see Fig. 6.2).

Apart from the FDI, mergers and acquisitions (M&As) are a critical form of investment. According to the Thomson One Banker database, which provides historical data of global M&As, from 1997 to 2018, China had acquired more than 30 local firms (see Table 6.2). The number is tiny compared to the rest of deals made by Chinese investors across the world, but the value involved in these acquisitions is particularly high. For instance, a single acquisition made by the Chinese energy giant, the *China National Petroleum Corporation* (CNPC) in 2013, reached a deal value of US $5 billion, which is four times more than the investment without involving M&A activities in the same period.

Moreover, M&As could reflect the trend of investment. By looking at the Chinese M&As in detail, one would observe three important features:

Table 6.1 Gross FDI from China, annual growth rate, and FDI ranking (2005–2017)

Year	FDI capital inflows	Growth rate, %	Ranking
2017	998.7	3.68	4
2016	961.9	12.84	3
2015	838.4	−121.99	3
2014	1,861.2	−20.67	2
2013	2,246.0	−7.51	2
2012	2,414.6	29.88	2
2011	1,693.1	−1.45	2
2010	1,717.6	45.45	2
2009	936.9	15.34	3
2008	793.2	44.64	5
2007	439.1	2.87	6
2006	426.5	49.24	5
2005	216.5	–	14

Source: Authors' own processed data based on National Bank of Kazakhstan

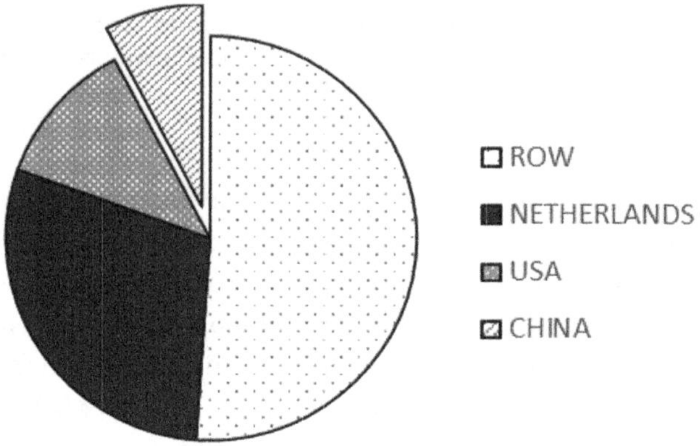

Fig. 6.2 Share of the total amount of FDI (from 2005 to 2017) shares of top investment countries. (Source: Authors' own processed data based on National Bank of Kazakhstan)

(a) Most acquisitions are focused on the energy industry, particularly the O&G sectors. This reflects significant investment imbalance existing between the energy and non-energy sectors.
(b) The interest from Chinese investors in this region is constantly rising, demonstrated in the rapid increasing deal value of M&As (see Fig. 6.3).

Table 6.2 Chinese M&As in Kazakhstan (1997–2018)

Date	Acquirer	Target	Target industry	Value of($mil)
12/11/2018	China Natl Mach Imp & Exp	SaryarkaAvtoProm LLP	Industrials	–
11/22/2018	Xiamen Tungsten Co Ltd	Severnyi Katpar LLP	Materials	40.20
08/30/2018	Xinhuaxia Intl Energy Dvlp Co	TNG Holding LLP	Energy	19.06
04/25/2018	China Nonferrous Metal Industry	KAZ Minerals PLC-Koksay Dep	Materials	70.00
07/28/2017	Schlumberger Holding II Ltd	Soak Oil & Gas LLP	Energy	214.00
05/15/2017	Investor Group	KTZE-Khorgos Gateway-Dry Port	Industrials	–
04/12/2017	CNMIE Co	Gruppa Kompanii Alliur	Retail	–
11/03/2016	Investor Group	Altyn Bank AO	Financials	80.98
01/14/2016	CEFC Natural Gas (Shanghai)	Petroleum TOO	Industrials	100.30
01/07/2015	Investor Group	Galaz & Co LLP	Energy	100.00
01/06/2015	Geo-Jade Petroleum Corp	KoZhaN	Energy	349.49
12/31/2014	Anhui Huaxin Intl Hldg Co Ltd	Dostyk Gas Terminal LLP	Energy	36.00
10/30/2014	Baotou Tomorrow Tech Co Ltd	KoZhaN LLP	Energy	–
04/09/2014	Shanghai Youlong Invest Mgmt	North Caspian Petroleum LLP	Energy	37.50
11/01/2013	SinoHan	Tethys Kazakhstan SPRL	Energy	105.00
09/07/2013	CNPC	Kashagan Oilfield	Energy	5000.00
04/16/2013	PRC	NCOC BV	Energy	–
02/14/2011	Palaeontol BV	Emir Oil LLP	Energy	170.00
09/28/2010	China Petrochemical Corp	Caspian Invest Resources Ltd	Energy	–
04/26/2010	Jinchuan Group Co Ltd	Kazakhmys PLC-Aktogay deposit	Materials	120.00
09/30/2009	Fullbloom Investment Corp	RD KMG AO	Energy	939.00
08/24/2009	Xinjiang Guanghui Ind Co Ltd	Tarbagatay Munai LLP	Energy	–
03/17/2009	CNPC	Mangistaumunaigaz JSC	Energy	–

(*continued*)

Table 6.2 (continued)

Date	Acquirer	Target	Target industry	Value of($mil)
09/30/2008	China Zhenhua Oil Co Ltd	Kuat Hldg Co	Energy	–
11/01/2007	Investor Group	OAO MangistauMunaiGaz	Energy	2603.90
12/30/2003	Shengli Oilfield	Big Sky Energy Kazakhstan Ltd	Energy	2.30
09/19/2003	CNPC	N Buzachi Oilfield, Kazakhstan	Energy	200.00
08/15/2003	CNPC	N Buzachi Oilfield, Kazakhstan	Energy	–
05/07/2003	CNPC	Aurado Expl Ltd-Liman Block	Energy	–
03/11/2003	China Petrochemical Corp	NCOC BV	Energy	615.00
03/07/2003	CNOOC Ltd	NCOC BV	Energy	615.00
06/05/1997	CNPC	Uzenmunaigaz	Energy	–
06/04/1997	CNPC	Aktyubinskmunaygaz	Energy	325.00

Source: Authors based on Thomson One Banker SDC database

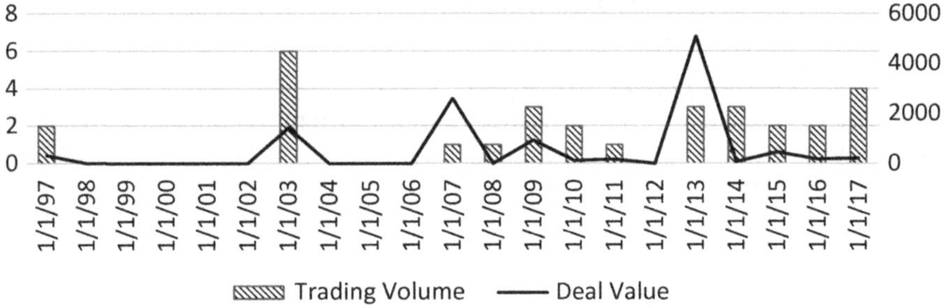

Fig. 6.3 Trading volume and deal value of Chinese M&As in Kazakhstan (1997–2017). (Source: Authors based on Thomson One Banker SDC database)

(c) Recent deals made by Chinese firms indicate a sign of growing interest in the construction area, represented by the deals between industrial firms such as *Gruppa Kompanii Alliur* and *KTZE-Khorgos Gateway* and Chinese firms during 2016–2017.

To sum up, China is among the top investment countries to Kazakhstan. Since 2006, China's investment has steadily increased despite a short-term decline from 2013 to 2016. By looking at the M&As taken by China alone, one could easily find that Chinese investment in Kazakhstan is highly resource-based. However, with more cooperation accompanied with BRI projects, it is highly possible that Chinese investment could rise again and gradually flow to non-resource areas.

BRI and Its Motivations

During the visit to Astana in 2013, the Chinese president Xi Jinping proposed the rudiments of BRI, calling for the joint development of the Silk Road Economic Belt (SREB), and in a later speech made at the congress of Indonesia, he initiates the twenty-first-century Maritime Silk Road. The two initiatives—SREB and twenty-first-century Maritime Silk Road—constitute the grand BRI.

BRI is a joint development proposal rather than a concrete action plan. According to the speech addressed by President Xi at Kazakhstan's Nazarbayev University on September 7th, 2013 (Ministry of Foreign Affairs of the People's Republic of China, n/d), the aims of the BRI include the following "enhancing": enhancing the cooperation on policies and regulations, enhancing the infrastructure and network building, enhancing the trade cooperation, enhancing the currency circulation and enhancing the communication of people, ideas and culture.

Covering 65 countries, 4.6 billion population, with over 1 trillion estimated investment, BRI is the single biggest development plan that ever exists in human history. Since its unveiling, BRI has received enormous attention both in China and from overseas. Domestically, it is listed as one of the most important chapters in the 13th Five-Year Plan, where it particularly emphasizes the importance of developing the SREB and pledges to construct a series of economic cooperation corridors, including China-Mongolia-Russia, China-Middle Asia-West Asia, China-Indochina, New Eurasian Continental Bridge and China-Pakistan (Fig. 6.4). Globally, some view BRI as a new model of international cooperation, and China aims to profit from the long-term prosperity of its

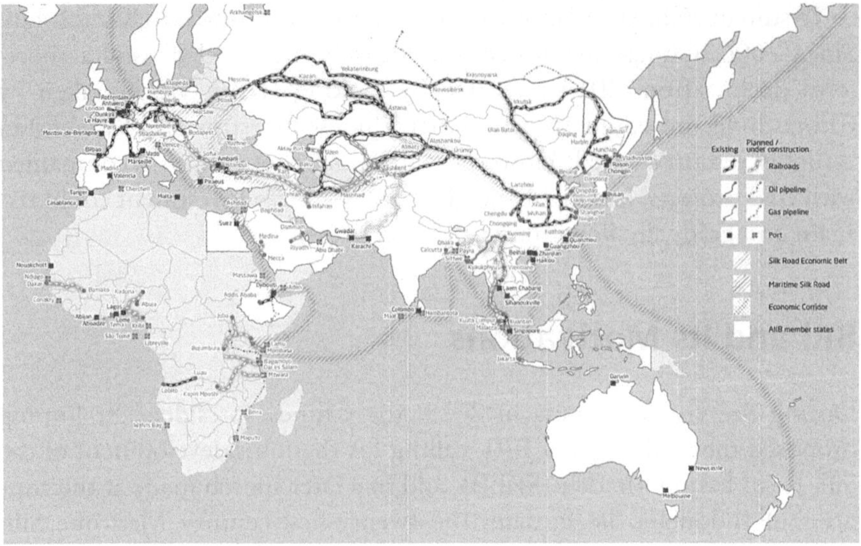

Fig. 6.4 Belt and Road Initiative. (Source: Merics.org., 2018)

neighboring countries. In contrast, others believe it is a mechanism for exporting the *China model*, a clear evidence of Chinese ambition to challenge the incumbent superpower, the US.

Discussion on the motivation of BRI has never stopped, as it fundamentally decides what China intends to gain from other countries and what benefits could be obtained by its cooperating partners. As a strategic node on the SREB, it is of vital importance to Kazakhstan to figure out the motives behind the Chinese grand plan. Thus, in order to achieve a better understanding of why China has formulated BRI at this very moment, it is essential to have a look at what kinds of challenges are faced by the Chinese government. Overall, there are three major challenges of China being the antecedents of BRI.

Overproduction of Infrastructure-Oriented Goods

After decades of infrastructure building and urban modernization, China has built extremely strong raw material production capacity, especially in the cement and steel industry. According to the U.S. Geological Survey

(2018), in 2017, China produced 2.4 billion metric tons of cement, while at the same time, the rest of world combined delivered only 1.7 billion metric tons. It is estimated that the cement used by China from 2011 to 2013 actually surpasses what the US used in the entire twentieth century. The huge capacity for producing raw material was not an issue during economic boom; in many ways, it reflects the strong economic performance and fast-paced development. However, with the economic slowdown as well as the economic transition, the domestic market is losing the appetite to consume the overproduced raw materials. Many European countries alongside the US have already expressed their concern about China's overproduction, as this potentially has a serious impact

Khorgos, the Biggest Dry Port in the World

The New York Times writes that the location of its latest big Chinese foreign investment has given a curious twist to the expanding ambitions of COSCO, the China Ocean Shipping Company (Higgins, 2018). The state-owned Chinese shipping giant became the 49% owner of a railway junction at a place called Khorgos more than 1600 miles away from the nearest ocean, at the border between China and Kazakhstan. According to *Forbes* magazine, on the Chinese side the US $3.25 billion new city of Horgos for 200,000 people is being built (Sheppard, 2018). On the Kazakhstan side is the Khorgos East Gate special economic zone, which includes Khorgos Gateway dry port, the recent Chinese FDI in the economy of Kazakhstan. The International Center for Boundary Cooperation, a duty-free zone, is connecting the two countries. However, this is a part of the country's attempt to diversify the economy through the transport and logistics industry, according to the State Program for Transport Infrastructure Development 2020 and another state program, Nurly Zhol, which puts emphasis on the formation of efficient transport and logistics infrastructure; a new city Nurkent in Kazakhstan with a projected population of 100,000 people is set to be built by 2035 to link together the various transportation and industrial projects of the Khorgos area (Higgins, 2018). According to *Forbes*, Nurkent is one of the five new cities in the world that are designed to challenge the future of how we view the economic potential of inland Eurasia (Perkins, 2015). The entire region around Khorgos is being transformed. According to *The Guardian*, construction will soon begin on an airport. Work is already underway on an industrial center, which will offer a rent holiday and zero taxation until 2035 (Watts, 2018). Eventually the region's

(*continued*)

(continued)

planners hope to attract IT and robotics companies. By 2025, they aim to create 25,000 jobs (Watts, 2018).

McKinsey suggests that the Belt and Road will remain the flagship international state-to-state collaboration program for building China-sponsored infrastructure around the world (Orr, 2017). Clearly the heads of relevant state-owned infrastructure companies are under strong pressure to deliver real projects, as the central government in Beijing has become frustrated at the slow pace of project realization. McKinsey also proposes that in 2018, multinationals focus more on what business opportunities result from the industrial free-trade zone in Kazakhstan than on gaining a major slice of the construction work (Orr, 2017).

on the global industry, and some countries even have pressured China to reduce the production and export. From China's perspective, however, multiple actions have been taken to eliminate excess capacity; overcapacity is not an issue that can be addressed in a relatively short period.

Pressure of Sustaining Economic Growth

China is a one-party state, the legitimacy of the ruling party—Chinese Communist Party (CPP)—roots in its competency (Li, 2013). Hence a decelerating economy posts a potential risk for the authority and social stability. On record, the CPP has successfully lifted over a billion of people out of poverty, creating one of the biggest economic miracles in history. From 1980 to 2015, the Chinese annual economic growth rate on average was 9.6%. During these 25 years, the GDP per capital significantly improved from US $200 to US $8000. However, after 2012, the economy started to show signs of deceleration; the annual GDP growth decreased to 7.85%, 7.75% and 7.29% in 2012, 2013 and 2014, respectively, and then dropped to 7% after 2015 (World Bank, 2018). While the reason for this is not entirely understood by scholars, most researchers (i.e., Huang, 2016) tend to agree that it is a structural rather than cyclical economic reasons. Perkins (2015) pointed out that the economic growth of China heavily relies on domestic investment led by the government, which is effective but not efficient nor sustainable in the long term. Moreover, despite being the international manufacturing powerhouse for many years, China is gradually losing the strength in manufacturing due to the increase in salaries and the aging society. Considering all these negative factors, it is difficult for China to sustain a relatively high growth rate without seeking new ground for economic growth.

Threat from Protectionism

2017 witnessed a critical turning point for the rise of "isolationism" and "protectionism." In Europe, the British people made a dramatic decision to leave the European Union (EU). In the US, Donald Trump surprisingly beat Hillary Clinton, with his famous slogan—*Make America Great Again*, accusing China and Mexico of taking advantage of the US and playing "unfairly" in trade. From speculation to reality, the *trade war* between China and the US has been escalating sharply since the beginning of 2018. On 25th of September 2018, the tariff imposed by the Trump administration on 200 billion Chinese goods marked a new high state of tensions between the two countries. It is hard to tell now which country could eventually claim victory, but China is under extreme pressure, given the trade imbalance existing between the US and China. To moderate the threat from US protectionism, China needs to build a much closer bilateral relationship with other countries, enhancing international cooperation and advocating globalization.

Challenges bring not only difficulties but also opportunities. To deal with the issues stated above, China needs to seek new markets to consume its overcapacity on raw material production, upgrade its industries, transfer the labor-intensive industries to neighboring countries and expand both trade and business areas with the international community. From Kazakhstan's perspective, it could be a great opportunity to develop its own domestic infrastructure, expand cooperation with China in related industries and build a much more solid partner relationship.

Kazakhstan's Opportunities

China's interest in Kazakhstan is constantly growing. A simple search of Google Trends using the keyword *Kazakhstan*, searched in the Chinese region, shows that the attention paid to Kazakhstan has risen sharply since 2013, the same year as the Chinese President Xi addressed the speech on building SERB (Fig. 6.5).

Being one of the closest neighbors of China, with a large landmass and favorable policies (*Kazakhstan 2050*—see Selmier, 2020, this volume), Kazakhstan is one of the best markets to consume the Chinese excess infrastructure materials; and infrastructure development has always been one of the primary objectives of the Kazakhstan government. Recognized by many economists (Firzli & Bazi, 2011), China's constant investment in infrastructure is one of the major reasons of why it outpaces other emerging countries. During the 1990s and 2000s, around 9% of the GDP was invested in infrastructure by the Chinese government, while the average figure in most emerging economies was 2–5%. This investment created the optimal condition for China's economic growth while "many underdeveloped economies suffered from various development bottlenecks" (ibid.). Since the beginning of the BRI, China has expressed its willingness to help Kazakhstan develop its infrastructure, and there is a great potential of collaboration from the two sides.

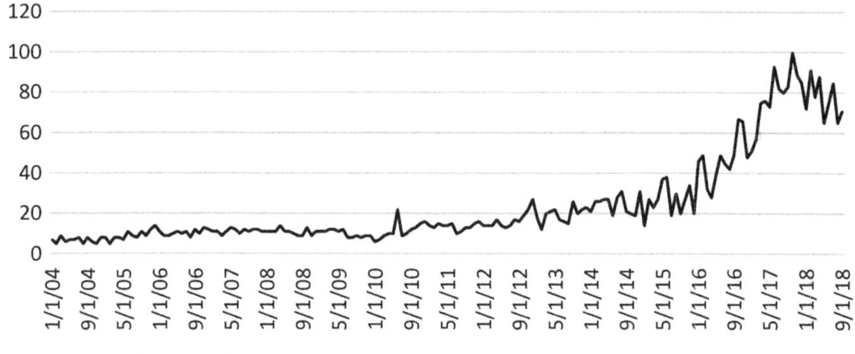

Fig. 6.5 Google Trends on searching "Kazakhstan" in China. (Source: Authors based on Google Trends)

Apart from the infrastructure construction, Kazakhstan could also benefit from the ongoing industrial upgrade of China, for instance, in the manufacturing industry. In order to move beyond the conventional economic development model and achieve sustainable growth, China has determined to move the country's manufacturing up the value chain and develop high-tech fields rather than labor-intensive industries, for which it issued a strategic plan called *Made in China 2025*. Meanwhile, Kazakhstan has robust manufacturing industries. In 2017, the manufacturing industry attracted roughly 5.2 billion gross FDI, ranking second in the FDI list of economic activities (see Table 6.3). Thus, in the processing of transferring the manufacturing industry from China to Kazakhstan,

Table 6.3 Gross FDI in Kazakhstan by economic activities (2015–2017)

Types of economic activities	2015	2016	2017
Agriculture, forestry, and fishing	71.8	50.1	26.1
Mining and quarrying	3485.3	7167.6	10,041.6
Manufacturing	2584.7	4079.6	5187.7
Electricity, gas, steam, and air conditioning supply	12.3	72.0	16.2
Water supply; sewerage, waste management, and remediation activities	−9.5	−1.9	1.1
Construction	791.4	826.9	205.5
Wholesale and retail trade; repair of motor vehicles and motorcycles	1510.8	2290.5	3129.4
Transportation and storage	479.0	504.3	720.1
Accommodation and food service activities	−50.7	12.7	72.7
Information and communication	40.6	391.8	144.8
Financial and insurance activities	470.0	384.5	417.9
Real estate activities	41.0	106.5	150.6
Professional, scientific, and technical activities	5562.7	4806.5	244.0
Administrative and support service activities	69.7	210.5	306.0
Public administration and defense; compulsory social security	0.0	0.0	0.0
Education; human health and social work activities; arts, entertainment, and recreation	20.8	23.3	2.1
Other service activities	89.7	24.5	99.6
Activities of households as employers; undifferentiated goods- and services-producing activities of households for own use	0.0	0.0	0.0
Activities, N.E.C.	0.0	0.0	0.0
Total	**15,170**	**20,949**	**20,765**

Source: Authors' own processed data based on National Bank of Kazakhstan

Kazakhstan is benefiting from attracting more Chinese companies to invest and set up factories and plants locally. Currently, there are plenty of cooperative projects in the automobile industry between the two countries. For instance, *China National Machinery IMP. & EXP. CORP* (CMC) has signed an agreement with Kazakhstan's local firm *Allur* on several projects at the Kostanay plant. China's *Dongfeng Auto Company* is also planning to set up factories in North Kazakhstan.

The trade dispute between China and the US urges China to expand and enhance its collaborative relationship with the other trading partners. In the foreseeable future, the cooperation between Kazakhstan and China will not only be limited in mining and manufacturing industries. In agriculture for example, there is also huge potential for the Chinese investors to step in.

Despite being the world's eighth largest wheat exporter, Kazakhstan's agriculture industry was largely established in the Soviet time—neither efficient nor advanced enough to support the needs of Kazakhs today. Reported by the *Financial Times* (2016), China had already engaged in talks with Kazakhstan to invest US $1.9 billion in agriculture projects in Kazakhstan in 2016. And according to Kazakhstan's Vice Minister of Agriculture, Gulmira Issayeva, China was planning to use US $40 billion Silk Road Fund on three projects; one of them to move three tomato processing plants from China to Kazakhstan. Other investments include US $1.2 billion in oilseed processing; US $200 million in beef, lamb, and horsemeat production; and US $80 million in tomato processing. Conclusively speaking, China's investment is no longer concentrated on just industrial products; with wider and deeper cooperation between the countries, we are very likely to see an expansion of interest to very diversified sectors.

Last but not least, cooperation in high-tech sectors is also promising. With decades of investment in technology areas, fostered by the dedicated subsidiary and national policies, China owns some of the best technology companies in the world. Among the top ten largest internet companies in the world, China owns four—*JD.com*, *Alibaba*, *Tencent* and *Baidu*. A booming digital economy is quickly happening in this country, reshaping the economic landscape with increasing application of artificial intelligence (AI), cloud computing and big data. Jack Ma, the founder of

Alibaba, stressed at the G20 summit that joining the electronic world trade platform (eWTP) and BRI is highly beneficial for facilitating free trade, enlarging the middle class, promoting social stability and developing the local economy. Recent research (Ambalov & Heim, 2018) suggests that local IT business supported by government participation will benefit from using FDI instruments to team up with a developed IT cluster of a country similar in culture and other parameters determining distance. Therefore, for Kazakhstan, cooperating with China on IT and e-commercial development establishes a new mechanism to improve the existing trade framework.

To sum up, there are many internal and external challenges faced by the Chinese government. Not only addressing these problems, BRI makes it possible to convert these challenges to opportunities, for both China

Huawei, a Pioneer for Digitalizing Kazakhstan's O&G Industry

In collaboration with Accenture, the World Economic Forum (2017) issued a white paper report on the digitalization of O&G industry. According to the report, the maturity of digitalization in the O&G industry is far behind that of other asset-heavy industries such as telecommunications, transportation, banking, and industrial manufacturing. Contrasting with other industries, the data used in the decision-making process of O&G is considerably limited. Assisted with informatic technologies, enterprises would be able to release their potential by providing predictive maintenance, remoting operations centers, establishing dynamic energy selection mode, building retailing channels and connecting service fields.

As a Chinese company, *Huawei Technologies* is a leading global provider of information and communications technology (ICT) equipment and services. It is the largest telecommunications equipment manufacturer in the world, ranked 72nd of Fortune Global 500 in 2018. Previously, *Huawei* provided many customer-tailored integrated solutions on digital upgrading of oilfields and pipelines. Sensing the needs of Kazakhstan's industrial upgrading and the increasing demand of Chinese energy supply, *Huawei* is one of the pioneer companies invested in Kazakhstan and has made a major contribution to deepening the digitalization of the country's O&G industry.

In June 2010, Huawei won the bid in the Kazakhstan natural gas pipeline project. The China-Kazakhstan natural gas pipeline stretches more than 2000 kilometers from the border between Uzbekistan and Turkmenistan, through Uzbekistan and Kazakhstan, and ends in Horgos, Xinjiang, China. Construction of the pipeline is led by *Asia Gas Pipeline* (AGP), a joint ven-

(*continued*)

(continued)

ture of the *Kazakhstan Oil* (KTO) and the *China National Petroleum Corporation* (CNPC). The entire project is divided into three parts: the pipeline system, station system and communications and control system, with *Huawei* responsible for the communication part.

The Kazakhstan segment of gas pipeline is mainly located in the desert areas, where it is designed to locate more than 60 valve chambers, 5 compressor stations and 2 metering stations. The rugged environment poses a variety of challenges for the implementation of the gas pipeline project. For safety concerns, high-standard explosion-proof grade and enclosure-protection class needed to be applied throughout the construction process. The quality of the projects requires the parameters of the gas pipeline needed to be transmitted in real-time communication without interruption. Also, considering the complexity of integrating various vendor systems and the harsh operating environment, there are technical issues which need to be solved by *Huawei*.

Applying the latest information and communication technology, the company provided an integrated communication system, allowing data, voice, and video to transmit in a backbone network. Building on this, *Huawei* established an open and flexible platform to connect various security and monitoring devices to provide systemic protection to the equipment alongside with the whole pipeline project. For security protection, *Huawei* set up a series of monitoring systems: an intelligent video surveillance (IVS) system, a station access control system, an intrusion detection system and an industrial-grade broadcasting system. This enables the relevant personnel to be alerted to potential problems. In order to ensure the real-time and uninterrupted transmission of supervisory control and data acquisition (SCADA) data, Huawei proposed a solution using optical transmission as the primary channel and satellite transmission as the auxiliary channel.

So far, with the state acceptance of SCADA (Line C), the project is nearly finished. According to the feedback from *AGP*, the communication network built by *Huawei* has made a major leap forward on the path of the digitalization of Kazakhstan's O&G industry.

Dahai Chang, Deputy General Manager of *AGP*, said (AGP, n/d):

> *The remote control and communication system of oil fields and pipelines have been established. With the help of this system site data could be collected and interchanged between sites and control center based in Beijing as well as pipelines are able to be under surveillance by Beijing head office thousand miles away.*

and Kazakhstan. As a strategic partner on SREB, Kazakhstan is a starting point for China to reach out to the world; more importantly, it can benefit from Chinese attention and investment. More Chinese investment into infrastructure, manufacturing, agriculture, and other non-O&G areas gives Kazakhstan the potential ability to upgrade its economy and reduce dependency on the energy sectors and makes concrete steps toward Kazakhstan 2050.

Conclusion

China is a strategic partner with Kazakhstan and a major contributor of FDI. With the fast-developing economy and a population of 1.3 billion people, China has huge demands on energy resources, contributing one of the driving forces of the Chinese investment in Kazakhstan. From the perspective of Kazakhstan, although natural resources played a significant role in economic development, the dependency on a resource-exploiting economy reduces the capacity to deal with the risks from the external environments, accompanied with sustainable issues in the long term. To step out of the O&G-based economic model, it is essential for Kazakhstan's government to attract more foreign investment in non-O&G sectors. Chinese BRI provides a great opportunity for both countries to expand the cooperation in a variety of economic areas, which fits with the vision of *Kazakhstan 2050*.

"If you want to be rich, build road first" is a well-known slogan often quoted by Chinese officials. Based on Chinese experience, transportation and network facilities are the key to achieving prosperity, contributing a main reason why the Chinese government put so much effort into pushing infrastructure construction in BRI-related countries. Although it is difficult to draw any conclusion on the long-term effect of BRI projects, at least at this stage, what China wants—addressing domestic and international challenges, achieving prosperity in the long term—fits with Kazakhstan's strategic goals. Henceforth, it is a win-win for both countries.

But the future cooperation between two countries should not and will not be limited just to infrastructure. What China can provide is not just cement, steel, and funds; the remarkable technological achievement by China opens the door of cooperation in much wider areas. Sectors such as agriculture, manufacturing, information technology, telecommunication and AI have great potential. With more projects like the digitalization of the pipeline led by *Huawei*, Chinese investment will be a major boost to Kazakhstan's economy and help it to integrate into the international trade and business network, enhance digitalization in the asset-heavy sectors and achieve a sustainable economic growth.

Bibliography

AGP. (n/d). Retrieved from: www.https://agp.com.kz

Ambalov, V., & Heim, I. (2018). Cluster nodes as a unit for value co-creation: The role of information technologies in competitiveness of Kazakhstan's oil and gas industry. In K. Liu, K. Nakata, W. Li, & C. Baranauskas (Eds.), *Digitalisation, Innovation and Transformation*.. Proceedings of 18th IFIP WG 8.1 International Conference on Informatics and Semiotics in Organisations, ICISO 2018, Reading, UK, July 16–18, 2018, Ch. 16 (pp. 155–163). Cham, Switzerland: Springer. https://doi.org/10.1007/978-3-319-94541-5

Asian Development Bank. (2018). *Kazakhstan accelerating economic diversification*. K. Anderson, G. Capannelli, E. Ginting, & K. Taniguchi (Eds.) Retrieved from: https://www.adb.org/sites/default/files/publication/445446/kazakhstan-economic-diversification.pdf

Data.worldbank.org. (2018). *GDP growth (annual %)*. Data [online]. Retrieved from https://data.worldbank.org/indicator/ny.gdp.mktp.kd.zg

Financial Times. (2016). *China seeking to revive the Silk Road*. Retrieved from https://www.ft.com/content/e99ff7a8-0bd8-11e6-9456-444ab5211a2f

Firzli, M. N., & Bazi, V. (2011). Infrastructure Investments in an age of austerity: The pension and sovereign funds perspective. *Revue Analyse Financière, 41*, 34–37.

Higgins, A. (2018). China's ambitious new 'port': Landlocked Kazakhstan. *The New York Times*. Retrieved from https://www.nytimes.com/2018/01/01/world/asia/china-kazakhstan-silk-road.html

Huang, Y. (2016). Understanding China's Belt & Road Initiative: Motivation, framework and assessment. *China Economic Review, 40*, 314–321.
Li, E. (2013). The life of the party: The post-democratic future begins in China. *Foreign Affairs, 92*, 34.
MacGregor, J. (2017). Determining an optimal strategy for energy investment in Kazakhstan. *Energy Policy, 107*, 210–224.
Merics.org. (2018). *Mapping the belt and road initiative: This is where we stand. Mercator Institute for China Studies*. Retrieved from https://www.merics.org/en/bri-tracker/mapping-the-belt-and-road-initiative
Ministry of Foreign Affairs of the People's Republic of China. (n/d). President Xi Jinping Delivers Important Speech and Proposes to Build a Silk Road Economic Belt with Central Asian Countries. Retrieved from: https://www.fmprc.gov.cn
Orr, G. (2017). What we can expect in China in 2018?. McKinsey&Company. Retrieved from: https://www.mckinsey.com/featured-insights/china/what-can-we-expect-in-china-in-2018.
Perkins, D. (2015). *The economic transformation of China*. Hackensack, NJ: World Scientific.
Selmier, W. T., II. (2020). Kazakhstan as logistics linchpin in the belt and road initiative. In I. Heim (Ed.), *Kazakhstan's diversification from the natural resources sector: Strategic and economic opportunities*. London, UK: Palgrave Macmillan.
Sheppard, W. (2018). Five new cities that are set to shake up the future for better or worse. *Forbes*. Retrieved from https://www.forbes.com/sites/wadeshepard/2018/03/29/5-new-cities-that-are-set-to-shake-up-the-future-for-better-or-worse/#746da8227250
U.S. Geological Survey. (2018). *Mineral commodity summaries 2018: U.S. Geological Survey*. Retrieved from https://minerals.usgs.gov/minerals/pubs/mcs/2018/mcs2018.pdf
Watts, J. (2018). Follow the new silk road. *The Guardian*. Retrieved from: https://www.theguardian.com/cities/ng-interactive/2018/jul/30/follow-new-silk-road-china-belt
WEF. (2017). *Digital transformation initiative. Oil and gas industry*. Retrieved from: http://reports.weforum.org/digital-transformation/wp-content/blogs.dir/94/mp/files/pages/files/dti-oil-and-gas-industry-white-paper.pdf

7

Kazakhstan as Logistics Linchpin in the Belt and Road Initiative

W. Travis Selmier II

Geography as (Logistics) Destiny

Historically, five overland routes led out of northern and western China. The sixth, the Karakoram Highway leading into Pakistan and Afghanistan, is a modern, six-lane engineering marvel billed as the world's highest highway in elevation terms. The other five are traditional routes along which traders and armies have traveled for millennia. Three of these routes run through or touch modern Kazakhstan; two—the more important, historically impactful—run just north and south of the Tianshan mountain range, a range which Niu Ruji called the "pivotal line of converging Asian Civilizations" (Aubakirova, Umirzakov, & Aitenov, 2017; Christian, 2000; di Cosmo, 2004: 72, 82; Lattimore, 1953; Niu, 2015). Some have contrasted the southern route, which constituted the Silk Road(s), and the northern route, which constituted the Steppe Road, but

W. Travis Selmier II (✉)
Department of Political Science, Indiana University, Bloomington, IN, USA
e-mail: wselmier@indiana.edu

I. Heim (ed.), *Kazakhstan's Diversification from the Natural Resources Sector*, Euro-Asian Studies, https://doi.org/10.1007/978-3-030-37389-4_7

these two routes were and remain tightly linked in terms of goods shipped and traded (Christian, 2000; di Cosmo, 2004; Frank, 1998: 120–22; Rossabi, 1990). Importantly, they are only integrated territorially within Kazakhstan's borders;[1] in fact, one of the key oil and natural gas pipelines is a modern manifestation of this integration of Silk and Steppe Roads (see Fig. 6.4 in Han & Ghobadian, 2020, this volume).

This chapter looks at the past and present in terms of logistics, reinforcing that reputed maxim of Mark Twain that "history does not repeat itself, but it sure does rhyme sometimes."[2] Kazakhstan's destiny is expected to rhyme with its past by providing major trading routes, but I predict it will become a modern logistics hub as well. These Silk and Steppe routes skirting the Tianshan range (literally Heaven Mountains) historically and in present day constitute main land trading routes into and out of China and East Asia, with the southern route traversing the desert in China's Xinjiang Province, and then westward through the Kyrgyz Republic and Uzbekistan into Iran. The northern route passes through the Junggar Pendi (Dzungar basin; see the Dzungar Gate in Fig. 7.1) in northern Xinjiang and into Kazakhstan, running north of the Western Tianshan at the mountains hugging the southeast corner of Kazakhstan. Professor Niu cites the seventh-century Buddhist Xuanzang who, dividing the "world into four parts: states dominated by elephants (India), by people (China), by horses (Mongolia and Central Asia), and by treasures (western Asia)," claimed all four parts could be seen by standing on top of Tianshan's peaks, and Xuanzang considered Tianshan to be the center of Asia (Niu, 2015: 6). Kazakhstan's southeastern border starts near the center of the Tianshan range; trading centers, oases, and the culture of the Silk Roads along both the Silk and Steppe Roads lie within Kazakhstan's present borders.

In the modern Silk Road development (sometimes called One Belt, One Road or Belt and Road Initiative), Kazakhstan will become a logistics linchpin. To understand why, to invest effectively and to minimize investment and operational risks, we must understand five critical elements: (1) the ancient and modern Silk and Steppe Roads' place in

---

[1] Kazakhstan is written in Cyrillic (Russian) as Казахстан and in Chinese (simplified) as 哈萨克斯坦.

[2] There is considerable debate about whether Mark Twain said this or if this was perhaps constructed from fragments of his writings and talks.

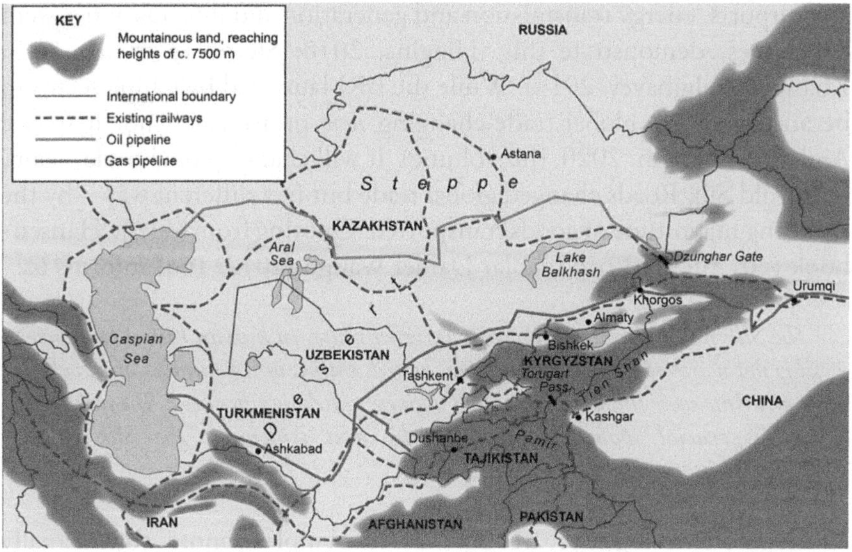

Fig. 7.1 The centrality of Kazakhstani logistics. (Source: Sternberg, Ahearn, & McConnell, 2017)

history; (2) Kazakhstan's role in this history; (3) how Kazakhstan's position between Russia and China provides great opportunities which the Kazakh government is attempting to maximize while minimizing threats and weaknesses; (4) the resulting relationship between China and Kazakhstan; and (5) why China's efforts to invest in maritime infrastructure facilities will likely run into many problems, which would push Chinese investment more toward land-based investment projects. The first four are given more weight in this chapter, in part because the fifth is partly based on the author's speculations (the fifth also does not involve Kazakhstani infrastructural and logistical development).

Total cost estimates for all planned, proposed and constructed projects under the Belt and Road Initiative (henceforth BRI) range between US $4 and US $8 trillion and span maritime- and land-based investments in Asia, Africa, Europe and beyond (Padilla, 2017; Selmier, 2018; Yu, 2017). Most of these projects fall under infrastructural investment, with a special focus on redevelopment or new construction of trade infrastructure; Kazakhstan's diverse projects, consisting of ports, railroads, roads and airports, energy transmission and generation and information system backbones, demonstrate this (Higgins, 2018; Sternberg et al., 2017; Zhang & Belgibayev, 2014). While the BRI launched by China seems to be an enormous, global trade-changing *new* project, it is not new (see Ambalov & Heim, 2020, this volume). It will change global trade, again, as the old Silk Roads changed global trade but in a different way—by the stunning magnitude of goods transported. Quoting from Valerie Hansen's book (2012), Silk Road scholar Daniel Waugh (2012: 164) informs us:

> "*The Silk Road was one of the least traveled routes in human history and possibly not worth studying—if tonnage carried, traffic, or the number of travelers at any time were the sole measures of a given route's significance." The qualifier here is crucial though, leading to the next sentence: "The Silk Road changed history.*"

While modern logistics are now more complex, more contractually defined, risk-managed, financially driven and business operation-optimized, the old Silk Road was quite complex as well, with contracts, an extensive range of goods traded, use of complex financing projects and impressive risk management strategies. By looking at the history of the old Silk and Steppe Roads we can glean modern lessons in each operational area of business, capture some advantage over less-prepared business competitors and perhaps impress our Kazakh business partners.

Then, as now, Kazakhstan (or rather what became Kazakhstan) provided not only important logistics hubs on the Silk and Steppe routes but also energy resources which contributed to China's economic development and to its security. Starting perhaps 3000 years ago and continuing for 2000 years, the steppes provided horses which were essential to China's energy needs, to its transportation and to its capacity to defend borders and secure them. In the present, those energy resources are oil and natural gas. Modern horsepower is delivered through these modern energy sources.

Section "Geography as (Logistics) Destiny" sketches a selective history of the old Silk and Steppe Roads with an emphasis on Kazakh influences and China's historical relationship to this influence. We should note that some political actors along the Silk Roads were imperial, while some were city-states which acted as entrepôts, and we must emphasize that modern Kazakhstan did not exist. The following section ("Kazakhstan Situated on Silk Roads and Steppe Roads") looks at the history of the area and the emergence of modern Kazakhstan along the New Silk Road/BRI, outlining the crucial role of Kazakhstan as transportation hub and energy producer and focusing on shipping costs, containerization, and capacity. Section "Shipping Costs, Containerization and Capacity" examines the four major issues facing Kazakhstan in her quest to become the logistics linchpin in the BRI: (1) small population in a very large country; (2) containerization development; (3) railroad gauge in the former Soviet Union countries is wider than the rest of the word; and (4) modern facilities must be developed. I introduce the logistic concept of the Four Rs (road, rail, runway and river/sea). Lastly, I touch upon international contention of the seas and how that may benefit Kazakhstan's unique position as the stable, land-based intermediary between East Asia and Europe.

Kazakhstan Situated on Silk Roads and Steppe Roads

In a sense, Kazakhstan has always been at the center of logistics. Horses for transport, first bred and trained for riding in Dereivka (present-day eastern Ukraine) beginning around 2000 BC, quickly spread westward across the steppe (di Cosmo, 2004) into what would become Kazakhstan. They were quickly adopted into steppe life; some scholars have called horses the "schooners of the steppe," as the vast waves of steppe grasslands resembled oceans. But the many easy paths which crossed those vast, similar-looking plains required the skills of a stargazer and necessitated specialized equipment to properly navigate.

Equestrian skills—and technologies involving reticulating bits, harnesses, saddles, and stirrups—were developed which allowed steppe-dwelling peoples to hunt, fight and literally live in the saddle. Various wheeled carts were also developed for specialized conveyances. Anthony and Vinogradov (1995) argue in an influential paper that the chariot was born on the steppe, spreading westward toward Egypt and the

Mediterranean and eastward into China. Ancient China fell in love with the horse not only for purposes of defense and transportation but, as time progressed, for the sheer beauty and power of the horse (di Cosmo, 2004; Liu, 2010). The area which was to become modern Kazakhstan was a key supplier into China, shipping horses and horse technology. Han Gu (32–92 CE), a Han Dynasty poet, historian and politician, rhapsodized both horses and the Tianshan region when he wrote, "A Heavenly Horse Soars across the Sky![3] (Hu, 2015). To fight against the nomads living in China's near-north and near-northwest more than 2500 years ago (Beng, 2014; di Cosmo, 2004; Wang, 2012), Chinese acquired these legendary "heavenly horses" of Central Asia by trading silk (of great use by light-traveling nomadic peoples on the cold, windy steppe). As the eminent historian Wang Gungwu wrote (2013: 10): "The only enemies of China who really were a threat and actually conquered China were the horsemen of the Steppe-Land. So, the Chinese built the Great Wall instead of a navy."

Why should a business investor want to understand the Chinese perspective toward the steppe, the Silk Roads old and new and Kazakhstan? First, China is the largest investor for Kazakhstan, inking nearly US $50 billion in contracts in 2015 (see Han & Ghobadian, 2020, this volume; Kambarov, 2015). In fact, China is Kazakhstan's most important partner in security (Contessi, 2015; Kembayev, 2018; Zhang & Belgibayev, 2014), energy projects (Heim, 2017; Hydrocarbons Technology, 2018; Kazakhstan-China Pipeline, LLC, 2018), infrastructural investment (Feng & Foy, 2017; Kenderdine, 2017; Uatkhanov, 2017) and finance and financial market development (Jenkins & Perzadayeva, 2018; Selmier, 2018; Voloshin, 2017). Second, China needs Kazakhstan for many reasons, and, realizing these reasons, Kazakh leaders seek to bind China and the Chinese industry to Kazakhstan while balancing Kazakh interests elsewhere. This idea is developed throughout the rest of the chapter, but let us sketch in here why this may lower political and investment risks in Kazakhstan for all investors. In Chinese leaders' viewpoints, Kazakhstan presents a stable, willing, resource-endowed, well-off, and welcoming business partner in the world where these five attributes rarely

---

[3] 天马行空, tian ma xing kong, author's translation.

exist for China (Aubakirova, et al., 2017; Kazakhstan 2050, 2016; Selmier, 2018). Diplomatically skilled Kazakhstan sits between China and Russia with critical border crossings to each while providing key pathways to Europe. China will seek to bolster this stable, neutral-but-friendly partner; Kazakhstan will continue to embrace this role, as discussed below (Contessi, 2015; Kirişci & Le Corre, 2015; Nixey, 2012).

Third, China's modern attempt at a modern global trading network is merely a repeat of past periods of "Pax Sinica." When China could—that is, when it was powerful, stable, and rich—it extended governance far to its West over these land-based trade routes. There is almost a clockwork nature to this pattern of power extension. Every seven centuries or so the Chinese government then in power, at the height of its power, worked its political and development magic on this trade network. During the mid-Han Dynasty (around the birth of Christ), the mid-Tang Dynasty in the early eighth century AD, the Yuan Dynasty in the fourteenth century and presently, we find a powerful China building infrastructure, establishing logistical and trading centers and seeking to govern and improve the existing trading system (for historical perspectives, see Frank, 1992; Hansen, 2012; Liu, 2010; Rossabi, 1990).

And hence, fourth, in marketing terms the Chinese have claimed "naming rights" on the Silk Road. Their effort was helped by nineteenth-century German geographer Ferdinand von Richthofen. He coined the term *die Seidenstrasse*—the Silk Road—because the Greeks and Romans valued silk highly and called China *Serica*, the land of silk (Hansen, 2012; Liu, 2010; Waugh, 2007, 2012), even though the roads also transported jade, horses, agricultural goods, art, ideas and people and slaves (Elverskog, 2010; Hansen, 2012; Liu, 2010). That a Chinese "brand name" was established is due in part to the European perspective of what goods were most important, but modern China has claimed ownership of the brand. But this claim is only partially true; over their 2500-year history, the trading routes were most completely and competently managed during two periods, and not by China, by the Abbasid Caliphate (roughly later eighth to later twelfth century AD) and the Mongol Empire (late thirteenth into mid-fourteenth century AD), when a "Pax Mongolica" (Elverskog, 2010: 162) created a continent-wide trading system which stretched across Asia into Europe:

through imposition of peace, religious tolerance and … an elite cohort of wide-ranging Muslim merchants by issuing them official certificates … backed by a powerful, well-administered [Mongol] state (Frank, 1998*: 255–7) complete with an extensive system of postal stations. (Rossabi,* 1990*: 353) and the tolerance, even encouragement, of travel across Asia and from Europe* (quoted from Selmier, 2018: 262)

Central Asians above all are cognizant of these ebbs and flows of the Silk and Steppe Roads. Economic and political cycles help modern businesspeople to understand why the peoples of Central Asian countries have seen all of this before, and their histories remind Central Asians of when they were once rich and at the center of the world's trading system rather than on the periphery and presently re-emerging onto the world stage.

And while the Silk and Steppe Roads were interlinked over this history, trade through the steppe routes increased at the expense of the Silk Roads in the eighteenth century for three reasons: the powers and economic health of Iran/Persia, the key intermediary on the Silk Roads and the Ottoman Empire both began to decline (Esfahani & Pesaran, 2009; Keddie, 1972; Palmer, 1994). As they declined, the growing Russian economy pulled trade and travelers toward the north through the steppe routes (Christian, 2000; Frank, 1998; Rossabi, 1990). Competing with both Iran and the Ottoman Empire, Russia actively tried to weaken the southern trade routes while capturing more trade and riches from the northern steppe routes passing into Russia.

But Russia found it could not compete effectively with European economies and their colonization efforts in other parts of the world and so looked south toward Central Asia and west toward Siberia as Russia recovered from the Napoleonic Wars: "by the mid-19th century economic interests, a fear of falling behind Europe after the Crimean War disaster, and the search for more land catalyzed Russian conquest of Central Asia" (Selmier, 2018: 263). While Russia struggled to control Central Asia (Allworth, 1995; d'Encausse, 1995a; Saray, 1982), inward-looking China chafed under internal turmoil and barbarians encroaching from the eastern seas rather than the western steppes; Iran atrophied as the English effectively turned it into a colony. Trade along the Silk Roads and Steppe Roads nearly disappeared. Although Russia built some railroad infrastructure, established large farming efforts, and developed some mining, aside from cotton exports, Central Asia under Russian control slid further into economic oblivion (d'Encausse, 1995a; Saray, 1982). The Soviet Union continued selected investment but found it difficult to achieve political stability, particularly in Uzbekistan, the most populous of the Central Asian countries. Then came World War II, and Central Asia underwent a period of extremely rapid industrial growth.

Correctly fearing that German troops would overrun the heavy industrial complexes in eastern Ukraine and southwestern Russia, 300 entire industrial plants and material processing units were disassembled, shipped then reassembled in southern Central Asia, particularly in Uzbekistan and Kazakhstan; this rapidly enlarged industrial base required equally rapid investment in railroads, mines and mineral processing facilities, more industrial plants and power plants (d'Encausse, 1995b; Matley, 1995). Plants were also shifted from areas around Moscow—in fact, from many plant sites west of the Urals—and moved east of the Urals and into Central Asia. World War II also brought a less-appreciated increase in human capital. Stalin's concern about loyalty led to forced inward migration by Russians, Ukrainians, Germans and Koreans who had settled in other parts of the Soviet Union, in the case of the Germans for centuries. These unwilling immigrants to Central Asia brought skills and, later, ties to their ancestral homelands (for instance, Korean firms and the Korean government are intensely interested in, and investing into, Kazakhstan).

The takeaways from this brief, selective history are the following: Kazakhstan is a richly endowed economy with strong industrial and extractive industry bases (as discussed throughout the book). With a diverse population and developed human capital, investment interest is strong, and this is enhanced by Kazakh citizens with ancestors from many other countries. Bordering the old Silk Roads with the old Steppe Roads running through it, its modern location could not be better situated for logistics. And interposed between Russia and China, significant land traffic simply has to pass through it. Russian political influences remained in Central Asia after the collapse of the Soviet Union in 1991 (Contessi, 2016; Nixey, 2012; Zhang & Belgibayev, 2014), and so Kazakhstan must finely balance its interests between China and Russia (Aubakirova et al., 2017; Contessi, 2015; Kembayev, 2018). Table 7.1 provides comparisons

Table 7.1 Demographic and economic comparison of China, Russia, and Kazakhstan

		China	Russia	Kazakhstan
Area (*1000 sq-km*)		9596	17,098	2724
Coastline (*km*)		14,500	37,653	0[a]
Selected demographic information				
Population (*mill*)		1379.3	142.3	18.6
Median age		37.4 years	39.6 years	30.6 years
Population growth rate		0.41%	–0.08%	1.04%
Urban population		57.9%	74.4%	53.2%
Calculated population density[b]		~144/km^2	~8.3/km^2	~6.8/km^2
Life expectancy at birth		75.7 years	71 years	71.1 years
Total fertility rate (*children born/ woman*)		1.6	1.61	2.25
Literacy (*total population*)		96.4%	99.7%	99.8%
Economic overview				
GDP (PPP, in USD trillions)		$23.1	$4.0	$0.47
GDP—real growth rate		6.8%	1.6%	3.3%
GDP—per capita (PPP)		$16,600	$27,900	$26,100
GDP by composition	**Agriculture**	8.2%	4.7%	4.8%
	Industry	39.5%	32.4%	34.4%
	Services	52.2%	62.3%	60.8%
GINI index		46.5 (2016)	41.2 (2015)	26.3 (2013)

Source: Authors' own processed data based on CIA Handbook (2017)

The original key for Table 7.1 read as follows: "Sources: From CIA Handbook, 2017. All figures are 2017 estimates unless noted

[a] Borders Aral Sea and Caspian Sea

[b] Author's calculation based on CIA figures

between these three counties, and here we note four important points: Kazakhstan has a younger and much smaller population than Russia or China, with roughly half living in cities. It is a highly educated, relatively high-earning, long-living population. Although Kazakhstan has no ocean coastline, there is 700 kilometers (roughly 470 miles) of coastline in the Caspian Sea which is being developed into an important transportation hub as discussed below. And Kazakhstan is geographically large and diverse, with an area more than a quarter the size of China, the United States or Brazil.

Shipping Costs, Containerization and Capacity

Far-flung European colonial establishment pulled attention from land to sea during the eighteenth and nineteenth centuries, and this shift naturally developed sea-going trade at the expense of land-based trading routes such as the Silk Roads and Steppe Roads. The goods which were transported also became increasingly heavy, fragile, and voluminous, pushing goods transport toward large ship holds rather than into smaller packs carried on camel or horse. Now, as then, shipping costs were increasingly driven by the number of times a good is handled (Crainic, Dell'Olmo, Ricciardi, & Sgalambro, 2015; Roso, Woxenius, & Lumsden, 2008; Vinokurov & Tsukarev, 2018). Land routes on the New Silk Road—the BRI—are still challenged by handling costs. But China's physical geography stimulates considerable land-based shipping. Production in the western provinces and their demands for energy sources must either be shipped to and from eastern seaboard ports, or sent and received from further west of these populous, fast-growing provinces. There are three international transport route options to and from China's west: southwest along the Karakoram Highway and through Pakistan; directly west along the rail over parts of the old Silk Roads skirting Kazakhstan's southern border and into Iran; and northwest through Khorgos and into Kazakhstan along the old Steppe Roads. Each route poses logistical, transport-economic, and political challenges.

Understanding these logistical, transport-economic, and political challenges helps firms to develop robust, resilient logistics networks. The middle route, toward China's crucial trading partner Iran, is under constvruction or being upgraded, providing a land route across the width of Asia (Erdbrink, 2017). Asghar Fakhrieh-Kashan, the urbane Deputy Minister for Roads and Urban Development, commented "if they (Chinese government and investors) want to save time and money, they will choose the shortest route. … There are also political advantages to Iran, compared to Russia" (Erdbrink, 2017). But both Russia and the United States are actively resisting this "shortest route" (Kim & Indeo, 2013; Nixey, 2012), and this resistance creates considerable political and operational risks for logistic chains.

Pakistan and Kazakhstan provide a powerful comparison, as Pakistan offers direct seaport access at Gwadar on the Indian Ocean while Kazakhstan offers access to Europe, through either the Caspian or through Russia, after passage through the Khorgos Dryport or Dostyk, both on Kazakh's eastern border (see Fig. 7.2). The China-Pakistan Economic Corridor (CPEC) links Xinjiang's Kashgar with Pakistan's deep-water port of Gwadar over the Karakoram Highway and through a massive rail/road/LNG pipeline/data backbone running down the spine of Pakistan to Gwadar. In energy transportation terms, Kazakhstan and Pakistan are each important to western China's energy needs: the Kazakhstan-China Oil Pipeline, a 50:50 joint venture between China National Petroleum Corporation (CNPC) and KazMunayGas, the Kazakh national oil company, pumped 12.2 million tons of oil from fields near Atasu to CNPC's complex in Alashankou, Xinjiang, in 2017 (Hydrocarbons Technology. (2018)., LLC, 2018. Also see Ambalov & Heim, 2020, this volume, for more details). In October 2017, Kazakhstan also began shipping natural gas from western Kazakh gas fields through another LNG pipeline. When the CPEC is completed, LNG could be pumped, and electricity wheeled into western China. But the Pakistani project is fraught with issues of

Fig. 7.2 Major transport routes through Kazakhstan. (Source: JEX Corporation (Japan Eurasia Express), 2018)

high debt, high-risk, massive engineering requirements in heavily populated areas and considerable local resistance. Selmier (2018: 270) sums up:

> *If Pakistan's prospects for the Initiative [BRI] from a Chinese perspective are potentially problematic, complex and complicated by Islamic economic considerations, Kazakhstan's prospects are simpler, secular and conditioned by pragmatic foreign policy.*

Kazakhstan's foreign relations has been following a "balancing" strategy through a well-engineered portfolio of foreign policy tactics (Contessi, 2015, 2016), and China has become the key partner in Kazakhstan's efforts. While Chinese investment into Kazakhstan and other Central Asian countries has increased Russian concerns about growing Chinese influence (Kirişci & Le Corre, 2015; Nixey, 2012; Tang, 2000), both Kazakhstan and China have tried to alleviate Russian concerns (Aubakirova et al., 2017; Kembayev, 2018; Makarov & Sokolova, 2016). We can see why both China and Russia are intensely interested in Kazakhstan merely by glancing at the borders shown in maps in Figs. 6.4 and 7.1. At 4254 mi (6846 kms), Russia and Kazakhstan share a border matched only by the Canadian-US border in rough length; the Sino-Kazakh border is over 1100 mi (1783 km) long.[4]

The map in Fig. 7.2 shows a rough tracing of Kazakh logistics by sketching Kazakhstan's major road/rail lines with key Kazakh cities and international border crossings. Scanning the map from east to west, we see the two key entry points between Kazakhstan and China at Dostyk (through the Dzungar Gate, with Baktu Port on the Chinese side) and Altynkol Station (where the Chinese side, Khorgos, has been developed into the largest dryport in the world). The more important northern entry points into Russia pass through Nur-Sultan (former Astana), the Kazakh capital, and then onto Pavlodar (Novosibirsk-bound), Petropavlovsk (east to Omsk, west toward Chelyabinsk) and Kustenay/Rudny (northeastward toward Orenburg and then onto Samara). Toward the south, a short spur crosses the border to Tashkent, Central Asia's

[4] Kazakh Ambassador to China Shakhrat Nuryshev notes their "common border do not separate our nations, but bring them closer together. … [W]e managed to create an exemplary model of interstate relations" (quote in Sabayeva, 2015).

largest city (2.4 million) in Uzbekistan, Central Asia's largest country (33 million).[5] Western exit points enter Russia near Orai (formerly Uralsk) heading toward large Volga-based cities such as Samara, Saratov and Volgograd and Caspian ports at Aqtau/Aktau (and possibly Atyrau/Aktyrau, both discussed in more detail below).

Four Major Issues in Becoming a Logistics Linchpin

From a physical geography perspective, Kazakhstan simply could not be better placed to gain advantages and capitalize on opportunities in logistics along the New Silk Road, and BRI investments bear out this fortuitous location. But there are at least four major issues in Kazakhstan's quest to become the logistics linchpin in the BRI. Each could be partially or completely addressed through investment and development and understanding each helps us to more accurately estimate risks and more effectively target investment. In increasing order of the capacity of investment to deal with these bottlenecks, the four are as follows: (1) Kazakhstan has a small population in a very large country; (2) containerization in all its manifestations is underdeveloped; (3) the railroad gauge in Kazakhstan (and throughout the former Soviet Union countries) is wider than in China and Europe; and (4) facilities for transportation, handling, processing, administration and financing are still underdeveloped. Each bottleneck increases transportation costs, inherently makes logistic chains more complex and pushes transshipment toward other networks. Let us look at each in turn.

The issue for Kazakhstan which is least easy to solve or address is that Kazakhstan has a small population spread across a very large area. The very nature of this vast steppe-situated country results in sparse population. For instance, the US CIA's comparative map shown in Fig. 7.3 superimposes Kazakhstan over what the CIA considers comparable parts

[5] Kabul and Urumqi are larger in population terms, but I have used Central Asia as a modern term in this chapter to denote the five former Soviet Union countries of Kazakhstan, Kyrgyzstan, Tajikistan, Turkmenistan and Uzbekistan.

Fig. 7.3 Kazakhstan superimposed over "representative" United States. (Source: CIA Handbook 2017)

of the United States, the Great Plains and part of the Midwest. But the population of three metropolitan areas subsumed within the American sampled area—Chicago, St. Louis, and Dallas-Ft. Worth—adds up to Kazakhstan's entire population. Returning to Table 7.1, we can see that the population densities depict this as well. China's population density is roughly 144 people per square kilometer, while sparsely populated Russia with its vast Siberian spaces west of the Urals is roughly 8.3 people per square kilometer (for comparative purposes, the United States is roughly 33 people per square kilometer). Kazakhstan is one of world's less-densely populated countries at roughly 6.8 people per square kilometer.

Continuing with map 4's comparison, we can employ Thill and Lim's (2010) examination of continental US' intermodal linkages in which they determine regional access variation to export via US ports. Taking into account the ports situated along the Great Lakes and St. Lawrence waterway, we might loosely suggest that the United States is surrounded by ports with access to the sea as Kazakhstan is isolated from seaports. Thill and Lim's maps show us the considerable advantages of a highly developed intermodal system providing export opportunities, while the Great Plains and Northern Rocky Mountain regions rank more lowly on access to seaports (see Thill & Lim, 2010), extensive construction of inland container ports and development of container terminals along Lake Superior, Michigan, and on eastward through the St. Lawrence waterway improve access considerably (ibid.).[6]

The United States has highly developed logistics systems and transportation networks. Importantly, it is five times as densely populated as Kazakhstan. To examine logistics difficulties in similarly sparsely populated areas with highly developed transportation networks, we can look to Scandinavia. For instance, Solvang and Hakam (2010) analyze the challenges of developing sustainable logistics networks in an area of Norway even more sparsely populated than Kazakhstan (4.3 people per square kilometer). They note three important generic differences between how densely and sparsely populated areas influence logistics networks: (1) denser populations allow "the network to take the advantages of both economy-of-scale and economy-of-scope"; (2) shorter distances in denser populations enable "mass-customized logistics service(s) with diverse focuses"; and (3) "sparsely populated area(s are) usually situated in a peripheral region of a country" (Solvang & Hakam, 2010). For Kazakhstan, the first point may be much more important than the last two, as the point of this chapter is to sketch out how Kazakhstan may act primarily as a transit zone for transshipments between China and Russia/Europe/Mediterranean rather than describe complex delivery networks for domestic consumers (as Solvang & Hakam analyze). So, population density may not matter as much as container facilities. Also, intermodal transportation may be relatively less important in comparison to more complex intermodal networks as train transport is what matters across Kazakhstan. Even in a highly developed transportation network such as

[6] Because this chapter is meant as a thematic survey, I have purposefully removed the econometric studies used in logistics and transportation analysis. Readers are invited, and encouraged, to look at the cited studies.

Scandinavia, many OD pairs (Origin-of-good to Destination-of-good) are served by a single mode (Rich, Kveiborg, & Hansen, 2011).

However, wherever a shift toward "seamlessness" in transportation is to be engineered (Capineri & Leinbach, 2006) it will require "the emergence of a system of inland intermodal transfer terminals" at key points (Thill & Lim, 2010: 532) and the infrastructural backbone which underpins this. Thill and Lim (2010) analyzed the *internal* US transportation network capacity to improve export-oriented trade, but their analysis applies to Kazakhstan as nearly all trade is export-oriented.

In a sense, then, Kazakhstan as a transit country is not as damaged by perceived intermodal weaknesses, nor is its logistics systems analyzed effectively by OD models as a very limited number of intermodal transfer terminals are required. The map in Fig. 7.4—a view of Kazakhstan from space—gives a sense of the vast steppe which a transportation system must cross. Yet there are relatively few transfer points required (as the map in Fig. 7.2 shows). But whether the unimodal or intermodal transfer is required, transportation will only be successful through standardization, and standardization for non-bulk goods requires *containerization* (Capineri & Leinbach, 2006; Levinson, 2016).

In the words of Vinokurov and Tsukarev (2018: 93), the BRI will be the "story of the container." The United States has a highly developed

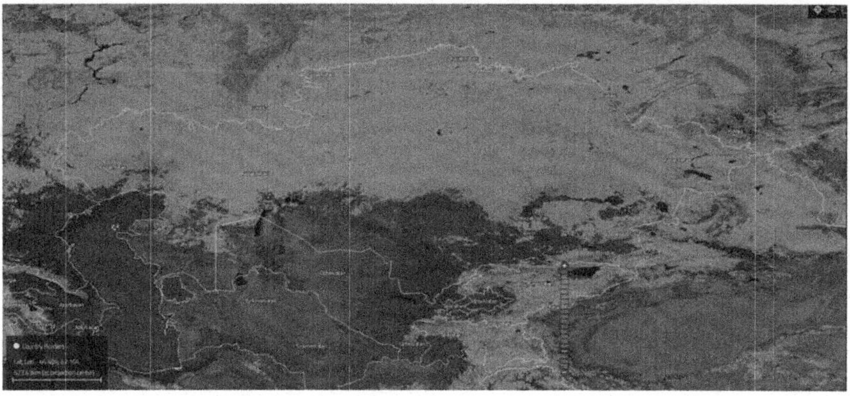

Fig. 7.4 Kazakhstan from space. (Source: Image courtesy of the Earth Science and Remote Sensing Unit, NASA Johnson Space Center)

transportation system for containerization, but containerization is still quite low in Central Asia (Makarov & Sokolova, 2016; Vinokurov & Tsukarev, 2018; Xinhua, 2017). Comparing Russia's 100 rail stations capable of modern container handling (admittedly, with some less modern than others) with less than ten presently in Kazakhstan, Vinokurov and Tsukarev (2018) comment that:

> *there is not a single facility, either in Kazakhstan or at any station on the border between [Dostyk in] Kazakhstan and Russia, that offers full-scale container services, including train marshalling, redirection, shipment storage and customs clearance.*

Containerization involves not only Chinese shipping containers across the border at Dostyk or Khorgos, but the "full-scale" facilities needed to add logistics value within Kazakhstan, optimally directing each container toward its destination. China's development effort at Baktu (dry)port across the border from Dostyk demonstrates a strong Chinese commitment to Kazakh logistics (Liu, Fang, & Ren, 2016). But even by late 2017, the amount of railroad carriage through Kazakhstan was still quite small: "when the current throughput capacities of the various China-to-Europe landbridge rail routes are combined, the total doesn't exceed that of four mega container ships that presently serve China's trade with Europe" (Tsuruoka, 2018, quoting logistics expert Doug Procak).

Thill and Lim (2010: 532) note: "The success of intermodalism requires a more tightly integrated process of transportation and logistics, so that modal networks are interconnected through minimal seams at transfer terminals." But ***different railroad gauge*** increase transportation costs (Silin, Kapustina, Trevisan, & Drevalev, 2018; Vinokurov & Tsukarev, 2018; Wu, 2017). Tsarist Russia, fearing that European trains could carry European invaders directly into Russia, established a wider-gauge standard for trains in the Soviet Union (1.520 meters in Russia versus the international standards, 1.435 m). This legacy is problematic in that goods must either be transferred onto cars running over the wider gauges or specialized cars which can change gauges must be used (Makarov & Sokolova, 2016; Tsuruoka, 2018; Wu, 2017). The present, costly, solution is to off-load containers at the Sino-Kazakh border and then reload onto trains running on the wider gauges (and reverse this process when containers exit the wide tracks of the former Soviet Union railway systems). This is part of the reason the China-to-Europe landbridge rail costs are roughly ten times what maritime shipping might be (Tsuruoka, 2018; see also Wu, 2017). As Kenderdine (2017) notes, there is no *present* alternative to gauge-changing:

> *The Mongolia-Russia-Belarus route is also long, and also involves Russia. The same is true of the Kazakhstan-Russia-Belarus route. The Kyrgyz route passes through five jurisdictions and requires two rail gauge changes: one from China to Kyrgyzstan, and another from Turkmenistan to Iran.*

But a purely cost-benefit analysis which ignores politics would misunderstand the importance of the China-to-Europe landbridge. Makarov and Sokolova (2016) correctly point to China's motivation coming from the "need to diversify export risks in the face of deteriorating military and political conditions in the sea rather than by perceived commercial benefits" (see also Padilla, 2017; Silin et al., 2018; Wang, 2013). Kazakhstan is well-situated here as an intermediary; assuaging China's worries about safe passage, calming the steppe "waters" between China and Russia and developing a transportation and energy infrastructure which bolsters each economy (Aubakirova, et al., 2017; Kembayev, 2018; Selmier, 2018).

Issues 2 and 3 (*containerization* and *different railroad gauge*) provide part of the impetus behind an alternative route through Kazakhstan which does not continue transit through Russia. The requirement for massive investment in Kazakh transport infrastructure gives more options to Kazakh policy planners as legacy infrastructure need not be quite so important. The difference in railroad gauges make the former Soviet Union into a "wide-gauge island" as noted above, requiring a change not only at the Chinese border but when the wide gauge encounters an international gauge railroad in the West (Europe, Iran, elsewhere). The option of a route across the Caspian, with Kazakh railheads terminating at a Caspian ferry port at Aqtau (and possibly Aktyrau), is being pursued (Kenderdine, 2017; Makarov & Sokolova, 2016; Silin et al., 2018). Presently two container ferries are carrying cargo onto Baku, from which trains run westward through Azerbaijan toward Georgia and Turkey.

Makarov and Sokolova (2016) estimate transportation facilities investment of some US $8 billion is required to bring this plan to full fruition on the Kazakh Caspian coast.

In January 2017, the first train finished an 18-day journey over the China-to-Europe landbridge from Yiwu, China, to London, carrying 24 containers (Wu, 2017). Both train and the tiny cargo were symbolic, bringing up broader questions about needs for *transportation, handling, processing, administration and financing facilities* which are still underdeveloped. The best-known facility under development is the Khorgos Gateway project; this, the largest dryport in the world, has been developed on the Chinese side of the border (Feng & Foy, 2017; Higgins, 2018). Chinese leaders have suggested Shenzhen as a model, but this is an incomplete analogy. Shenzhen developed as a manufacturing hub first, then as a financial and logistics center. Khorgos is perhaps better seen as a throughput hub where containers are shifted from one gauge to another, export processing and information management may be accomplished here and routing along to Central Asia and the Caspian route achieved. Ongoing discussions of converting some Kazakh rail lines to the international standard width continue (Silin et al., 2018).

The Khorgos Gateway is an international port which has the potential for high-volume customs clearance as well as transportation, handling, and data administration of transshipments. Khorgos breaks the mold where a dryport has been as near a seaport:

> *as inland freight terminal directly connected to one or more seaports with high-capacity transport means, where customers can drop and pick up their standardized units as if directly at a seaport* (Crainic et al., 2015: 518; see also Roso et al., 2008)

But this is not to say that Khorgos is not connected to a seaport; Khorgos is linked to Lianyungang some 4200 kilometers away, with COSCO Shipping handling the logistics of Kazakh goods transported to that port (Sabayeva, 2015; Uatkhanov, 2017) while Dubai World handles portions of Khorgos Dryport operations.

Logistics of the New Silk Road/BRI will necessitate developing the "four critical forms of distribution: runway, road, rail and river/sea" (Cox,

2009: 150). Including the Caspian Sea ferry route, Kazakhstan will offer all Four Rs, but not at the same place. This lack of co-locational transportation options may lessen, but will not remove, the logistic benefits Kazakhstan has to offer. But investors and others seeking to establish logistics hubs in Kazakhstan will need to understand the steppes and nature of Kazakh feelings about distance. Perhaps Australians and Russians come closest to this sense that a few hours' drive may be considered nearby. In this regard, at or near Khorgos (near in Kazakh terms), three of Cox's "Four Rs" transport systems may come together in a Kazakh co-locational sense: road, rail and runway.

Looking again at Shenzhen's gradual integration into the developing Pearl River Delta region, it began as a low-cost production center with design, marketing, management, transportation, and financial servicing tied to Hong Kong. Travel times between the two required sometimes three hours or more as roads, customs, immigration, and other facilities were underdeveloped and cumbersome. In comparison, present driving times for the 300 kilometers from Khorgos to Almaty require a bit more than four hours, but this could be shortened with higher speed railway and highway development. Almaty is the logical place for logistics HQs as it is the largest city, largest airport and has well-developed banking and business services. Khorgos in combination with Almaty offers the possibility of a massive freeport:

> *In some cases, the free port can become the main driver of national economic development, as the case of Dubai illustrates by combining port, airport and real estate development and creating a free port in a relatively closed regional context.* (Lavissière & Rodrigue, 2017: 6)

Modern freeports are usually seen as seaports, but being a seaport is not a necessary condition. However, developed finance and business services are required (Lavissière & Rodrigue, 2017) to develop synergies through interlinkages between logistics and finance (Kasarda, 2015; O'Connor, 2010; Selmier, 2017). The Almaty-Khorgos linkage would provide the package of transport, logistics and finance which Shenzhen and Hong Kong achieved in the earlier decades of Shenzhen's development and which continues today.

A hub airport is also a key part of a dynamic modern freeport such as seen in Dubai and Istanbul (Kasarda, 2015; Selmier, 2017). Both Kazakhstan and China may benefit from investing in a hub airport at Almaty (or perhaps Nur-Sultan). Almaty and Nur-Sultan combine the advantages of optimal location between Europe and East and Southeast Asia, sound diplomatic relationships between Kazakhstan and China and Russia, well-developed business services and land transport options and the possibility for robust financial markets (many business travelers either work in finance or travel to negotiate financial contracts). To gain a sense of air travel logistics and the centrality of Almaty, Table 7.1 above gives a rough estimate of flying times between important East Asian, Gulf and European destinations with present flights now available through Almaty. It is important to note that jet fuel, landing fees and operational costs are relatively high at present in Kazakhstan but that addressing these higher costs is a focus of Kazakh government officials.

Although Almaty may be a more logical choice for a logistics hub given proximity, financial and business services and a larger airport, the Kazakh government has been attempting to pull more business functions toward the capital of Nur-Sultan. The Astana International Financial Centre (AIFC) officially opened on January 1, 2018. The AIFC provides additional inducements to the development of a wide-footprint Kazakh freeport, including financial operations under British legal standards (nearest alternatives would be Singapore, Hong Kong, offshore operations in UAE and Europe), the Shanghai Stock Exchange as a key strategic partner (holding a 25% ownership share) and trading platform technology provided by NASDAQ (Jenkins & Perzadayeva, 2018; Norton Rose Fulbright, 2018; Voloshin, 2017). To create the logistics and business services of a freeport would necessitate tight coordination between Khorgos, Almaty and Nur-Sultan, which is quite conceivable.

Silk Road Logistics and Politics

> *The Silk Roads were originally defined by Richthofen narrowly and since have become such a ubiquitous term that one wonders what it really means. Obscurity can help a concept as well as hurt it, and so the Chinese (and Americans and others) have adopted it for their own meanings.* (Selmier, 2018: 271)

Politics and governance have always been a key determining factor on land-based Silk Roads ancient and modern and on the maritime routes which have become associated with the modern concepts surrounding the Silk Roads. China's efforts to develop a "string of pearls" of maritime logistics centers (and possible naval bases) have garnered considerable controversy from perspectives involving strategy (Beng, interviewing Wang, 2014: 170–71; Padilla, 2017), incurrence of debt (Hurley, Morris & Portelance, 2018; Lloyd & Partners, 2017) and cultural conflict (Kirişci & Le Corre, 2015; Selmier, 2018). On the one hand, Tony Padilla (2017) has suggested Americans still revere Admiral Mahan's thought—Mahan, the naval strategist whom Teddy Roosevelt followed to build the modern American Navy—that "the destiny of the world will be decided in these (Indian Ocean) waters." On the other hand, China is emerging as an anxious seapower (Wang, 2013) which has caused fears that it seeks to encircle the Indian Ocean.

Logistics experts will factor in this maritime political turbidity to their calculations, realizing that contention on the seas and oceans will increase risks while land-based transport, even if more expensive, may provide a more tranquil setting. And China will also consider this calculus. Even if land transport is more expensive, Chinese firms and the Chinese government will invest in land transport and logistics to hedge bets and provide other transportation routes, thereby lowering transportation costs and underpinning an emerging transportation infrastructure. Kazakhstan, as an island of relative calm in more turbid terrestrial times, will benefit.

Bibliography

Allworth, E. A. (1995). Encounter. In E. A. Allworth (Ed.), *Central Asia: One hundred thirty years of Russian dominance, a historical overview* (pp. 1–59). Durham, NC: Duke University Press.

Ambalov, V., & Heim, I. (2018). Cluster nodes as a unit for value co-creation: The role of information technologies in competitiveness of Kazakhstan's oil and gas industry. In K. Liu, K. Nakata, W. Li, & C. Baranauskas (Eds.), *Digitalization, innovation and transformation* (pp. 155–163). Proceedings of 18th IFIP WG 8.1 International Conference on Informatics and Semiotics in Organisations, ICISO 2018, Reading, UK, July 16–18, 2018, Ch. 16. Cham, Switzerland: Springer. https://doi.org/10.1007/978-3-319-94541-5_16.

Ambalov, V., & Heim, I. (2020). Investments in the digital Silk Road. In I. Heim (Ed.), *Kazakhstan's diversification from the natural resources sector: Strategic and economic opportunities*. London, UK: Palgrave Macmillan.

Anthony, D. W., & Vinogradov, N. B. (1995). Birth of the chariot. *Archaeology, 48*(2), 36–41.

Aubakirova, A., Umirzakov, U., & Aitenov, N. (2017). New silk road: Opportunities and threats for Central Asia (A view from Kazakhstan). *Central Asia & the Caucasus, 18*(4), 7–20.

Beng, O. K. (2014). *The Eurasian core and its edges: Dialogues with Wang Gungwu on the history of the world.* ISEAS–Yusof Ishak institute. Retrieved from https://muse-jhu-edu.proxyiub.uits.iu.edu/book/39808/

Capineri, C., & Leinbach, T. R. (2006). Freight transport, seamlessness, and competitive advantage in the global economy. *European Journal of Transport and Infrastructure Research, 6*(1), 23–38.

Christian, D. (2000). Silk roads or steppe roads? The silk roads in world history. *Journal of World History, 11*(1), 1–26.

CIA. (2017). *The World Factbook*. Retrieved from https://www.cia.gov/library/publications/the-world-factbook/

Contessi, N. P. (2015). Foreign and security policy diversification in Eurasia: Issue splitting, co-alignment, and relational power. *Problems of Post-Communism, 62*(5), 299–311.

Contessi, N. P. (2016). Central Asia in Asia: Charting growing trans-regional linkages. *Journal of Eurasian Studies, 7*, 3–13.

Cox, L. D. (2009). Evolving the Memphis Aerotropolis. *Airport Management, 4*(2), 149–155.

Crainic, T. G., Dell'Olmo, P., Ricciardi, N., & Sgalambro, A. (2015). Modelling dry-port-based freight distribution planning. *Transportation Research Part C, 55*, 518–534. https://doi.org/10.1016/j.trc.2015.03.026

D'Encausse, H. C. (1995a). Systematic Conquest, 1865–1884. In E. A. Allworth (Ed.), *Central Asia: One hundred thirty years of Russian dominance, a historical overview* (pp. 131–150). Durham, NC: Duke University Press.

D'Encausse, H. C. (1995b). The national republics lose their independence. In E. A. Allworth (Ed.), *Central Asia: One hundred thirty years of Russian dominance, a historical overview* (pp. 131–150). Durham, NC: Duke University Press.

Di Cosmo, A. T. (2004). *Ancient China and its enemies: The rise of nomadic power in east Asian history*. Cambridge, UK: Cambridge University Press.

Earth Science and Remote Sensing Unit, NASA Johnson Space Center. (2018). *Photo of Kazakhstan*. Retrieved from https://issearthserv.jsc.nasa.gov/lunaserv.html

Elverskog, J. (2010). *Buddhism and Islam on the silk road*. Philadelphia, PA: University of Pennsylvania Press.

Erdbrink, T. (2017, July 25). For China's global ambitions, 'Iran is at the center of everything'. *New York Times*. Retrieved from https://www.nytimes.com/2017/07/25/world/middleeast/iran-china-business-ties.html?emc=eta1

Esfahani, H. S., & Pesaran, M. H. (2009). The Iranian economy in the twentieth century: A global perspective. *Iranian Studies, 42*(2), 177–211.

Feng, E., & Foy, H. (2017, December 20). China-Kazakhstan border woes dent silk road ambitions. *Financial Times*. Retrieved from https://www.ft.com/content/1606d70a-9c31-11e7-8cd4-932067fbf946

Frank, A. G. (1992). *The centrality of Central Asia*. Amsterdam, The Netherlands: VU University Press.

Frank, A. G. (1998). *ReORIENT: Global economy in the Asian age*. Berkeley, CA: University of California Press.

Han, T., & Ghobadian, A. (2020). Chinese investments across the new silk road. In I. Heim (Ed.), *Kazakhstan's diversification from the natural resources sector: Strategic and economic opportunities*. London, UK: Palgrave Macmillan.

Hansen, V. (2012). *The silk road: A new history*. Oxford, UK: Oxford University Press.

Heim, I. (2017). Local content policies: Global versus national? In M. Munoz (Ed.), *Globalization alternatives* (pp. 73–84). Dallas, USA: Business Expert Press.

Higgins, A. (2018, January 3). China's ambitious new 'port': Landlocked Kazakhstan. *New York Times*. Retrieved from https://www.nytimes.com/2018/01/01/world/asia/china-kazakhstan-silk-road.html.
Hu, Yuanbin. (胡元斌). 2015. *Historical vignettes of idioms*, first series (成语故事·第一辑). Beijing, China: Nanwen Educational.
Hurley, J., Morris, S., & Portelance, G. 2018. *Examining the debt implications of the belt and road initiative from a policy perspective*. CGD policy paper. Washington, DC: Center for Global Development.
Hydrocarbons Technology. (2018). *Kazakhstan-China crude oil pipeline*. Retrieved from https://www.hydrocarbons-technology.com/projects/kazakhstan-china-crude-oil-pipeline/
Jenkins, C., & Perzadayeva, S. (2018, January). *Law of Astana International Financial Centre*. Moore & Van Allen PLLC. Retrieved from http://www.mvalaw.com/news-publications-547.html
JEX Corporation (Japan Eurasia Express). (2018). *International transport to Kazakhstan (map)*. Retrieved from http://www.jexpress.co.jp/english/logi_kazakhstan.html
Kambarov, B. (2015, December 15). Kazakhstan, China Sign $50 Billion Worth of Deals in 2015, Ambassador in Beijing Says. *Astana Times*. Retrieved from http://astanatimes.com/2015/12/kazakhstan-china-sign-50-billion-worth-of-deals-in-2015-ambassador-in-beijing-says/
Kasarda, J. (2015). China's dynamic airport economic zone. *Site Selection*, November, 74–77.
Kazakhstan 2050. (2016). *China intends to strengthen party-to-party ties with Kazakhstan*. Retrieved from https://strategy2050.kz/en/news/32380
Keddie, N. R. (1972). The economic history of Iran, 1800–1914, and its political impact an overview. *Iranian Studies, 5*(2/3), 58–78.
Kembayev, Z. (2018). Implementing the silk road Economic Belt: From the Shanghai cooperation organisation to the silk road union? *Asia Europe Journal, 16*(1), 37–50.
Kenderdine, T. (2017, September 14). *Caspian Sea is China's best bet for belt and road*. Nikkei Asia Review. Retrieved from https://asia.nikkei.com/Politics/Caspian-Sea-is-China-s-best-bet-for-Belt-and-Road
Kim, Y., & Indeo, F. (2013). The new great game in Central Asia post 2014: The US "new silk road" strategy and Sino-Russian rivalry. *Communist and Post-Communist Studies, 46*(2), 275–286.
Kirişci, K., & Le Corre, P. (2015). *The great game that never ends: China and Russia fight over Kazakhstan*. Brookings. Retrieved from https://www.brook-

ings.edu/blog/order-from-chaos/2015/12/18/the-great-game-that-never-ends-china-and-russia-fight-over-kazakhstan/

Lattimore, O. (1953). The new political geography of inner Asia. *The Geographical Journal, 119*(1), 17–30.

Lavissière, A., & Rodrigue, J-P. (2017). Free ports: Towards a network of trade gateways. *Journal of Shipping and Trade 2, Article number: 7*. Retreived from https://jshippingandtrade.springeropen.com/articles/10.1186/s41072-017-0026-6.

Levinson, M. (2016). *The box – How the shipping container made the world smaller and the world economy bigger* (2nd ed.). Princeton, NJ: Princeton University Press.

Liu, H., Fang C., & Ren Y. (刘海猛;方创琳; 任宇飞). (2016). Silk road economic belt China-Kazakhstan international cooperation demonstration zone logistics industry development and cross-border E-commerce platform construction (丝绸之路经济带中国-哈萨克斯坦国际合作示范区物流业发展与跨境电商平台建设). *Arid Land Geography* (干旱区地理), *5*, 951–958.

Liu, X. (2010). *The silk road in world history*. Oxford, UK: Oxford University Press.

Lloyd & Partners. (2017). *One belt, one road. Credit, political and security risk*. Retrieved from https://www.lloydandpartners.com/our-insights/risk-outlook/one-belt-one-road-opportunities-and-risks

Makarov, I., & Sokolova, A. (2016). Coordination of the Eurasian economic union and the silk road Economic Belt: Opportunities for Russia. *International Organizations Research Journal, 11*(2), 29–42.

Matley, I. M. (1995). Industrialization (1865–1964). In E. A. Allworth (Ed.), *Central Asia: One hundred thirty years of Russian dominance, a historical overview* (pp. 309–348). Durham, NC: Duke University Press.

Mercator Institute for China Studies (MERICS). (2017). *China aims to build a global infrastructure network*. Retrieved from https://www.merics.org/sites/default/files/2017-08/170515_MERICS_China_Mapping_BRI_March_2017_0.jpg

Niu, R. (牛汝极). (2015). The Tianshan mountain range: The pivotal line of converging Asian civilizations. *Journal of Asian History, 49*(1–2), 5–18.

Nixey, J. (2012, June). *The long goodbye: Waning Russian influence in the South Caucasus and Central Asia*. REP RSP BP 2012/03. London, UK: Chatham House.

Norton Rose Fulbright. (2018). *Inauguration of Astana's international financial Centre*. Norton Rose Fulbright Publication, April. Retrieved from http://www.nortonrosefulbright.com/knowledge/publications/165542/inauguration-of-astanas-international-financial-centre

O'Connor, K. (2010). Global city regions and the location of logistics activity. *Journal of Transport Geography, 18*(3), 354–362.

Padilla, T. (2017). Analysis: China to shape international trade via belt and road. *The Journal of Commerce*. Retrieved from https://www.joc.com/international-trade-news/infrastructure-news/china-infrastructure-news/analysis-china-shape-international-trade-belt-and-road_20170609.html

Palmer, A. (1994). *The decline and fall of the Ottoman empire*. New York, NY: Barnes & Noble.

Rich, J., Kveiborg, O., & Hansen, C. O. (2011). On structural inelasticity of modal substitution in freight transport. *Journal of Transport Geography, 19*(1), 134–146.

Roso, V. (2008). Factors influencing implementation of a dry port. *International Journal of Physical Distribution & Logistics Management, 38*(10), 782–798. https://doi.org/10.1108/09600030810926493

Roso, V., Woxenius, J., & Lumsden, K. (2008). The dry port concept: Connecting container seaports with the hinterland. *Journal of Transport Geography, 17*(5), 338–345.

Rossabi, M. (1990). The 'decline' of the central Asian caravan trade. In J. D. Tracy (Ed.), *The rise of merchant empires – Long distance trade in the early modern world 1350–1750* (pp. 351–370). Cambridge, UK: Cambridge University Press.

Sabayeva, G. (2015, May 18). Border does not divide Kazakhstan and China, but brings them closer, says Kazakh Ambassador in Beijing. *The Astana Times*. Retrieved from http://astanatimes.com/2015/05/border-does-not-divide-kazakhstan-and-china-but-brings-them-closer-says-kazakh-ambassador-in-beijing/

Saray, M. (1982). The Russian conquest of Central Asia. *Central Asian Survey, 1*(2–3), 1–30.

Selmier, W. T., II. (2017). *Power of the modern caravanserai: Dubai and the new silk road initiative*. Baltimore, MD: Presented at International Studies Association Convention.

Selmier, W. T., II. (2018). The belt and road initiative and the influence of Islamic economies. *Economic and Political Studies, 6*(3), 257–277.

Silin, Y., Kapustina, L., Trevisan, I., & Drevalev, A. (2018). The silk road economic belt: Balance of interests. *Economic and Political Studies, 6*(3), 293–318.

Solvang, W. D., & Hakam, M. H. (2010). Sustainable logistics networks in sparsely populated areas. *Journal of Service Science and Management, 3*(1), 72–77.

Sternberg, T., Ahearn, A., & McConnell, F. (2017). Central Asian 'characteristics' on China's new silk road: The role of landscape and the politics of infrastructure. *Land, 6*(3), 55. https://doi.org/10.3390/land6030055

Tang, S. (2000). Economic integration in Central Asia: The Russian and Chinese relationship. *Asian Survey, 40*(2), 360–376.

Thill, J.-C., & Lim, H. (2010). Intermodal containerized shipping in foreign trade and regional accessibility advantages. *Journal of Transport Geography, 18*(4), 530–547.

Tsuruoka, D. (2018, January 9). China's landlocked 'port' in Kazakhstan doesn't need water to succeed. *Astana Times*. Retrieved from http://www.atimes.com/article/chinaslandlocked-port-kazakhstan-doesnt-need-water-succeed/

Uatkhanov, Y. (2017, May 16). COSCO Shipping to invest in Khorgos-eastern gate free economic zone. *The Astana Times*. Retrieved from https://astanatimes.com/2017/05/cosco-shipping-to-invest-in-khorgos-eastern-gate-free-economic-zone/

Vinokurov, E., & Tsukarev, T. (2018). The belt and road initiative and the transit countries: An economic assessment of land transport corridors. *Area Development and Policy, 3*(1), 93–113.

Voloshin, G. (2017). Is Kazakhstan's new financial centre for real? *fDi Intelligence*. Retrieved from https://www.fdiintelligence.com/Locations/Asia-Pacific/Kazakhstan/Is-Kazakhstan-s-new-financial-centre-for-real

Wang, G. (2013). Continental power – An interview with Wang Gungwu. *Global ARC Quarterly Spring, 2013*, 10–19.

Wang J.-S. (王缉思). (2012, October 17). Marching West, China's Geo-strategic Re-balancing (西进，中国地缘战略的再平衡). *Huanqiu Times (环球时报)*. Retrieved from http://opinion.huanqiu.com/opinion_world/2012-10/3193760.html

Waugh, D. C. (2007). Richthofen's 'silk roads': Toward the archaeology of a concept. *The Silk Road, 5*(1), 1–10. Retrieved from http://www.silkroadfoundation.org/newsletter/vol5num1/srjournal_v5n1.pdf

Waugh, D. C. (2012). Destroyed, (the silk road) is no more. *The Silk Road, 10*, 164–167. Retrieved from: http://www.silkroadfoundation.org/newsletter/vol10/SilkRoad_10_2012_waugh_reviewofhansen.pdf

Wu S.-S. (2017, February 4). *Frictions on the new silk road*. Xinhua Silk Road Information Service. Retrieved from: http://en.silkroad.news.cn/2017/0204/10455.shtml

Xinhua. (2017, November 16). Baku-Tbilisi-Kars railway transportation costs for 2018 reduced. *Xinhua Silk Road Information Service*. Retrieved from http://en.silkroad.news.cn/2017/1116/69724.shtml

Yu, H. (2017). Motivation behind China's 'one belt, one road' initiatives and establishment of the Asian infrastructure investment Bank. *Journal of Contemporary China, 26*(105), 353–368.

Zhang, X., & Belgibayev, M. (2014). China's Eurasian Pivot. Asan institute for policy studies. Retrieved from http://www.theasanforum.org/chinas-eurasian-pivot/

Part IV

Kazakhstan: Economic Opportunities

The authors of the chapters in this section discuss the internal sources of economic diversification. Sabirov and Shakulikova research the government policy to support the development of the national industry in the oil and gas sector. Jumasseitova focuses on the development of the entrepreneurial ecosystem in Kazakhstan with regard to their connectedness with the companies from the countries-members of the Eurasian Economic Union. Authors of the concluding chapter consider the advantages of information technologies in the promotion of online tourism (e-tourism) in Kazakhstan and the opportunity to diversify its economy based on the extractive sector into the growing tertiary sectors, including the tourism industry.

8

Diversification and Local Industry Development

Beibit Sabirov and Gulzada Shakulikova

Introduction

This chapter discusses why local industry development is critical for diversification of the economy in resource-rich countries. If we analyze statistical information for the past 20 years, it can be concluded that natural resource mining products comprise two-thirds of the export structure of Kazakhstan and have done for the past 20 years. At the same time, two-thirds of imports comprise goods with high added value—machinery, equipment, and products of the chemical industry (Committee on Statistics of the Republic of Kazakhstan, n/d). The imports are machinery equipment needed for extracting and refining natural resources and products and chemical products, which could potentially be

B. Sabirov
Karachaganak Petroleum Operating BV, Nur-Sultan, Kazakhstan

G. Shakulikova (✉)
Atyrau University of Oil and Gas, Atyrau, Kazakhstan
e-mail: rector@aogu.edu.kz

I. Heim (ed.), *Kazakhstan's Diversification from the Natural Resources Sector*, Euro-Asian Studies, https://doi.org/10.1007/978-3-030-37389-4_8

produced in Kazakhstan from these natural resources using this equipment. This shows that Kazakhstan exports mostly raw materials and imports high technological products, and the economy of the country is not able to process raw materials into final products. This means that despite numerous attempts to diversify the economy, Kazakhstan has still not been able to get away from natural resource dependency.

How then can the economy of Kazakhstan be balanced in order to produce high-technological equipment? A tool for creating a more diversified economy would be an effective policy to support national business and the development of cooperation in the oil and gas (O&G) sector, coupled with the focused efforts of the mining companies themselves in this matter. The rapid development of the O&G industry could become a driving force for growth, creating a multiplier effect on other sectors of the economy.

This research makes several contributions to the literature. First, we review government policy on supporting the development of national industry in the O&G industry. Second, we analyze the approaches of the largest O&G operators in developing local industry and in supporting Kazakhstani producers. Finally, we attempt to make recommendations to improve the effectiveness of government policies.

Based on the analysis of the reports of companies on purchased goods, works and services (GWS) accumulated in the System for Receiving Reports of Subsoil Users of the Ministry of Energy of the Republic of Kazakhstan, we identify the share of local products and services in procurement of the major O&G consortiums operating in Kazakhstan. In order to analyze the procurement structure and determine products for potential production in Kazakhstan, we identify the ten most frequently procured goods, works and services produced in Kazakhstan and the ten items most frequently imported by largest O&G operators.

According to our hypothesis, due to the technical complexity of the development of the O&G deposits, as well as the complexity of the industry's value chain, a significant amount of the goods needed by operators are GWS of high technology, and such goods are imported. We also assume that the GWS which are most frequently purchased from local suppliers are low-tech GWS. To test these hypotheses, we analyzed the reports of the three largest operators provided to the state authorities on purchased GWS. We assume that such "gaps" exist in terms of supporting and developing R&D and innovation.

Development of the Indigenous Firms in the Energy Sector

Kazzazi and Nouri (2012) argue that while local content (LC) is a common phenomenon and a universally accepted term for the O&G industry, there is still very little research on this topic in academic literature. The authors of this article concluded that the most significant variable for the development of LC in the O&G sector is government policy. In addition, there are some other important policies, which are the policies of municipal authorities, the policies of O&G companies to support local suppliers, the potential and skills of the companies themselves, as well as the policies for R&D of local companies. These policies are important since the local industry can develop only if the matrix of all these policies is in place (Nygaard, 2010, 2012; Heim, 2019).

The key empirical study on lower economic growth in resource-dependent economies (the phenomenon which has been called *resource course*) was undertaken by Sachs and Warner (1995), who analyzed data from 95 countries from 1970 to 1990 and found that countries with a high share of raw materials in exports showed slower GDP growth than countries that did not have an extensive stock of raw materials. Based on this research, Auty (2002) discovered that it is countries with a high share of hydrocarbons in exports that show the slowest GDP growth. Bulte, Damania and Deacon (2005) used an empirical method to prove a negative relationship between the country's raw material reserves and the development level of the state apparatus or "good institutions", which in turn affects the indicators of its human development.

Chang (2002) in his study used numerous historical examples to prove that the application of protective measures for local producers for the cultivation of promising industries is expedient and empirically confirmed. Al-Kasim (2006), in his extensive work, tells the story of the formation of the Norwegian oil industry from the discovery of the Ekofisk field to the present day. The author pays particular attention to clarifying the features of the Norwegian government's policy regarding the management of its natural resources. Barroso and Macedo (2009) reviewed government policies to regulate LC in Brazil. Okuneva (2016) in her research article lists the main causes of the economic and political crisis in Brazil including corruption scandals surrounding the Petrobras National Company. The research projects mentioned here justify the viewpoint that regulation in the O&G dependent economies is necessary to support diversification.

The issue of the need to diversify the economy and support domestic industry through the protection of the domestic producers and LC policies is also considered by Kazakhstani researchers. Thus, Madiyarova (1999), analyzing the foreign economic policy of various countries, indicated that the export policy of developing countries should be complex. It should provide for customs protection, for financial and fiscal stimulation, as well as for the creation of other conditions to support competitiveness.

Other research on the influence of the O&G industry on the economy concluded that Kazakhstan follows the *resource course* scenario due to the clear raw material orientation of the economy and the complete dependence on world oil price volatility (Gymranova, 2016). Therefore, Temirbekova and Temirbek (2014) suggested that the policy of local industry development is a matter of national economic security since with the creation of new industries and new jobs there is an increase in competencies and ultimately the well-being of the population. However, the authors noted that the most developed countries have moved away from strict regulation of the O&G industry and adhere to a policy of increasing the investment attractiveness of the manufacturing sector, the development of technology and the introduction of innovations. As a next step, Idrisov (2015) proposed that the development of the manufacturing industry through technology and innovation will bring Kazakhstan human capital to a different level of quality. Amangeldy and Esengalieva (2017) also connected the future of Kazakhstan with the development of O&G engineering cluster in the West Kazakhstan region. Karenov (2017) in his work on the specifics of the industrial and innovative potential of Kazakhstan called for expanding policy to develop the knowledge-based model of the economy based on human capital. Overall, Kazakhstani researchers agree on the fact that adjustments in policy toward support of R&D and innovations are necessary. The aim of this chapter is to give suggestions on design of future policy.

Data collection for the study was part of this work. Regulatory acts of Kazakhstan and other resource-driven economies, including the experience of countries that have overcome their dependence on the energy sector (UK and Norway), were studied closely. Specialized literature and research articles as well as government business support programs were reviewed. The list of laws studied included, for example, the Code of the Republic of Kazakhstan *On Subsoil*, Law of the Republic of Kazakhstan On Subsoil and Subsoil Use (expired), Law of the Republic of Kazakhstan *On Oil* (expired), Law *On introducing amendments and additions to some legislative acts of the Republic of Kazakhstan on issues of Kazakhstan content*, the Unified methodology for calculating LC by the organizations when purchasing GWS, as well as the Rules for the acquisition of GWS by subsoil users and their contractors.

The primary data were collected from the compilations of the Statistics Committee of the Ministry of National Economy of the Republic of Kazakhstan and analytical data from the Ministries of National Economy and Energy, the Information and Analytical Center of Oil and Gas, and the Union of Oil Service Companies of Kazakhstan. Moreover, the present research used documents stored in the Central State Archive of the Republic of Kazakhstan (correspondence between state bodies, minutes, and abstracts of government meetings).

To calculate the LC in the O&G sector of Kazakhstan as well as to identify the GWS which are purchased with the highest frequency by *Tengizchevroil*, *Karachaganak Petroleum Operating* and *North Caspian Operating Company*, we used the data of subsoil users' reports for the last quarter of 2017 (annual report on purchased GWS) accumulated in the System for Receiving Reports of Subsoil Users of the Ministry of Energy of the Republic of Kazakhstan. These reports are submitted in electronic form to the competent authority body—the Ministry of Energy—on a quarterly basis in accordance with the Law on Subsoil and Subsoil Use. The report for the fourth quarter presents data on the results of the reporting year. The accuracy of the data is carefully checked by the competent authority. Access to the electronic system is allowed for authorized users only.

Local Procurement in the Energy Sector of Kazakhstan

According to the Ministry of Energy of the Republic of Kazakhstan, the total volume of purchases of mining companies in the energy sector in 2017 amounted to 4.9 trillion tenges (in terms of the weighted average exchange rate of the tenges of the National Bank of the Republic of Kazakhstan it amounts to US $15.1 billion); these huge figures indicate the potential of the Kazakhstani market. If domestic companies bid more tenders placed by subsoil users, this would have a powerful impact on the development of Kazakhstan's business.

Table 8.1 shows the main indicators of LC in the procurement of subsoil users of the energy sector. At present, the average share of local companies in procurement is 43.13%.

Considering the material and service segmentation of purchases, there is a significant imbalance in the specific gravity of each segment. So, in the period of 2017, the procurement of the Kazakhstan service sector (work and services) accounted for 93% of all purchases or 1971.6 billion tenges, while the purchases of the Kazakhstan manufacturing sector accounted for 7.17% or 152.3 billion tenges.

Purchases of GWS by the three largest subsoil users, namely *TCO*, *KPO* and *NCOC*, account for a large share of the total volume of procurement of the entire energy sector (the share of three companies in 2017 amounted to 68% or 3331.3 billion tenges). The indices of LC of these companies are significantly lower than industry-average indicators

Table 8.1 Share of LC in GWS procurement of subsoil users in 2017, thousand tenges and % of total

	Total	Goods	Works	Services
Total purchased	4,924,931,532	616,837,994	2,409,832,182	1,898,261,356
Local	**2,123,903,133**	**152,301,091**	**1,001,059,051**	**970,542,991**
Import	2,801,028,398	464,536,903	1,408,773,131	927,718,364
Share of local of total purchased, %	**43.13**	**24.69**	**41.54**	**51.13**

Source: Authors' own processed data based on data from the Ministry of Energy of Kazakhstan

Table 8.2 Purchase of GWS by three subsoil users, TCO, KPO and NCOC, in 2017, thousand tenges

	Total	Goods	Works	Services
Total purchased	3,331,310,997	189,133,400	1,869,927,557	1,272,250,039
Local	**1,022,387,844**	**15,972,487**	**583,090,540**	**423,324,815**
Import	2,308,923,153	173,160,913	1,286,837,016	848,925,223
Share of local	**30.69**	**8.45**	**31.18**	**33.27**

Source: Authors' own processed data based on data from the Ministry of Energy of Kazakhstan

(see Table 8.2) and this is primarily associated with technological complexity and high content of hydrogen sulfide and other corrosive materials from the developing deposits.

So, if the industry average indicator of the LC in goods is 24.69%, then the three "pillars" of the O&G market have 8.45% of the LC between them. The industry average indicator in the works is 41.54% and in the services is 51.13%, while the operators of the development of Kashagan, Tengiz and Karachaganak have 31.18% and 33.27%, respectively. These significant differences can be explained in several objective ways.

An analysis by the authors showed that low-tech products predominate in the procurement of goods from local suppliers. Among the works and services procured from Kazakhstani manufacturers, auxiliary services also occupy a significant place; they are the services in the field of hiring personnel and dealing with transport, construction services and catering.

The data on the top ten most frequently imported goods of each of the three largest operators for total imports for 2015–2017 were studied. These goods potential can be produced in Kazakhstan, to meet the demand from the three largest O&G operators in 2015–2017.

The top ten most frequently imported items of expenditure for the *TCO* accounted for 36.2% of the company's total imports of goods for 2015–2017 (see Table 8.3).

The top ten most frequently imported items of expenditure of *NCOC* accounted for 96.3% of the company's total imports of goods for 2015–2017 (see Table 8.4).

In order to eliminate distortion of the analysis results under the influence of equipment replacement in 2015–2016 at the Kashagan field, a

Table 8.3 Top ten most frequently imported goods by TCO in 2015–2017, Bln tenges

Type of goods/statistical code	2015	2016	2017
Drilling pipes, 24.20.11.321B	12.1	5.7	4.5
Fittings, 25.62.10.310A	4.4	7.7	4.6
Diesel fuel, 19.20.26.500A	3.9	6.6	4.4
Casing, 24.20.11.322B	4.3	2.6	6.0
Professional clothes, 14.12.30	2.2	4.3	4.7
Air conditioning equipment, 28.25.12	8.3	1.3	1.6
Throttle, 28.14.13.750A	0.9	6.4	3.8
Parts of electric motors and generators, 27.11.61	1.6	6.2	2.9
Tools, 25.73.60	3.6	4.1	2.9
Pipes, different diameters, 24.20	4.1	4.3	2.0

Source: Authors' own processed data based on data from the Ministry of Energy of Kazakhstan

Table 8.4 Top ten most frequently imported goods by NCOC in 2015–2017, Bln tenges

Type of goods/statistical code	2015	2016	2017
Pipes, 28.99.20.900A	–	54.2	–
Pipes, 22.21.29.400A	39.0	–	–
Pipes, 26.30.30.300A	31.5	–	–
Pipes, 33.20.70.000A	29.8	–	–
Pipes, 24.51.11.500A	24.5	1.0	–
Pipes, 22.19.73.400A	20.7	–	–
Gas compressors, 28.13.27.300A	–	2.0	1.3
Gas compressors, 28.12.12.350A	2.8	–	–
Gate valve, 28.14.13.300A	–	–	2.5
Flow meter, 26.51.52.350A	–	–	1.5

Source: Authors' own processed data based on data from the Ministry of Energy of Kazakhstan

more detailed analysis of the company's imports for 2017 was carried out. The ten most frequently imported goods were identified, representing 88% of the total *NCOC* import of goods in 2017 (see Table 8.5).

The analysis revealed that the top ten most frequently imported items of expenditure of *KPO* accounted for 66.4% of the company's total imports of goods for 2015–2017 (see Table 8.6).

Table 8.5 Top ten most frequently imported goods by NCOC in 2017, Bln tenges

Type of goods/statistical code	2017
Stop valves (28″ and 18″ pipe valves), 28.14.13.300A	2482.4
Electronic flow meters, 26.51.52.350A	1545.7
Gas compressors and flash evaporation compressors, 28.13.27.300A	1278.0
Licensed software, 26.11.30.500A/26.11.30.990 B	310.6
Oil transformers 10/0, 27.11.41.550B	166.5
Industrial uniform, 14.12.11.390A	162.4
Fittings for 28″ and 18″ pipe valves, 22.19.30.700A	80.8
Assembled filters from any material, 26.70.21.900A	58.5
Self-regulating heating cable, 27.51.29.000A	58.0
Hydraulic oils, 19.20.29.520A	54.0

Table 8.6 Top ten most frequently imported goods by KPO in 2015–2017, Bln tenges

Type of goods/statistical code	2015	2016	2017
Parts for pumps and compressors (spare parts for pumps and compressors), 28.13.3	6.0	10.0	1.4
Other industrial products (supply of expansion kits, spare parts for generator, for servers, for storage hardware, UPS, spare parts of various materials), 32.99	5.4	5.5	3.9
Taps and valves (supply of ball valves, nipple/throttle valves), 28.14	1.7	6.8	5.6
Fittings for pipes, small tubes, hoses, sleeves made of plastic (supply of pipes and bends), 22.21.29.700A	5.2	7.0	0.0
Casing, tubing and drill pipes for drilling oil and gas wells (supply of tubing and drill pipes), 24.20.11.320A	2.8	6.5	1.7
Gas turbine parts (supply of spare parts for gas turbine), 28.11.33	1.4	4.8	1.6
Distribution valves, slide gates, ball valves and other (supply of ball valve), 28.14.13	1.3	3.4	0.0
Oil and gas well drilling services (supply of wellhead equipment and fountain fittings, drill bits), 09.10.11.000A	1.4	1.8	1.3
Gaskets and seals similar of sheet metal in combination with other materials (supply of rushing rings, rings for mechanical sealing), 28.29.23	0.8	1.9	0.8
Other construction services (supply of chemical reagents), 43.99.90.000A	3.3	0.1	0.0

Source: Authors' own processed data based on data from the Ministry of Energy of Kazakhstan

Based on the analysis of the most imported articles of goods of *KPO*, *TCO*, and *NCOC*, the following categories of goods were identified:

1. Taps, valves, and their spare parts (average annual import of three operators in the amount of US $34.1 million):
   (a) ball, nipple/throttle valves;
   (b) supply of spare parts for valves.
2. Compressors and spare parts (US $21.4 million, while the calculation did not take into account the import of *NCOC* in 2015–2016 to exclude the effect of increased demand due to the replacement of equipment):
   (a) compressors of gas of instant evaporation (rotor);
   (b) spare parts for compressors, pumps.
3. Parts of electric motors and generators (US $19.8 million):
   (a) parts of electric motors and generators, in particular spare parts for a gas turbine generator;
   (b) electrical components—wires/cables.
4. Equipment for air conditioning (US $15.3 million)
5. Work clothes, including personal protective equipment (US $12.5 million):
   (a) industrial winter uniforms (jackets, gloves);
   (b) industrial summer uniforms (overalls, safety shoes).

It is necessary to understand that due to the fact that the main areas of the purchases of the energy sector of Kazakhstan fall on the “three pillars” of the O&G sector, operators of the development of the Kashagan, Tengiz, and Karachaganak fields, the greatest result in increasing the LC in the industry can be achieved by working with three operators directly and motivating them, in turn, to attract local suppliers to tenders.

Steps Taken by Three Major O&G Consortiums Toward Local Industry Development

Future Expansion Project of TengizChevrOil (TCO)

As part of TCO's Future Growth Project (FGP), there is a plan to build a new oil refining plant with a capacity of 12 million tons per year and crude gas re-injection facilities with a capacity of 9.4 billion m^3/year. This will involve constructing a new well production system and pressure boosting facilities, as well as infrastructure and support facilities. The cost is estimated at US $36.8 billion, and the commissioning of FGP facilities is scheduled for July 2022. This year, the project started the active phase of implementation. The projected Kazakh content in the implementation of FGP is 32% (or about US $11.8 billion).

According to the Ministry of Energy of the Republic of Kazakhstan, *TCO* has established a requirement for all major construction contracts for a minimum LC of 50%. *TCO* practices the mechanism of "long-term contracts", that is conclusion of contracts for a period of more than one year that provides the manufacturer with a stable order flow and allows planning the business several years in advance. Organization of a partnership with a Kazakhstan company is one of the main conditions for concluding a long-term contract with a foreign supplier for FGP. In August of this year, *TCO* announced the interim results of its work at FGP. Thus, since the beginning of the project the actual purchase amount from Kazakhstani companies amounted to US $4.5 billion (or 31%).

North Caspian Operating Company (NCOC)

NCOC is the operator of the first major offshore O&G development project in Kazakhstan, and its Local Content Development Policy focuses on training local companies and facilitating international certification according to international standards in the field of management, goods and services. It also provides financial support for its certification according to the requirements of the American Society of Mechanical Engineers and the American Petroleum Institute.

NCOC provides specialized vocational training for local company employees. The company focuses on training related to:

- electronic systems and their assembly;
- work in confined spaces;
- industrial safety rules.

In addition, as part of the Kashagan field development project, a number of joint ventures have already been created between Kazakhstan and foreign companies that operate successfully in Kazakhstan.

Karachaganak Petroleum Operating (KPO)

Karachaganak Expansion Project (KEP) is one of the largest most promising O&G projects which will be managed by the international consortium *Karachaganak Petroleum Operating (KPO)*. The goal of the project is to increase the volume of recoverable liquid hydrocarbons through the installation of additional gas treatment facilities, gas re-injection facilities and the removal of production restrictions.

At the end of 2015, *KPO* updated the Local Content Policy and developed a two-year Local Content Development Program that supports the implementation of state programs for the industrialization and development of mechanical engineering, as well as assisting in the creation of an oilfield cluster around the Karachaganak project, contributing to the development of the economy of the West Kazakhstan region and the Republic of Kazakhstan.

As part of the *KPO* corporate program for the development of LC, the following measures have been identified to support local suppliers:

- tenders with local suppliers or tenders only among joint ventures;
- holding of early tenders;
- assisting in the establishment of joint ventures with local suppliers and ensuring technology transfer;
- extension of existing contracts in exchange for the development of production/localization of goods and materials;
- procurement from a single source (on a non-competitive basis) for local goods and materials.

In order to develop LC, the practice of "early tenders" has been introduced in Karachaganak, which means that companies that receive a contract with *KPO* in advance undertake to establish the production of necessary products in Kazakhstan. After the launch of production, this company already has a sales market guaranteed. As part of this process, there is already a pilot bid for the supply from local companies, including supply of drill bits from *ZhigerMunayService LLP*, supply of caustic soda from *JSC Caustic* and supply of barite from *Karazhal Operating Ltd*. The process of placing a pilot bid for cement at *JSC Shymkent Cement* was resumed, and a long-term contract was signed with *Edil-Oral Ltd* for repair and rewind of explosion-proof electric motors.

In order to facilitate the development of Kazakhstani suppliers, subject to the availability of a sufficient number of local suppliers, *KPO* accepted tender from Kazakhstani suppliers. By the end of 2018, *KPO* initiated 85 Kazakhstan tenders for a total of US $264 million, and 53 such contracts were concluded for a total of US $104 million (the remaining tenders are at the stage of realization).

At the same time the company began implementing a number of large-scale projects. For each of the projects, *KPO* has developed and agreed strategies and a plan for the development of local companies, as well as determined targets for the level of LC.

While developing this plan and strategy, *KPO* realized that to carry out large volumes of design and construction works within the framework of projects, Kazakhstan companies do not possess enough of their own technical, human and financial resources, as well as not having access to new technologies. Thus, in accordance with the approved Strategies and Plan for LC of projects, *KPO* introduced mandatory requirements for foreign companies to create joint ventures and consortia with the participation of Kazakhstan partners in order to maximize the involvement of local producers and oilfield service companies to perform more sophisticated and complex works.

The company also continues to develop the potential of WKO machine-building plants by facilitating training and certification according to international standards ASME and API (for the manufacture of vessels under pressure). Two WKO machine-building enterprises from WKO, *Aksaigazservice JSC* and *Zenit Ural Plant JSC* successfully passed a preliminary assessment of an independent audit company for subsequent preparation for certification according to ASME standards. This will allow local companies to improve the quality of their products to win more tenders in the future.

All of the above measures over the past few years have allowed *KPO* to increase the share of LC in *KPO* purchases from 47.5% in 2014 to 54.1% in 2017.[1]

Public-Private Initiatives

In addition to individual initiatives, large O&G operators are taking joint actions in the field of LC development. On September 25, 2012, three major O&G consortiums, *NCOC*, *KPO* and *TCO*, and *JSC National Company KazMunayGas* signed a declaration ("Aktau Declaration on Joint Actions for the Development of the Kazakhstan Oil Service Industry") that contains the following key initiatives:

- unification and simplification of the registration/prequalification procedure of Kazakhstani companies;
- development of a common database of suppliers "Alash";
- harmonization of procurement processes;
- joint planning of future procurements;
- definition of goods and services for the localization of production.

All major operators are working on a synergy of efforts to develop Kazakhstani production, one of the mechanisms of which is holding joint forums aimed at familiarizing market participants with the demand for goods that are subject to localization and at explaining technical requirements and standards. The major operators also work with specialized associations and chambers of commerce, with the aim of attracting leading foreign companies to create joint production of new equipment and materials with the Kazakhstan party and in Kazakhstan. This not only allows the creation of new jobs but also facilitates the transfer of

[1] KPO report on sustainable development in 2017

technologies and the development of new production capabilities in Kazakhstan. Furthermore, it enables local companies to expand their markets by entering international markets in the future.

Conclusions and Implications

International O&G companies (IOCs) make a significant contribution to local industry development by:

1. Planning for procurement from local manufacturers
   Consortiums cooperate with the regions to study the capabilities of local oilfield services and engineering companies. They hold early tenders, place pilot orders and conclude long-term contracts.
2. Creating a base of local suppliers
   As part of the Aktau Declaration between NCOC, KPO, TCO and KMG, a common database of *Alash* suppliers was developed and launched in February 2016. Project operators use *Alash* permanently as one of the sources of information to search for potential suppliers when conducting market research. However, *Alash* is not used as a tool for prequalification and qualification of companies, due to the fact that each operator has its own processes and procedures for conducting prequalification. Unification of industry standards could be a potential solution.
3. Developing R&D and introducing new technologies in domestic production
   According to the standard contract model of subsoil use, there are provisions on supporting R&D in Kazakhstan allocating 1% for R&D from the annual budget of subsoil users. However, no significant technological breakthroughs in the oil and gas industry of Kazakhstan have so far been noted. This means that the further development of R&D and the introduction of new technologies in the domestic production are necessary for Kazakhstan.
4. Indirect financial support for business
   Consortiums help to attract foreign investment in the WKO, as well as provide training to Kazakhstani companies according to inter-

national standards. They reimburse part of the cost for local companies through cooperation with the EBRD. Kazakhstani Bank of Development (KBD) could also contribute to this activity.

5. Partnerships between international and local suppliers

   Partnerships between international and local suppliers are also being facilitated and established by all three operators. This type of cooperation needs to be further promoted by the policymakers through public-private projects.

To conclude, the LC in the O&G industry in 2017 was 43%, a good result. However, when considering the material and service segmentation of purchases, we established a significant imbalance in the specific gravity of each segment. In 2017, procurement of the Kazakhstan service sector (work and services) accounted for 93% of all purchases, while purchases of the Kazakhstan manufacturing sector accounted for 7.2%. It should be noted that this indicator only partially reflects the actual volume of Kazakhstani purchased goods and does not take into account Kazakhstani goods purchased through work contracts (e.g., construction works or drilling works), where subsoil user contractors purchased Kazakhstan's construction or chemical products independently, and such goods in subsoil users' reports on LC are indicated as the "work" category. It should also be noted that not all manufacturers are able or willing to receive CT-KZ certificates on time and this has negative impact on the statistics on LC in goods.

This fact reveals the service orientation of the business environment of Kazakhstan, and leads to the problem of low volumes of procurement of local goods by subsoil users of the O&G sector. A low LC indicator for goods indicates the absence or shortage of necessary machine-building production capacities in the country. Taps, valves and their spare parts, compressors and their spare parts, parts of electric motors and generators and air conditioning equipment are all in long-term demand from O&G operators—all these commodity items are currently fully imported, which confirms our hypothesis in Introduction that the main share of goods purchased by O&G companies is imported. International experience of leading countries shows that investing in promising technologies and production leads to the development of the domestic industry, which in turn leads to an increase in the share of LC in goods, but such a process may take some time to obtain results.

If we examine the dynamics of the structure of goods, works and services purchased from local manufacturers in more detail, it becomes obvious that Kazakhstani enterprises for 27 years of independence have not begun to produce high-technology equipment and high-tech products or to provide services that require special knowledge and competencies.

At the same time, historical reporting on local content does not yet reflect the work being carried out by O&G operators to purchase technologically more complex equipment and materials, for example, *KPO* already uses a number of high-tech products (pressure vessels, drill bits, modular substations, metal structures) that are available on the market, and these products have not yet been reflected in subsoil user reporting.

The analysis of the reports of the three largest operators showed that low-tech products predominate in the purchase of goods from local suppliers, for example fuel, lubricants, timber, cables/wires, nitrogen and personal protective equipment. Among the works and services procured from Kazakhstani manufacturers, a significant share of auxiliary services can be identified; these are the services in the field of hiring personnel, transport, construction services and catering. However, it should be noted that in 2017 a notable degree of work, namely design and engineering, to the amount of 123.8 billion tenges, was carried out by the Kazakhstan company *KPJV LLP*—a joint venture between the *Kazakhstan Institute of Oil and Gas, Kazgiproneftetrans JSC* and foreign companies *Worley Parsons* and *Fluor*. Thus, the introduced hypothesis was only partially confirmed, since there is progress toward inclusion of local partners in a work and service project which requires significant knowledge and, therefore, provides transfer of knowledge from a foreign partner to a local one, as well as high profit margins for local companies.

The state, as a regulator of the subsoil use sphere, has set strict limits regarding LC, but these strict "rules of the game" do not apply to the main purchasers of the industry—operators of the Tengiz, Kashagan and Karachaganak deposits, which accounted for 68% of all purchased goods, works and services in the industry at the end of 2017. The reason is agreements with shareholders of the operators with special provisions concluded more than 20 years ago. As the analysis reveals, the LC indicators of the three largest operators are significantly lower than the industry average, due to a number of factors.

First of all, there is a lack of obligations for LC in production-sharing agreements (PSAs). However, it should be noted that all operators work on the principle of good faith in the development of LC demonstrating commitment toward local industry development. In view of the terms of the PSA, which guarantee the stability of their provisions in case of any changes in legislation, the government is not in a position to amend the PSAs in order to meet the requirements of new legislation.

The second contributing factor is compliance with international standards. Taking into account the high content of hydrogen sulfide (5–15%), high pressure of extracted O&G (up to 700 bars), corrosive environment, as well as large subsoil users, standards require all manufacturers/suppliers to comply with international standards and certification of international institutions. However, Kazakhstan manufacturers have little financial interest in modernization or in training their own personnel to comply with international standards. Few Kazakhstani suppliers have a sufficient level of technology, knowledge, and competencies to meet these standards. An additional factor hindering the production of domestic goods, according to the requirements of large oil and gas companies, is the lack of specialized independent laboratories that can certify Kazakhstani goods according to international standards. Due to this fact, Kazakhstan companies cannot provide necessary certificates.

Another factor which needs to be considered is the price factor. The provisions of the agreements for the Kashagan and Tengiz projects provide for exemption from customs duties and VAT on the import of goods, while VAT is applied to the purchase of domestic products. As a result, there is a situation when it is more profitable to purchase imported products without paying fees and VAT than purchasing from a Kazakhstan manufacturer, who has VAT included in the cost of components and raw materials for the production of such products.

The next factor which has an important impact is affiliation. Foreign investors try to purchase products from their subsidiaries, global and/or proven suppliers in the market, which can provide a competitive price and delivery time, due to the well-developed system of sub-suppliers.

Due to the closed procedures of procurement by large subsoil users *TCO*, *KPO*, and *NCOC*, each operator has its own tender procedures, and procurement is performed in accordance with this. In order to take part in *TCO* and *NCOC* tenders, suppliers have to pass a rather complicated prequalification process; however, this does not guarantee them participation in the operator's tenders.

Finally, contractors and subcontractors of *TCO*, *KPO*, and *NCOC* do not comply with the norms of Article 77 of the Law of the Republic of Kazakhstan "On Subsoil and Subsoil Use" that stipulates the obligation of subsoil user contractors to comply with the procedure for acquiring goods, works and services approved by the government. Thus, contractors of the three operators and their subcontractors make purchases at their discretion.

The factors discussed above need to be taken into consideration by the policymakers when planning the scope of work on the development of LC with *TCO*, *KPO* and *NCOC* companies, since these are the operators who will increase the oil production in the coming years and who have planned for investments in the construction and modernization of existing capacities. Due to the late stage of development and significant depletion of reserves in other fields, a decrease in the level of hydrocarbon production is observed. Already, *TCO*, *KPO* and *NCOC* are implementing a number of measures and mechanisms designed to ensure the placement of their orders with Kazakhstani suppliers. For example, these are mechanisms of early tenders and long-term contracts. These also include tenders only among Kazakhstani suppliers and assistance in finding foreign partners to create a joint venture. At the local level, support in enhancing the competencies of local businesses, in passing certification in accordance with international standards, is required.

Policy implications in this research include the following. Firstly, it is the development of R&D in the O&G industry and, secondly, the transfer of technology and knowledge. According to the Global Competitiveness Index of the World Economic Forum for 2018, Kazakhstan took 87th place among 137 countries, indicated by the *Innovation indicator* (with a total score of 32.1 out of 100), 94th place according to the *R&D expenses indicator* (0.2% from GDP). These facts demonstrate the underinvestment in R&D capabilities in Kazakhstan (see Ambalov & Heim, 2020, this volume). This is the "growth point" that can help Kazakhstan to radically change the structure of non-primary production and the economic development model.

According to the Global Competitiveness Report of the World Economic Forum for 2017–2018, in terms of the indicator "Direct foreign investment and technology transfer", the indicator that shows how much foreign investment brings new technology to the country, Kazakhstan was in 93rd place among 137 countries (4.0 points from 7). The indicator "Use of the latest technologies at the company level" is also interesting: Norway is in 7th place (5.8 points out of 7); Kazakhstan is only 81st (4.3 points out of 7). As we can see, despite the significant volumes of direct foreign investments made in the economy of Kazakhstan, their volumes do not correlate with the transfer of technologies to Kazakhstan, and domestic companies are significantly behind the companies in developed countries of the world in terms of technological equipment. The transfer of knowledge and technology is still insufficient for building high technological industrial capacity.

At the company level, the development of R&D and the introduction of new technologies in domestic production, meaning the involvement of the local business in this process, are lagging behind. If measures are taken to support science-intensive areas, as well as increasing competitiveness, along with working to raise competence and growth of the local industry with a focus on the O&G industry, R&D and innovations can become a driving force of related industries, for example, steel, chemical or other manufacturing industries.

Bibliography

Al-Kasim, F. (2006). *Managing petroleum resources: The "Norwegian model" in a broad perspective.* Oxford, UK: Oxford Institute for Energy Studies.

Amangeldy, T. N., & Esengalieva, S. M. (2017). State and problems of development of machine-building production in Kazakhstan. *Science and education: a new time, 5*(22), 244–250. Амангелды Т.Н., Есенгалиева С.М. (2017). Состояние и проблемы развития машиностроительного производства в Казахстане. *Наука и образование: новое время*, *5* (22), 244–250.

Ambalov, V., & Heim, I. (2020). Investments in the digital Silk Road. In I. Heim (Ed.), *Kazakhstan's diversification from the natural resource sector: Strategic and economic opportunities*. London, UK: Palgrave Macmillan.

Auty, R. (2002). *Sustaining development in mineral economies: The resource curse thesis*. London, UK: Routledge.

Barroso, H. R., & Macedo, M. (2009). Local content in Brazilian oil industry. *T &B Petroleum, 28*, 64–68.

Bulte, E. H., Damania, R., & Deacon, R. T. (2005). Resource intensity, institutions, and development. *World Development, 33*(7), 1029–1044.

Chang, H. J. (2002). *Kicking away the ladder: Development strategy in historical perspective*. London, UK: Anthem Press.

Committee on Statistics of the Republic of Kazakhstan. (n/d). Retrieved from: http://stat.gov.kz/

Gymranova, G. I. (2016). The impact of the oil and gas industry on the economy. *Financial Herald, 2*(33), 101–108. Гимранова Г.И. (2016). Влияние нефтегазовой промышленности на экономику. *Финансовый вестник, 2*(33), 101–108.

Heim I. (2019). *Local content policy and value co-creation: adopting information technologies in the oil and gas industry* (Unpublished doctoral dissertation). University of Reading, Reading, UK.

Idrisov, M. M. (2015). The program of industrial and innovative development of the Republic of Kazakhstan for 2015–2019. *Economics, Entrepreneurship and Law, 5*(4), 253–272. Программа индустриально-инновационного развития Республики Казахстан на 2015–2019 годы. *Экономика, предпринимательство и право, 5*(4), 253–272.

Karenov, R. S. (2017). Industrialization is one of the key areas of development of Kazakhstan in the new economic reality., *Bulletin of the Karaganda University, Series Economics, 4*(88), 91–100. Каренов Р.С. (2017). Индустриализация—одно из ключевых направлений развития Казахстана в новой экономической реальности, *Вестник Карагандинского университета, Серия Экономика, 4*(88), 91–100.

Kazzazi, A., & Nouri, B. (2012). A conceptual model for local content development in petroleum industry. *Management Science Letters, 2*(6), 2165–2174.

Madiyarova, D. (1999). *Strategy for the formation of foreign economic activity.* Almaty (Kazakhstan): Economics. Мадиярова Д. (1999). *Стратегия формирования внешнеэкономической деятельности*. Алматы, Казахстан: Экономика.

Nygaard, C. (2010). Russia's oil and gas policy. In A. Gawrich, A. Franke, & J. Windwehr (Eds.), *Resources from energy as a curse? Rentierism and energy policy in post-soviet states*. Opladen/Farmington Hills, MI: Barbara Budrich Publishers.

Nygaard, C. (2012). Regulating property and exploitation rights of natural resources. In A. Heinrich & H. Pleines (Eds.), *Challenges of the Caspian resource boom: Domestic elites and policy making*. Basingstoke, UK: Palgrave Macmillan.

Okuneva, L. S. (2016). Impeachment of the president of Brazil: Conclusions and thoughts. *Latin America, 10*, 5–22. Окунева Л.С. (2016). Импичмент президента Бразилии: выводы и размышления. *Латинская Америка, 10*, 5–22.

Sachs, J., & Warner, A. M. (1995). *Natural resource abundance and economic growth*. NBER working paper series. Working paper 5398. Cambridge, UK: National Bureau of Economic Research.

Temirbekova, A. B., & Temirbek, E. B. (2014). *Support for domestic producers through the development of Kazakhstani content, materials of MNPK. Scientific discussion of the post-soviet space: Problems and prospects* (pp. 168–171). Taraz State Pedagogical Institute. Темирбекова А.Б., & Темирбек Е.Б. (2014). Поддержка отечественных производителей путем развития казахстанского содержания, материалы МНПК. Научная дискуссия постсоветского пространства: проблемы и перспективы, Таразский государственный педагогический институт, с. 168–171. Retrieved from: https://www.almau.edu.kz/upload/pdf/статья_в_Тараз_Темирбек.pdf

9

Building Entrepreneurial Ecosystems: Effects of Economic Integration

Assel Jumasseitova

Introduction

Entrepreneurial ecosystems (EEs) are defined as a set of interdependent actors and factors coordinated in such a way that they enable productive entrepreneurship within a particular territory (Stam & Spigel, 2017). The main difference with other related concepts such as *industrial district, cluster, innovation system*, and *business ecosystem approach* is that EEs consider small fast-growing businesses as central players (leaders) in the creation of the system and in keeping the system healthy (Feldman, 2014), rather than larger, more established firms or slower growing SMEs. In cluster and industrial districts, high growth start-ups are not necessarily included (Markusen, 1996). Start-ups are explicitly placed in the center of the ecosystem. Entrepreneurial employees are of great importance not only for new value creation in developed economies like Europe (Bosma,

A. Jumasseitova (✉)
Kazakh-British Technical University, Almaty, Kazakhstan
e-mail: a.dzhumaseitova@kbtu.kz

I. Heim (ed.), *Kazakhstan's Diversification from the Natural Resources Sector*, Euro-Asian Studies, https://doi.org/10.1007/978-3-030-37389-4_9

Stam, & Wennekers, 2012; Stam, 2013) but also for resource-rich developing countries, due to their attempt to overcome the *middle-income trap* and diversify from resource industries to the new service industries. These problems are particularly relevant for Kazakhstan striving to build its entrepreneurial ecosystems (Jumasseitova & Bigabatova, 2017). This research considers how economic integration with the EEA affects the development of the entrepreneurial ecosystem in Kazakhstan.

Economic Integration

Integration can be defined as a process of "the grouping together of units or factors to form a single whole. Integrated development may, therefore, mean either the integration of a number of regions or increased cohesion between sectors, regions and social classes" (Perroux, 2010). In this research, we focus on the integration of sectors between countries, in particular, the transportation and digital industries. The key point in the discussion about international economic integration is the degree of state participation. Some argue that the market is the most effective regulator of the economy and therefore see integration as a creation of a single economic space based on free foreign trade and monetary policies (e.g., Friedman, 2009). Other economic schools attempted to find a compromise between market mechanisms and the role of the state in the coordination of economic policies (e.g., Chang, 2002). In this research, we believe that unless a national state exists, it is not possible to achieve integration without the participation of member states. Therefore, when the full integration of the economic systems of member countries is not the aim, integration is achieved based on the principles of the market mechanism with the coordinating role of the state.

Trade-facilitating integration agreements encompass two parts: a definition of the underlying trade facilitation principles and a set of specific, binding, and enforceable trade facilitation measures (Wille & Redden, 2007). Balassa (1961) differentiated five stages of economic integration: a free trade zone, the customs union, which then moves into a single market, economic union, and finally full economic integration. There are various degrees of integration, depending on the type of agreement made between the trading countries and the degree to which barriers between them are removed. Economic integration has both positive and negative (access to new markets and increased foreign competition respectively) effects on the local companies' development (Nguyen & Enderwick, 2016). However, foreign competition forces domestic firms to become more innovative, and productive, and as a result more competitive (Kyophilavong, Vanhnalat, & Phonvisay, 2017). Research suggests that the industrial SMEs integrate and internalize more quickly and reactively with the help of advanced technologies (Huin, Luong, & Abhary, 2003). The regional digital economy has the potential to expand further (Pitakdumrongkit, 2018). The implementation of a cooperative policy between regional states may assist enterprises to grow internationally (Soesastro & Basri, 2005).

Research on recent economic integration initiatives, such as China's Belt and Road Initiative (BRI), finds that it has provided Chinese firms with significant incentives to speed up the pace of internationalization, having a positive formal institutional effect on the export performance of Chinese SME's firms that target the *Belt* countries (see Ribberink & Schubert, 2020, this volume; Li, Liu, & Qian, 2019). Previous economic integration initiatives such as the European Union (EU) and the Association of Southeast Asian Nations (ASEAN) simplified export and import procedures and expanded the market for SMEs.

To summarize, economic integration initiatives can have a significant effect on economies of participating countries, including its small- and medium-sized sectors. Kazakhstan is situated in the region with high integrative activity. Currently, two major integration projects such as the EEA and the BRI are emerging. In the next sections of this chapter, we will observe the development of the EEA project, which has currently reached the stage of single market integration.

Eurasian Economic Union

Recent global economic and geopolitical trends have led to the need to review the development strategy of Kazakhstan by evaluating regional integration processes in Eurasia. The process of Euro-Asian integration began after establishing the Commonwealth of Independent States (CIS), following the dissolution of the Soviet Union in 1991. The concept of the

Eurasian Economic Union was originally proposed by the former President of the Republic of Kazakhstan Nursultan Nazarbayev in 1994. The aim of this initiative was a voluntary, equitable integration, to pursue joint political and economic development of the post-Soviet economies, in order to take a leading position in the global economy (Dragneva & Wolczuk, 2012). That concept presented the principles, objectives, and mechanism of formation of the Eurasian Union provided the establishment of a number of coordinating supranational structures, setting out the basic premise of cooperation. It includes cooperation in the economy, scientific exchange, cultural cooperation, educational cooperation across countries, and joint environmental initiatives. The participation in integration unions is a priority for Kazakhstan, as the country sees great opportunities to develop capabilities based on regional integration. The main goal of integration is considered to be a stable, economic development and security in the region. Table 9.1 shows the evolution of economic integration within the Eurasian Economic Union.

Table 9.1 Evolution of the Eurasian Economic Union

Union	Period	Type	Main principles	Member countries
Eurasian Economic Community (EurAsEC)	2000–2014	Free trade area	No trading barriers	Belarus Kazakhstan Kyrgyzstan Russia Tadjikistan
Eurasian Customs Union (EACU)	2010	Customs union	No customs, common tariff on all import goods	Armenia Belarus Kazakhstan Russia
Eurasian Economic Space (EES)	2012	Single market	Free movement of people, goods, services, and capital	Armenia, Belarus Kazakhstan Kyrgyzstan Russia
Eurasian Economic Union (EAEU)	2015	Single market	Free movement of people, goods, services, and capital; common macroeconomic policies; transport, industry, and agriculture; competition and antitrust regulation	Armenia Belarus Kazakhstan Kyrgyzstan Russia

Source: Author

Table 9.2 shows the geographic and economic characteristics of member countries. As can be observed, Russia has dominated in terms of area, market size, and national income.

The Eurasian Economic Area was established in 2012 for the purpose of a common market that provides the free movement of persons, goods, services, and capital. The Eurasian Economic Space initially consisted of Belarus, Kazakhstan, and Russia and was expanded by Armenia and Kyrgyzstan joining in 2015 (Tarr, 2016). The key aim at this stage was the creation of a common market, in particular, the market of energy resources. The EAEU introduced the free movement of goods, capital, services, and people, and it provided common policies in the spheres of macroeconomics, transport, industry and agriculture, energy, foreign trade and investment, customs, technical regulation, and finally competition and antitrust regulation. The Eurasian Economic Union is designed to achieve a number of objectives. The economic objectives include improving resource allocation, efficiency in production, competition, reduction in prices for consumers and expansion of consumer choice, as well as an increase in investment by firms that want to take advantage of the larger market size.

Table 9.2 Selected economic and geographic indicators of member countries (2017–2018)

Country	Area, Tkm^2	Population, Mln	Life expectancy at birth, total (years)	Adjusted net national income per capita	
				Current US$	Annual % growth
Armenia	30	2952	74.8	3412	9.1
Belarus	208	9485	74.1	4980	3.4
Kazakhstan	2725	18,276	73.0	6378	0.9
Kyrgyzstan	200	6316	71.2	971	7.1
Russia	17,125	144,478	72.1	8519	2.0
Tajikistan	142	9101	71.2	793	–

Source: Author's own processed data based on the World Bank

The methodology in this research was a survey of companies (Ritchie & Spencer, 2002), based on a group of companies operating in Kazakhstan which was selected to determine the effect of EAEU on their activity. The survey questionnaire was administered to 204 small and medium-sized firms from different sectors of the economy in Kazakhstan. We received 184 fully completed answers, with a response rate of 90%. The questionnaire aimed to explore whether SMEs in Kazakhstan feel the effect integration in EAEU. Closed-end-type questions were used. Respondents could choose from a choice of answers to help find an association (positive, negative, neutral) between economic integration and the company's activity. To assess companies' sensitivity toward Eurasian economic integration, we asked the executives whether integration had an impact on their respective businesses and whether this impact was positive or negative. Positive effects included companies' intentions for regional expansion, increasing sales, and whether they were acting to improve their competitiveness to take advantage of integration. Examples of the questions: "Are there suppliers from the following countries among your partner companies?" "Are there buyers from the following countries among your partner companies?" "If exporting abroad, indicate which country" "New markets have opened for you in the following countries: (list of countries)".

The companies in our study represented a wide range of industries, including energy, industrial goods, construction, financial services, catering, retail, IT, and telecommunications. Following the classical view of the three-sector theory developed by Fisher (1939) we divided the respondents into three sectors of activity: extraction of raw materials (primary), manufacturing (secondary), and services (tertiary). The primary sector includes extraction of raw materials, mining, and agriculture. The secondary/manufacturing sector is concerned with the production of final goods. The tertiary sector is related to offering services such as trade, IT, logistics, telecommunication, retail, tourism, banking, and entertainment.

The focus of our research was the development of small and medium-sized organizations in Kazakhstan as one of the possible ways of the diversification of the economy. The Law of the Republic of Kazakhstan *On private entrepreneurship* defines a small business as one with no more than 50 employees. A medium-sized business is a company with between 51 and 250 employees. Large businesses are defined as separate legal entities carrying out the entrepreneurial activity with more than 250 employees. The majority of the companies in this research are small enterprises—63% of respondent companies, 25% medium enterprises, and 11% large enterprises representing all three sectors of the economy. Pearson's chi-square test was applied to test the independence of categorical variables. The coefficient of the test proves that the observed distribution of data fits well with the distribution that is expected, and the variables are independent.

Discussion and Further Directions of Research

Although the integration process on post-Soviet space has a long history, the Eurasian Economic Union is a relatively young institution. Therefore, it may be too early to expect to see the effects of integration on the entrepreneurial ecosystem. However, in fact, trends can be identified. To suggest further directions of research, this research provided the following results. The share of total trade between Kazakhstan and EAEU member countries has increased since 2015, which shows that countries are using the opportunities provided by integration and non-tariff trade for their benefit. However, the results are different across the sector. Most companies from the tertiary sector did not experience any effect of the Eurasian Economic Union on their businesses; most of them are small enterprises (84.3%) that provide mostly services. This can be explained by the small scale of their activity. Medium-sized businesses are the most sensitive to the integration effects among the companies we surveyed. About half (48.6%) of these companies responded that there was an impact on their business after joining the Eurasian Economic Union. These findings show that more research needs to be done to understand how entrepreneurial ecosystems function and what institutions can be developed to support SMEs in emerging countries. Despite their importance for the economy, entrepreneurial ecosystems are a relatively new topic in the literature on international business (Autio, Nambisan, Thomas, & Wright, 2018; Brown & Mason, 2017). As ecosystems can be geographical and online, it is especially interesting how regional integration and digital technologies can support the development of SMEs. The directions of further research with respect to the possible diversification in Kazakhstan could be the following: how are digital entrepreneurial ecosystems developing in the emerging countries' context? What is the role of regional integration in fostering such entrepreneurial ecosystems? What kind of government policy helps or hinders entrepreneurial ecosystems?

Bibliography

Autio, E., Nambisan, S., Thomas, L. D., & Wright, M. (2018). Digital affordances, spatial affordances, and the genesis of entrepreneurial ecosystems. *Strategic Entrepreneurship Journal, 12*(1), 72–95.

Balassa, B. (1961). Towards a theory of economic integration. *Kyklos, 14*(1), 1–17.

Bosma, N. S., Stam, E., & Wennekers, S. (2012). Entrepreneurial employee activity: A large scale international study. *Discussion Paper Series/Tjalling C. Koopmans Research Institute, 12*(12).

Brown, R., & Mason, C. (2017). Looking inside the spiky bits: A critical review and conceptualisation of entrepreneurial ecosystems. *Small Business Economics, 49*(1), 11–30.

Chang, H. J. (2002). *Kicking away the ladder: Development strategy in historical perspective*. London, UK: Anthem Press.

Dragneva, R., & Wolczuk, K. (2012). *Russia, the Eurasian Customs Union and the EU: Cooperation, stagnation or rivalry?* Chatham house briefing paper REP BP, 1.

Feldman, M. P. (2014). The character of innovative places: Entrepreneurial strategy, economic development, and prosperity. *Small Business Economics, 43*(1), 9–20.

Fisher, A. G. (1939). Production, primary, secondary and tertiary. *Economic Record, 15*(1), 24–38.

Friedman, M. (2009). *Capitalism and freedom*. Chicago, IL: University of Chicago press.

Huin, S. F., Luong, L. H. S., & Abhary, K. (2003). Knowledge-based tool for planning of enterprise resources in ASEAN SMEs. *Robotics and Computer-Integrated Manufacturing, 19*(5), 409–414.

Jumasseitova, A., & Bigabatova, M. (2017). Eurasian economic integration: The challenges for small and medium companies. *Central Asian Economic Review, 119*(1), 110–121.

Kyophilavong, P., Vanhnalat, B., & Phonvisay, A. (2017). Lao SME participation in regional economic integration. *Journal of Southeast Asian Economies, 34*, 193–220.

Li, J., Liu, B., & Qian, G. (2019). The belt and road initiative, cultural friction and ethnicity: Their effects on the export performance of SMEs in China. *Journal of World Business, 54*(4), 350–359.

Markusen, A. (1996). Sticky places in slippery space: Typology of industrial districts. *Economic Geography, 72*(3), 293–313.

Nguyen, H. T. N., & Enderwick, P. (2016). The perceptions and responses of Vietnamese firms towards deeper regional economic integration: Case studies from the food processing industry. *Journal of Southeast Asian Economies, 33*(1), 65–82.

Perroux, F. (2010). *A new concept of development: Basic tenets.* London, UK: Routledge.

Pitakdumrongkit, K. (2018). *Addressing digital protectionism in ASEAN: Towards better regional governance in the digital age.* Policy report. Nanyang Technological University, S. Rajaratnam School of International Studies. Retrieved from: https://www.rsis.edu.sg.

Ribberink, N., & Schubert, L. (2020). Infrastructure investment and development alongside the belt and road initiative. In I. Heim (Ed.), *Kazakhstan's diversification from the natural resources sector: Strategic and economic opportunities.* London, UK: Palgrave Macmillan.

Ritchie, J., & Spencer, L. (2002). Qualitative data analysis for applied policy research. In A. Bryman & R. G. Burgess (Eds.), *Analyzing qualitative data* (pp. 187–208). London, UK/New York, USA: Routledge.

Soesastro, H., & Basri, M. C. (2005). The political economy of trade policy in Indonesia. *ASEAN Economic Bulletin, 22*(1), 3–18.

Stam, E. (2013). Knowledge and entrepreneurial employees: A country-level analysis. *Small Business Economics, 41*(4), 887–898.

Stam, E., & Spigel, B. (2017). Entrepreneurial ecosystems. In R. Blackburn, D. De Clercq, J. Heinonen, & Z. Wang (Eds.), *Handbook for entrepreneurship and small business.* London, UK: Sage.

Tarr, D. G. (2016). The Eurasian economic union of Russia, Belarus, Kazakhstan, Armenia, and the Kyrgyz Republic: Can it succeed where its predecessor failed? *Eastern European Economics, 54*(1), 1–22.

Wille, P., & Redden, J. (2007). A comparative analysis of trade facilitation in selected regional and bilateral trade agreements and initiatives. In ESCAP, Trade Facilitation Beyond the Multilateral Trade Negotiations: Regional Practices, Customs Valuation and Other Emerging Issues - a study by the Asia-Pacific Research and Training Network on Trade, 27–76. New York (NY): United Nations.

10

Development of the e-Tourism Industry in Kazakhstan

Sayabek Ziyadin, Raigul Doszhan, and Gulvira Akybayeva

Introduction

What is the role of the tourism industry in the economy of Kazakhstan? Can Kazakhstan diversify its economy from the primary sector into the growing tertiary sectors, such as the tourism industry? What is the role of online services and digital technologies in the development of the modern tourist infrastructure? The literature suggests that the tourism sector of the economy is one of the most promising industries in the global economy. For example, according to the United Nations World Tourism Organization (UNWTO), 2016 was the seventh continuous year of steady growth after the global financial and economic crisis of 2008. Indeed, such a period of stable growth has not been observed since the 1960s. As a result, in 2016 the number of international tourists traveling

S. Ziyadin (✉) • R. Doszhan
Al-Farabi Kazakh National University, Almaty, Kazakhstan

G. Akybayeva
Astana IT University, Nur-Sultan, Kazakhstan

I. Heim (ed.), *Kazakhstan's Diversification from the Natural Resources Sector*, Euro-Asian Studies, https://doi.org/10.1007/978-3-030-37389-4_10

the world grew by 300 million compared to the pre-crisis level of 2008. Revenues from international tourism in 2016 amounted to $1.22 trillion (UNWTO, 2017). The tourism industry, one of the fastest-growing sectors of the world economy, accounts for 10.4% of GDP in 2018 (WTTC, 2019). The tourism industry in Kazakhstan continues to actively develop. Forms and methods of travel logistics are being improved, new forms of tourism are emerging, and more favorable conditions for the sustainable development of tourism are being created and developed. Diversification from the energy resource sector in Kazakhstan to new industries such as tourism will lead to sustainable development, which in this context meets the needs of the present without compromising the ability of future generations to meet their own needs (WCED, 1987). The future of tourism will continue to be impacted by the multidimensional implications of four megatrends, including evolving visitors' demand, sustainable tourism growth, enabling technologies, and travel mobility (UNWTO, 2017).

In 2018, the former President of Kazakhstan, Nursultan Nazarbayev, in his annual Address to the Nation of Kazakhstan, *the New Development Opportunities in the Context of the Fourth Industrial Revolution*, noted that one of the more important conditions for the sustainable development of Kazakhstan is the further expansion of digital technology (Nazarbayev, 2018). The development of the new digital economy is one of the main drivers of economic globalization, mobile communication, and a wide range of information (see Ambalov & Heim, 2020, this volume). When the earlier stage of economy digitization could have been characterized by increased diffusion of internet technologies, the next stage will be the development of a wide range of digital services, products, and platforms into a single cyber-physical system. This transition to the new digital economy can potentially lead to radical transformations within many sectors of the economy.

Indeed, the academic literature suggests that there is currently a tendency to digitize all industries, including tourism (Philbeck & Davis, 2019). The modern development of the tourism industry would be impossible without the associated modernization of touristic infrastructure. It assumes, along with the construction of modern roads, airports, and hotels, the increasingly widespread use of information and communications technology (ICT). It is rapidly becoming a prerequisite for successful work, a guarantee of efficiency, reliability, accuracy, and effectiveness of management decisions. It has been found that tourist activities are increasingly being shaped by price comparison and a combination of technologies; new applications for mobile devices that offer a wide range of opportunities are being developed; social networks are consolidating within a more transparent market; and changes in the concept of the value chain are producing new business models (Blanco, 2011).

New technologies have changed the entire landscape of the tourism industry (Opara & Onyije, 2013). As a result of its growing influence on the efficiency of tourist institutions, ICT can now be considered a fundamental aspect of modern tourism (Stiakakis & Georgiadis, 2011). Aghaei, Nematbakhsh, and Farsani (2012) suggested that ICT represents a powerful tool that can benefit the development and strengthening of the tourism industry strategy and its operations. Consequently, the impact of ICT in the tourism industry cannot be underestimated as a decisive driving force in today's information society (Paraskevas, 2005). According to Buhalis and Law (2008), ICT affects the industry in terms of costs, market, competition, and regulation. Recently, a variety of websites dedicated to the development of the tourism industry, travel agencies, sanatoriums, boarding houses, hotels, and so on can be found in the Kazakhstani segment of the internet (Malska & Khudo, 2012).

How can the emergence of digital technologies in the tourism sector of Kazakhstan be used to build a sustainable economy based not only on energy resources but also on a diversified balanced economic structure? This research suggests that Kazakhstan, possessing unique natural wealth, has great potential for the development of tourism in the internal and regional markets. The development of tourism will allow Kazakhstan to seamlessly integrate into the international tourism market and allow for intensive development of tourism in the country. This will ensure a steady increase in employment and income, stimulating the development of related industries and increasing the flow of foreign investment into the national economy.

The Tourism Industry in Kazakhstan

In this section, we examine the current state of the tourism industry. Tourism is one of the top priorities of state policy (Bisakayev, 2019). In 2010, Kazakhstan introduced the *Program for the development of the promising areas of the tourism industry for 2010–2014* and in 2014 introduced the *Concept for tourism development in Kazakhstan until 2020*. The concept was revised in 2017 and extended until 2025, after the transformation of the Ministry of Culture and Sports and the Committee on Tourism Industry. Nevertheless, industry representatives are not satisfied with the pace of the changes and note problems associated with infrastructure and excessive government intervention in business, but at the same time, they emphasize the importance of increasing government funding for tourism development (Albekova, 2017).

Kazakhstan, despite rich touristic potential, is characterized by an unfortunately low level of touristic development (see Table 10.1). According to the index of competitiveness of travel and tourism, in 2017 Kazakhstan ranked 81st out of 136 countries and in 2015 ranked 85th of 141 countries. Kazakhstan has since improved its position by the only four places to 81st in the latest World Economic Forum's (WEF) Travel and Tourism Competitiveness Index (2017).

About 4.5 million people visit Kazakhstan annually and spend an average of $336 each. Kazakhstan's travel and tourism industry contributes to GDP US $3 billion annually, which comprises 1.6% of the total GDP. The industry employs about 150,000 people or 1.7% of the population. Due

Table 10.1 Key touristic indicators for Kazakhstan, 2017

Key indicators	Score
International tourist arrivals, number of tourists	4,559,500
International tourism inbound receipts, US$ million	1533.6
Average receipts per arrival, US$ million	336.4
T&T industry GDP, US$ million	3077.5
T&T industry GDP, % *of total*	1.6
T&T industry employment, number of jobs	150,585
T&T industry employment, % *of total*	1.7

Source: Authors' own processed data based on the Travel and Tourism Competitiveness Index 2017 (WEF)

to a low HIV-positive population and the absence of malaria, the index in health and hygiene is the highest. The second-best ranking is for price competitiveness. This category examines ticket taxes and airport charges, hotel prices, purchasing power parity, and fuel prices. Kazakhstan demonstrates good results in the business environment ranking, 36th in the world. The information and communications technology (ICT) readiness is ranked 52nd for safety and 58th for security. Human resources and the labor market ranked 47th. International openness, which includes visa requirements, the openness of bilateral air service agreements, and the number of regional trade agreements in force, is ranked at 113th place in the world. Environmental sustainability was assessed as being poor (99th place), mainly due to low indicators in environment treaty ratification and baseline water stress. The tourist service infrastructure is in 97th place. This is mainly due to the poor quality of tourist infrastructure and the lack of car rental services.

Comparing the ranking with other Eurasian countries, Kazakhstan follows Russia (43rd place), Georgia (70th place), and Azerbaijan (71st place). Kazakhstan was followed by Armenia (84th), Tajikistan (107th), and the Kyrgyz Republic (115th). The share of tourism industry in the GDP (calculated for accommodation and food services only) in 2015 was about 0.3%, and the gross value added created directly by tourism was 406.4 billion tenges, or 1.0%, of Kazakhstan's GDP, which is relatively low. For comparison, the contribution of the tourism sector to the GDP in Turkey is 10.9%, while in the UAE it is 14.3%.

The issue of the need to diversify in the tourism industry in Kazakhstan was raised a long time ago. However, unlike developed countries, tourism in Kazakhstan, as well as in Russia and other CIS countries, is still not perceived as an important sector of the economy. In general, the concept of *tourism* in Kazakhstan is still associated with sports and health and not with the economy in terms of generating significant revenues. Indeed, tourism in the country exists more in a de facto sense than a *de jure*. Of course, one can refer to the shortage of proper information about the tourist opportunities of Kazakhstan abroad. The main reason here, however, is the absence of investments in the tourism sector (Erdavletov & Koshkimbaeva, 2006).

Table 10.2 Number of visitors in terms of entry and exit, million people (2014–2016)

Indicator	2014	2015	2016
Total number of tourists	16,782	17,731	16,263
Outbound tourism, among them	10,450	11,301	9755
CIS countries	9375	10,355	8959
%	89.7	91.6	91.8
Outside the CIS	1075	946	796
%	11.3	8.4	8.2
Inbound tourism, among them	6332	6430	6508
CIS countries	5655	5835	5935
%	89.3	90.7	91.2
Outside the CIS	677	595	573
%	10.7	9.3	8.8

Source: Authors' own processed data based on the Ministry of the National Economy of the Republic of Kazakhstan Committee on Statistics

It is sufficient to consider the dynamics of the industry in terms of the number of inbound and outbound tourists (see Table 10.2).

As can be seen in Table 10.2, the main share of tourism is outbound tourism, while the CIS countries' destinations, both in terms of outbound and inbound tourism, occupied a leading position with more than 90% in 2016.

The most visited countries by Kazakhstani tourists in 2016 among the CIS countries were:

- Russian Federation—51.5%;
- Kyrgyzstan—31.3%;
- Uzbekistan—15.9%;
- Other countries—1.3%.

The choice of Kazakhstani tourists in terms of visiting countries outside the CIS in 2016 was as follows:

- China—27.3%;
- Turkey and Iran—26.5%;
- Developed countries—16.8%;
- Other countries—29.4%.

Kazakhstanis have shown an increasing interest in the following destinations: Thailand, the Netherlands, Austria, Malaysia, South Korea, the Czech Republic, and India. A decreasing interest has been observed in tourism to Egypt, Israel, the USA, Tunisia, Greece, and Latvia. According to the statistics published by the Committee on Statistics of the Ministry of National Economy, Kazakhstan has a rich tourist potential but accounts for less than 1% of the worldwide tourist arrivals. At present, tourists from Kazakhstan spent US $1.8 billion abroad annually. This includes tourism as well as business and other trips; that is, they export abroad and buy imported tourist products.

In terms of the total contribution of the tourism industry to GDP, Kazakhstan ranks 129th worldwide. For three years, revenues from tourism decreased by 22.21%, and by the end of 2016, the direct contribution of the tourism industry to the GDP of Kazakhstan amounted to US $7.9 billion. Analysis of incoming tourist flows in Kazakhstan shows that the country is still not attractive for foreign tourists. Kazakhstan ranks 101st in the world in terms of export of tourist services (World Data Atlas, 2016).

The number of enterprises in the tourism industry in Kazakhstan is constantly growing. In 2016, there were 2754 companies engaged in tourist activities in Kazakhstan. Of the total number of types of accommodation, 62.4% were in hotels, of which 16.1% had a category (star rating) and 83.9% were without categories, while 37.5% were other types of accommodation. The presence of international hotel chains in the Kazakhstan tourist market is relatively low, and all of them are located in four main business destinations, namely Astana, Almaty, Atyrau, and Aktau. Prices for accommodation facilities with a good level of hotel services are much higher in Kazakhstan than in similar hotels in the leading tourist destinations of other countries. The price of a room for international branded hotels of category 5* in the cities of Astana and Almaty is two to three times higher than in Europe. Prices for services in other types of accommodation—houses, tourist camps, shelters, camping, hostels for visitors, and others—are much lower (see Fig. 10.1).

Overpricing is associated with low booking rates, a lack of competitive offers, and strong dependence on business tourism. The tourist services offered, including hotel accommodation, provide limited services and are

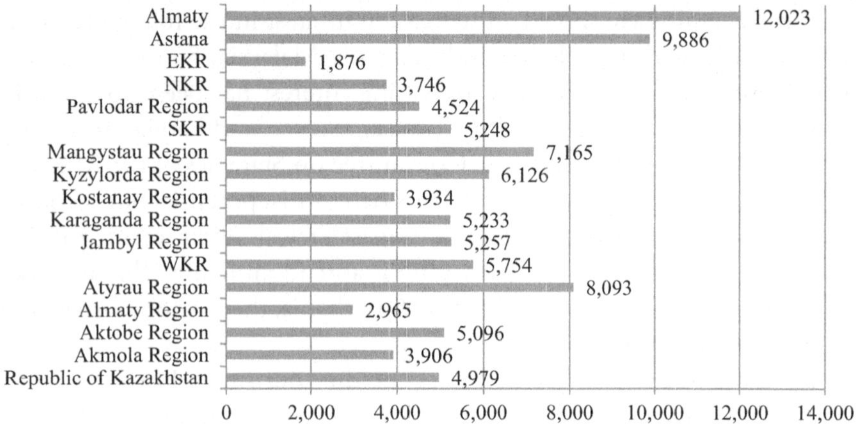

Fig. 10.1 Average price of bed-days, tenges, 2016. (Source: Authors' own processed data based on the Ministry of National Economy of the Republic of Kazakhstan Committee on Statistics)

of poor quality. It is also necessary to develop a regulatory framework for the industry and standards in line with the requirements of international visitors.

The high price of accommodation and air tickets significantly increases the cost of a trip to Kazakhstan and, accordingly, reduces its competitiveness on the international market. Kazakhstan ranks 70th in the World Economic Forum out of 140 countries in terms of the amount charged for air travel. There are no low-cost airlines in the Kazakhstan air market (low fares).

Hotels, boarding houses, houses, and recreation centers, as well as sanatoria and resort facilities, are in state of deterioration. To date, due to the lack of a category (star rating) in the vast majority of hotels, the quality of services offered to tourists does not meet international requirements. In practice, there is no single system for classifying hotels according to the level of comfort and services offered. There are international hotel chains in the market that have built hotels in Astana and Almaty, for instance, Holiday Inn, Radisson Blu, InterContinental, and Hyatt. The provision of hotel rooms in Kazakhstan is a quite low level (ranking 87th out of 140 in the World Economic Forum rating).

The main problems that hamper the development of the tourism industry in Kazakhstan include:

- insufficiently developed legal and regulatory framework;
- high prices for accommodation with fairly low levels of development of the tourist infrastructure;
- persistent concerns among potential tourists about their safety;
- poor development of the leisure and entertainment infrastructure in tourist centers;
- a lack of information available for potential tourists;
- a lack of coordination among the representatives of the tourism industry and the local authorities to promote regional tourism products;
- a lack of highly skilled personnel.

Analyzing the reasons for the low level of domestic tourism, Yulia Yakupbaeva, Deputy Chairman of the Board of the National Chamber of Entrepreneurs, said (Albekova, 2017):

> *Regional tourism is developing. … To date, there are independent tourism departments only under the akimats of Almaty, Almaty, Akmola and Mangistau, and East Kazakhstan regions. In other regions, this is either the tourism department in the business administration, or the department of industrial and innovative development, sports, foreign relations, but not tourism.*

Nevertheless, state and private institutions are conducting systematic work on the development of recreational areas. Khorgos International Center for Cross-Border Cooperation (ICBC), which received the first tourists in 2012, is worthy of special attention by both private and public sectors. The basic principle laid down in the creation of a zone of cross-border cooperation is the free movement of the citizens of Kazakhstan, China, and other countries within its borders without the need for visas. The main goal of the creation of the Center is to facilitate cooperation between Kazakhstan and China based on modern transport, logistics, and tourism infrastructure development (see Ambalov & Heim, 2020, this volume). According to predictions, the number of visitors reached six million people by 2018. This is one of the most impressive regional projects in Central Asia, as it creates the conditions not only for the development of the transit potential of Kazakhstan and the Almaty region in the East-West direction but also for the development of international tourism (Ableeva, Aktymbayeva, & Zhilkibaeva, 2017).

Kazakhstani tourist facilities, despite the recreational potential of the country, are still not included in the international tourism industry value chains. One of the reasons for this is the lack of reliable information about the market conditions and the standards of service expected by the typical client. Features of the implementation of the tourist product do not allow us to consider a full-fledged market without adequate supporting information. It is information flow that provides links between the tourist service producers. These not only take the form of data streams but also those of services and payments. Services, such as spending a night in a hotel, renting a car, complex tours, and places on aircraft, are not being sent to travel agents, who in turn do not store them until they are sold to consumers. Information is transmitted and used regarding the availability, cost, and quality of these services between interested parties. Similarly, payments are transferred from travel agents to tour operators, and commissions are paid between travel agents. Therefore, tourism—both international and domestic—is within the sphere of the growing use of information technology.

Information Technology in the Structure of the Tourism Industry

Many participants in the tourism industry are vertically or horizontally involved in each other's activities. All this allows us to consider tourism as a highly integrated service, which makes it even more receptive to the use of information technology in its organization and management. Ikonnikov and Sadovskaya (2014) suggest that it is information flow, rather than goods, which build the links between the providers of tourist services.

Therefore, the management and development of the tourism business require particular attention being paid to the quality of ICT transmission facilities, as well as to information services. It is important to ensure a good data transfer rate. The quality of information, its reliability, its timeliness, and relevance for the end-user also plays an important role in information exchange. The various information technologies and systems used in tourism include both internal (deployed by the organizations) and external systems (platforms). These include global computer networks, satellite navigation systems, digital phone networks, global distribution systems (GDS), computer reservation systems (CRS), information and legal systems, business management systems, management information systems, e-commerce applications, electronic payment systems, accounting information systems, automated control systems, as well as electronic document and multimedia systems (Vetitnev, 2017).

These systems are often not deployed by travel agencies, hotels, or airlines individually, but shared by many organizations. Moreover, the deployment of the information technology system by each segment of the tourism industry is important to all other segments. For example, internal hotel management systems can be linked to internet-based global networks, which in turn provide the basis for communication with hotel reservation systems that can themselves be accessed by travel agencies through their computers. Consequently, we are dealing with an integrated system of information technology, which is spreading rapidly within the tourism industry. It becomes clear that digital disruption is currently taking place in the tourism industry for airlines, hotels and motels, car rental, tourist operators, restaurants, special tour operators, and travel agents (Hojeghan & Esfangareh, 2011).

Morozova, Morozov, Chudnovskij, Zhukova, and Rodigin (2014) suggested that the effects of information technologies on the industry are expected to be improved efficiency, quality of services, new and more flexible services, as well as dissemination of best practices through the management, delivery of services, and distribution and sales channels. According to the director of Saber Travel Network Central Asia, Alexey Yanshin, mobile technologies have taken tourism to a new level. With the increase in the number of users of smartphones and tablets, the demand for mobile travel applications is also growing. Tourists prefer to use smartphone apps as an integral part of the travel process. Tourism businesses have actively begun to use modern mobile technologies that make it possible to offer not only the best prices but also a personalized list of services, thereby earning trust and customer loyalty, which is crucial in conditions when technologies change the entire landscape of the tourism industry (Yanshin, 2018).

The global development of information technology gives tourism service providers new opportunities for the development of their businesses. Digital platforms have become the main carriers of marketing information, and the distancing of places of consumption from places of purchase, as well as the related need to move tourists in the direction of interest, leads to the fact that the tourism industry is becoming one of the biggest beneficiaries of the technological revolution and modern information transfer technologies. Due to the latter situation, even a small tourist region can not only acquire considerable popularity but also popularize and ensure the effective "sale" of everything that it can offer tourists—hotels, museums, festivals, festivities, congresses, and other elements offered to potential tourists around the world.

Conclusions and Policy Recommendations

The development of information technology has led to an increase in the number of tourists and contributes extensively to the ongoing process of globalization. In the globalization of the tourist market, the importance of the quality of information exchange between all participants of the tourist market is increasing. First, this refers to information exchange between travel agent, tour operator, and host tour operator. To ensure the competitiveness of a tourism enterprise, it is necessary to create a single information space "supplier–seller of a tourist product". The quality and relevance of the information exchanges directly affect the quality of the tourist services provided, since any inconsistency or inaccuracy of information provided to the end-user, for example about accommodation facilities or additional services, can negatively affect the experience that the end-user receives and thus the impression they gain. In addition, in modern conditions the quality of a tourist product is determined not only by the quality of the basic services provided but also by the availability and level of information support and information communicated.

In the tourist business, the quality of information exchange and information provided directly affects the competitiveness of not only tourism enterprises but also the competitiveness of tourist destinations. The processes of globalization, as well as further development of global tourism, have led to a significant expansion of the geography of tourist flow. As a consequence, competition between countries and regions (tourist destinations) for tourists is also increasing. In these conditions, each tourist destination is interested in providing the most complete and comprehensive information about the presence of unique and attractive tourist resources, as well as the level of development of the tourist infrastructure, and specific features of culture and customs. Moreover, this information is necessary both for professionals of the tourist business and for the end-users. Advertising on the internet has become one of the most effective tools for attracting tourists. Traditional printed advertising tools are usually limited both in the volume of information provided and in their relevance; therefore, the most effective information source, in this case, is the internet. Most foreign tourist destinations create and maintain their websites providing comprehensive information in several languages. Tourist destinations in Kazakhstan should also invest in information technology, infrastructure, as well as advertising. The policymakers in Kazakhstan need to consider policies supporting investments in the tourism industry. The country could potentially become a regional tourist destination for neighboring countries, such as China and Russia.

Modern computer technologies are being actively introduced into the sphere of the tourism business, and their application has become an integral condition for increasing the competitiveness of any tourism enterprise. A variety of modern computer technologies are currently used in the global tourism industry. The degree of their influence on the competitiveness of tourism enterprises and the development of the tourism industry is different. Modern computer technology impacts the promotion of travel products. This requires forming new digital marketing channels for promotion and sale of the travel product. Thus, in the field of advertising, direct distribution of tourist information via e-mail (direct mail) has become widespread.

The enterprises associated with the tourism industry should actively create their own websites, as well as use banner advertising. At present, e-commerce is beginning to penetrate the tourist market in Kazakhstan. There are already electronic tourist offices, which allow for online purchasing of tours, booking a seat on an aircraft or hotel, the purchase of tickets for events, and booking rental cars anywhere in the world. Many hotel companies' websites provide opportunities for booking and making payment for services online. Thus, computer technologies have provoked the creation and application of fundamentally new electronic marketing channels for the promotion and marketing of travel products.

Acknowledgments The authors thank all anonymous reviewers for their helpful comments. This research was supported by the BR05236689 "Diversification of tourism in the Republic of Kazakhstan in the transition to a digital economy: strategies and implementation mechanisms" scientific and technical program.

Bibliography

Аблеева, А. Г., Актымбаева, Б. И., & Жилкибаева, М. И. (2017). Формирование и развитие туристических деинстинаций в современных условиях. Международного Центра приграничного сотрудничества «Хоргос» – новое туристическое направление Казахстана. Белгород, Издательский дом "Белгород"., pp. 107–110/ Ableeva A. G., Aktymbayeva B. I., & Zhilkibaeva, M. I. (2017). Formation and development of tourist de-installations in modern conditions. The Khorgos International Center for Cross-Border Cooperation is a new tourist destination in Kazakhstan (pp. 107–110). Belgorod (Russia): Publishing House Belgorod.

Ветитнев, А. М. (2017). *Информационные технологии в туристической индустрии.* Москва: Издательство Юрайт./Vetitnev, A. M. (2017). *Information technologies in the tourist industry.* Moscow: Izdatel'stvo Yurajt.

Aghaei, S., Nematbakhsh, M. A., & Farsani, H. K. (2012). Evolution of the World Wide Web: From Web 1.0 to Web 4.0. *International Journal of Web & Semantic Technology, 3*(1), 1–10.

Albekova, A. (2017). *Kazakhstani tourism needs a reboot.* Retrieved from: https://inbusiness.kz/ru/news/kazahstanskij-turizm-nuzhdaetsya-v-perezagruzke

Ambalov, V., & Heim, I. (2020). Investments in the Digital Silk Road. In I. Heim (Ed.), *Kazakhstan's diversification from the natural resources sector: Strategic and economic opportunities.* London, UK: Palgrave Macmillan.

Bisakayev, U. (2019). *Tourism development, expansion of online platforms and top 10 places for recreation in Kazakhstan — Kazakh Tourism*. Retrieved from: https://www.government.kz/en/news/interviews/razvitie-vnutrennego-turizma-rasshirenie-online-platform-i-top-10-mest-dlya-otdiha-v-kazahstane-kazakh-tourism-18570

Blanco, J. (2011). Understanding and managing innovation and technological change: A major opportunity for tourism organizations. *World Tourism Organization (UNWTO) Affiliate Members AM-Reports – Technology in Tourism, 1*, 6–21.

Buhalis, D., & Law, R. (2008). Progress in tourism management: Twenty years on and 10 years after internet: The state of e-tourism research. *Tourism Management, 29*(4), 609–623.

Erdavletov, S. R., & Koshkimbaeva, U. T. (2006). Modern tourism of Kazakhstan and problems of its development. In *Proceedings of the international scientific and practical conference tourism and recreation: Fundamental and applied research*. (pp. 129–137). Retrieved from: http://www.geogr.msu.ru/cafedra/recr/conf/MSU_Tourism_Conf_I_2006.pdf

Hojeghan, S. B., & Esfangareh, A. N. (2011). Digital economy and tourism impacts, influences and challenges. *Procedia – Social and Behavioral Sciences, 19*, 308–316.

Иконников, В. Ф., & Садовская, М. Н. (2014). *Информационные технологии в индустрии туризма*. Минск: РИПО/Ikonnikov, V. F., & Sadovskaya, M. N. (2014). *Information technologies in the tourist industry*. Minsk: RIPO.

Malska, M. P., & Khudo, V. V. (2012). Turystychnyi biznes teoriia ta praktyka. Pidruchnyk. 2-vyd. pererob. Ta dop. – K.: Tsentr uchbovoi literatury, 2012. – 368 s.

Ministry of National Economy of the Republic of Kazakhstan Committee on statistics. (2017). *Tourism of Kazakhstan statistical collection 2012–2016*. Retrieved from: http://stat.gov.kz/

Morozova, M., Morozov, A., Chudnovskij, A. D., Zhukova, M. A., & Rodigin, L. A. (2014). *Tourism information support*. Moscow: Federal Agency for Tourism. Морозова Н. С., Морозов М. А., Чудновский А. Д., Жукова М. А., & Родигин Л. А. (2014). *Информационное обеспечение туризма*. М.: Федеральное агентство по туризму.

Nazarbayev, N. (2018). *New opportunities under the fourth industrial revolution*. Retrieved from: http://www.akorda.kz/

Opara, J. A., & Onyije, E. (2013). Information and communication technologies (ICT): A panacea to achieving effective goals in institutional administration. *International Journal of Management Science, 1*(1), 11–15.

Paraskevas, A. (2005). The impact of technological innovation in managing global value chains in the tourism industry. In *OECD Conference on Global Tourism Growth: A challenge for SMEs*, 6–7 September, Gwangju, Korea, pp. 1–17.

Philbeck, T., & Davis, N. (2019). The fourth industrial revolution. *Journal of International Affairs, 72*(1), 17–22.

Stiakakis, E., & Georgiadis, C. K. (2011). Drivers of a tourism e-business strategy: The impact of information and communication technologies. *Operational Research, 11*(2), 149–169.

World Commission on Environment and Development (WCED). (1987). *Our common future. World commission on environment and development*. New York, NY: Oxford University Press.

World Data Atlas. (2016). *Total contribution of the tourism industry to GDP 2016*. http://knoema.ru/atlas/

World Economic Forum. (2017). *The travel & tourism competitiveness report 2017*. http://ev.am/sites/default/files/WEF_TTCR_2017.pdf/

World Tourism Organization (UNWTO). (2017). *Tourism highlights*. Retrieved from: https://www.e-unwto.org/

World Travel and Tourism Council (WTTC). (2019). *Travel and tourism economic impact 2019 world*. Retrieved from: https://www.wttc.org/-/media/files/reports/economic-impact-research/regions-2019/world2019.pdf

Yanshin, A. (2018). *What is Kazakhstan missing for tourism development?* Retrieved from: https://kursiv.kz/opinions/2018-07/chto-ne-khvataet-kazakhstanu-dlya-razvitiya-turizma

Correction to: Investments in the Digital Silk Road

Vitaly Ambalov and Irina Heim

Erratum to

I. Heim (ed.), *Kazakhstan's Diversification from the Natural Resources Sector*, Chapter 5 in: Euro-Asian Studies, https://doi.org/10.1007/978-3-030-37389-4_5.

An entry was incorrect in the reference list. This has been corrected. The correct information is given below:

Heim, I., Kalyuzhnova, Y., Li, W. (V.) and Liu, K. (2019). Value co-creation between foreign firms and indigenous SMEs in Kazakhstan's oil and gas industry: the role of information technology spillovers. Thunderbird International Business Review, 61 (6):911-927. https://doi.org/10.1002/tie.22067

The updated online version of these chapters can be found at https://doi.org/10.1007/978-3-030-37389-4_11.

I. Heim (ed.), *Kazakhstan's Diversification from the Natural Resources Sector*, Euro-Asian Studies, https://doi.org/10.1007/978-3-030-37389-4_11

Index[1]

[1] Note: Page numbers followed by 'n' refer to notes.

I. Heim (ed.), *Kazakhstan's Diversification from the Natural Resources Sector*, Euro-Asian Studies, https://doi.org/10.1007/978-3-030-37389-4

The manufacturer's authorised representative in the EU is Springer
Nature Customer Service Centre GmbH, Europaplatz 3, 69115 Heidelberg,
Germany. If you have any concerns regarding our products, please
contact ProductSafety@springernature.com

Printed and bound by CPI Group (UK) Ltd, Croydon, CR0 4YY
30/09/2026
02225460-0005